Machado de Assis, Blackness, and the Americas

SUNY series, Afro-Latinx Futures

Vanessa K. Valdés, editor

Machado de Assis, Blackness, and the Americas

Edited by

VANESSA K. VALDÉS and EARL E. FITZ

Cover image of Machado de Assis from 1864, first published in Jean-Michel Massa, *La jeunesse de Machado de Assis (1839-1870): Essai de biographie intellectuelle.* vol. 2, 1969. Université de Poitiers, PhD dissertation.

Published by State University of New York Press, Albany

© 2024 State University of New York

For information, contact State University of New York Press, Albany, NY
www.sunypress.edu

Library of Congress Cataloging-in-Publication Data

Names: Valdés, Vanessa K., editor. | Fitz, Earl E., editor.
Title: Machado de Assis, blackness, and the Americas / edited by Vanessa K. Valdés and Earl E. Fitz.
Description: Albany : State University of New York Press, [2024] | Series: SUNY series, Afro-Latinx Futures | Includes bibliographical references and index.
Identifiers: ISBN 9781438498812 (hardcover : alk. paper) | ISBN 9781438498836 (ebook)
Further information is available at the Library of Congress.

To our families, past, present, and future

Contents

Acknowledgments

This study began with an email exchange during the summer of 2020: the world as we had known it was burning, between the onset of the global pandemic and the social justice uprisings spurred by the murders here in the United States of Ahmaud Arbery, Breonna Taylor, and George Floyd. The reckoning of 2020 wrought examinations of the conditions of Black life around the globe; two days before the annual US national celebration of independence, an invitation to reconsider the reception of this giant of Brazilian letters in the United States was issued and accepted. We thank Rebecca Colesworthy, senior acquisitions editor at SUNY Press, for all of her support since the moment of this project's inception. We thank each of our contributors for their participation and their patience, and we thank our anonymous readers whose recommendations strengthened the study before you. Finally, we thank our colleagues at SUNY Press across departments for their contributions to this volume, particularly Ryan Morris, who has shepherded into production all of Dr. Valdés's books published at SUNY Press.

Introduction

The Complexities of Disguise:
Machado de Assis and His Contemporary Moment

Vanessa K. Valdés and Earl E. Fitz

Joaquim Maria Machado de Assis (1839–1908) is even today regarded as Brazil's greatest writer. Along with his compatriots, Clarice Lispector and João Guimarães Rosa, Machado stands as a pillar of modern Brazilian literature. Yet even in Brazil he has remained a cypher in ways his compatriots do not. A great deal of what is contested about Machado has to do with race broadly and with Blackness specifically. Not surprisingly, this is also true for the growing legions of his admirers outside of Brazil. For those who do not read Portuguese, and who may not know the culture from which he arises, this confusion over how he is to be read may be attributed to the fact that much of his writing remains untranslated. Indeed, with a few exceptions, only his novels and stories have been re-created in other languages, leaving his abundant work in other genres, his "crônicas," literary criticism, theater, and poetry left to live on only in its original tongue. It is for this reason that his prose is the subject of this study. Yet even for a lusophone audience, Machado presents some complicating factors. He is enthusiastically lauded as a distinguished writer and intellectual and yet he is also said by many to be one whose lived realities as a man of African heritage are often ignored or minimized. In the United States, where the reception of Machado is the focus on this book, to speak and write about Machado de Assis is to come to grips with Brazil's own relationship with its vast population of Afro-descendants and its history of freedom and enslavement, of marginalization and erasure.

There is the reality of the sheer number of Africans trafficked to Brazil; as Calvin Baker writes: "More than a third of all Africans removed from their homeland from the early 1500s to the mid-1800s—more than 4 million people—were transported to Brazil," the claiming of which, by the Portuguese, dates from 1500 (98). This explains why today "Nigeria is the only country with a larger Black population than Brazil, and in the body of African American culture stretching from Harlem to Rio, the state of Bahia," in northeastern Brazil, "might be fairly viewed as its spiritual heart. Perhaps the heart of the entire Black world" (Baker, "No Novel," 98). It also explains why, already in the seventeenth century, the Jesuit priest Antônio Vieira could declare, of his beloved Brazil, that it had "the body of America and the soul of Africa" (quoted in Burns, 55). For North Americans who wish to understand Machado de Assis, it behooves them to know more about Brazil.

As a nation, for almost the last century Brazil has boasted an identity made up of "mixed-blood people," and for being an American culture in which miscegenation, cultural as well as biological, "was never a crime or a sin" (Ribeiro 321).[1] This is in contrast to the United States, which—while it boasts in its ideology of being a nation of immigrants, has continually struggled to acknowledge a history of miscegenation—indeed, has grappled with the inclusion of the histories of all groups that have contributed to the development of this country.[2] In Brazil, there has never been anything like the "one-drop rule" or any legal prohibition on interracial marriage, as there was in the United States until 1967 and the Loving v. Virginia Supreme Court decision.

This is not to imply that interracial marriage between white and Black populations in Brazil have somehow eased racial discrimination or strict racial hierarchies; rather, it is to highlight that a national ideology about racial mixture has provided an environment in Brazil that is more amenable to interracial marriage than in the United States.[3] All to say that when we discuss the racial status of a Brazilian writer, artist, intellectual, or political leader, we are engaging an issue of great complexity. We cannot assume that what we know about racism as it is known and practiced in the United States can be applied to Brazil. To do so is to ignore the details of each country's complex and nuanced histories. To be discussed as a Black writer in Brazil involves issues of slavery and oppression, yes, but also a wealth of cultural nuances that have made it difficult for many a

US reader to comprehend and appreciate. Still, these must be understood, for Brazil offers the would-be inter-Americanist an exceptional perspective from which to consider the hemispheric American experience.

First, race is taught and understood differently in the United States and in Brazil, in great part because the narratives regarding the founding of our nations differ, in spite of the shared histories of colonization led by the kingdoms of the Iberian Peninsula. Brazil, founded as a Portuguese colony in 1500, is only slightly older than the United States; Portuguese settlers raped and maimed first the Indigenous populations and, within the first four decades of its founding, trafficked enslaved Africans across the Atlantic Ocean. While the standard telling of United States history begins with British settlement and the establishment of the Thirteen Colonies, Spanish settlement on the land that would become the United States was occurring at the same time as the establishment of Brazil. Having established Ayiti-Kiskeya-Bohio (renamed La Española, i.e., Hispaniola) as their base in the hemisphere, Spaniards—including those of African descent, free and enslaved, would go on to seize the lands of Boriken (Puerto Rico) in 1508; Xaymaca (Jamaica) in 1509; Cubanascnan (Cuba) in 1511; and the lands of the Apalachi, Timucua, Ais, Tocobaga, and Calusa peoples (Florida) in 1513.[4] In 1526, Lucas Vázquez de Ayllón attempted to found a town, San Miguel de Guadalupe, in Sapelo Sound, along the eastern coastline between what is now South Carolina and Georgia. It failed, in part due to attacks from the Indigenous peoples there and an uprising by the enslaved Africans trafficked as part of the expedition. As Jane Landers notes, "the escaped Africans took up residence among the Guale, becoming the first maroons in what is today the United States, as many of their counterparts were already doing in Hispaniola, Puerto Rico, Jamaica, Cuba, and Mexico" (13). Two years later, in 1528, there was another attempt at settlement of what had already been named La Florida: Pánfilo de Narváez led hundreds of Europeans and Africans, landing near what is today Tampa Bay. It too failed. In 1565, the Spanish had success with the establishment of St. Augustine, Florida: free and enslaved Africans accompanied Pedro Menéndez de Avilés in this endeavor. Iberian settlement on this land has not yet entered our textbooks, and there remains a great need for work on Afro-Indigenous histories, particularly in this early colonial period.[5] While the 1619 Project has done a great deal to center African contributions to the development of the United States from the seventeenth century forward, there remains a reticence to embrace a history that challenges the English colonization project with which we are more familiar in the United States—one that may resemble histories of the rest of the continent.

This is to underscore that the histories of the Americas are rich and nuanced; students and scholars in the United States must remain cognizant, when studying Brazil, that it is not the same as Spanish America either. In large part, this is because, in the late fifteenth and sixteenth centuries, Portugal was different than Spain (Seed 100–48, 149–78). All these contrasts, including those that relate to race, religion, and social interaction, were brought to America where they produced substantially different cultures. On the question of race, for example, Brazilian anthropologist Gilberto Freyre pointed out almost ninety years ago that "a consciousness of race . . . was practically non-existent in the cosmopolitan and plastic-minded Portuguese," who, in contrast to the Spaniards (who had embraced an ideology of purity, in blood, religion, and thought), had long cultivated more harmonious relations with the Muslims and the Jews (3; see also Herring, 87–88; and Skidmore, 345–62). As the sixteenth century wore on, Brazil, thanks to Portugal's overseas trading network, also benefited from being part of a global commercial system. The social, political, and economic "formation of Brazil," Portugal's New World colony, "went forward without the colonizers being concerned with racial unity or racial purity" (Freyre 40). But, though in the main true, this assessment, too, is more complex than it might first appear to be.

A controversial figure, Freyre was interested in comparing Brazil's development to that of Spanish America, English America, and French America. He spent many years in the United States, first at Baylor University and then, for his doctoral studies, at Columbia, where he studied with Franz Boas. Freyre was shocked at the virulence and sadism of US racists. In 1933 and *The Masters and the Slaves*, he wrote that "the Portuguese, in addition to being less ardent in their orthodoxy than the Spaniards and less narrow than the English in their color prejudices and Christian morality," produced in Brazil a culture that was distinctive in the Americas (81; see also 185). Famously, he concluded: "Hybrid from the beginning, Brazilian society is, of all those in the Americas, the one most harmoniously constituted so far as racial relations are concerned" (82; see also 85). This assessment has been challenged in recent decades.[6] Still, what stands as hard fact is this: in terms of its racial history, Brazil is different than the United States. It is far from perfect, and it has never truly been the racial democracy that many have wished it were. Nonetheless, as far as race in the Americas is concerned, Brazil its own specific case, and this must be understood, especially by those who would undertake comparative studies of Brazil, its hemispheric neighbors, and its artists.

A singular writer, Machado challenged during his lifetime—and continues to challenge even today—thinking about the genius and intellect of African peoples and their descendants by successfully engaging in what Eduardo de Assis Duarte names as a "poética da dissimulação," a poetics of dissimulation.[7] For readers here in the United States, the question of how Machado should be interpreted offers an unexpected parallel to the controversy here, arising some sixty years ago, that swirled around Ralph Ellison, whom critic Irving Howe accused in a 1963 *Dissent* article of failing to be militant enough about racism and racial injustice here in the States (see Howe). Ellison's response, that the artist's first responsibility was to their art and not to a cause, no matter how just it might be, was one that Machado might well have embraced. He, too, wished to be known as an artist, one who was free to write however he liked about whatever he chose.

Peoples of African descent throughout the Americas have historically needed to conceal their true selves in order to survive a heterosexist white supremacist patriarchal environment intent on their destruction.[8] In this, Machado de Assis is no different. In his most well-known essay "The Negro Digs Up His Past" (1925), Arturo Alfonso Schomburg, renowned bibliophile and student of the global Black experience, observes: "by virtue of their being regarded as something 'exceptional,' even by friends and well-wishers, Negroes of attainment and genius have been unfairly disassociated from the group, and group credit lost accordingly."[9] Essays by Regina Castro McGowan and Paulo Dutra within this volume address the intentional divorce of Machado from the context in which he and his contemporaries—Africans and their descendants, free and enslaved—lived and died during his lifetime. Niyi Afolabi comes to terms with Machado's own agency in this process; indeed, for Machado, a man of considerable intellectual ability, he assessed the situation in which he lived and made decisions that facilitated the rise of his fortunes in Rio society. Machado de Assis lived in the city of Rio de Janeiro for the entirety of his life; in the course of his existence, from 1839 to 1908, Rio was first the capital of the Empire of Brazil (1822–1889) and then, following the abolishment of the monarchy, the capital of the Republic of the United States of Brazil (1889–1930). While students of politics and history may be concerned with the implications of the changing political structures of the country on its capital city, for the purposes of this book it is critical to know that undergirding those structures was the enslavement of African peoples. As Mary C. Karasch writes in her groundbreaking study *Slave Life in Rio de Janeiro, 1808–1850* (1987), "in the first half of the nineteenth century, slavery in Rio was at its height. Neither before 1808 nor after 1850 would slaves, especially African slaves, so dominate the life of the city. [. . .] Further, no other city in the Americas even approached Rio's slave population in 1849. [. . .] Thus, the years from 1808 to 1850 were the most important period in the history of slavery in Rio, and Rio had the largest urban slave population in the Americas."[10] Celso Thomas Castilho writes: "The port of entry for the overwhelming majority of African slaves arriving in Brazil in the nineteenth century, Rio's population doubled from the 1820s to the 1850s, reaching just over 200,000 in 1849; of these almost 40 percent, or an estimated 78,000 people, were enslaved. This was a staggering number: Rio's slave population exceeded the combined slave population in the ten largest cities of the US South."[11] Brazil was the largest slaveholding society in the Americas: it was the last country in the Americas to end the enslavement of Africans and their descendants, in 1888, and its capital city, in which Machado de Assis lived, was at the center of this endeavor.

Machado himself was born free: in the short entry for Machado de Assis in his *Dicionário Literário Afro-Brasileiro* (2007), Nei Lopes highlights that the writer was the great-grandson of a freed Black couple and the son of a mulatto father and an Azorean woman who was raised, from the age of ten, by his father and his Black stepmother.[12] Yet he was a man of visible African ancestry, as Castro McGowan analyzes in her essay, and the laws that governed populations of enslaved, freed, and free Black peoples were more similar than not. In her examination of the nightly curfew implemented in Rio from the 1820s until the 1870s, Amy Chazkel points out: "Though people of color in nineteenth-century Rio faced the indignities of racial animosity and a constant threat of illegal enslavement or re-enslavement, all residents, including those of African descent, generally enjoyed a customary right to move about the city by day. After dark, simply circulating or assembling in the streets became a crime, and the night vested the newly professionalized police with emergency powers."[13] In a straightforward manner, the author calls attention to the pervasive menace of enslavement for those who were legally free; while everyone was allowed to move in the daytime hours, at night, from the perspective of the police and other municipal authorities, the distinction between freed and enslaved blurred.[14]

Chazkel later notes: "A person of African descent became a presumed slave and public enemy abroad in the city streets, who posed a potential danger to society that eclipsed his or her rights. Each night at sundown, the law allowed for its own suspension, and police held the power to decide—ironically just as visual perception became more difficult—who deserved to be arrested, searched, and flogged."[15] In an environment in which Black peoples were more susceptible to violence simply because of their skin, it was they who were thought to pose a danger to this society. As Alejandro de la Fuente and Ariela Gross observe about three sites of enslavement in the Americas, "it was not a society's recognition of slaves' humanity, nor its racial fluidity, that marked the differences among Cuba, Virginia, and Louisiana. It was how successfully the elites of that society drew connections between blackness and enslavement, on the one hand, and whiteness, freedom, and citizenship, on the other.[16] While their study focuses on those specific geographies, it is not incongruent to expand and apply their astute observation to the entirety of the hemisphere in which the enslavement of African peoples and their descendants flourished, particularly in the nation that held then and that continues to hold now the largest population of peoples of African descent.

Returning for a moment to the poetics of dissimulation, for many, Machado's choice to evade a more obvious anti-racist stance is untenable. In his text *Literatura Negro-Brasileira* (2010), Cuti names Maria Firmina dos Reis (1822–1917); Luís Gama (1830–1882); João da Cruz e Sousa (1861–1898); and Afonso Henriques de Lima Barreto (1881–1922) as precursors of the literary movement in which he himself would later flourish as part of Quilombhoje, namely one in which a collective Black consciousness was expressed in Brazil. He makes no mention of Machado, who was their contemporary. Moving from the nineteenth century into the twentieth, Paulina Alberto notes that while there was a small group of writers of color who celebrated cultural practices rooted in Africa in the 1910s and 1920s, "many other upwardly mobile men of color, . . . , like the famous mulatto novelist Machado de Assis, quietly disavowed their African heritage."[17] This is her sole mention of Machado in a study dedicated to Black intellectuals of the twentieth century. His dissimulation worked perhaps too well: while he is held as a subject of genius, that talent is seen to have done little to affect the lives of millions with whom he shared a heritage.

It may be useful for our readers to contrast the experiences of Machado with those of his also talented contemporary, Lima Barreto. On the question of how central these two Brazilian writers make the subject of race in their work, they could hardly be more different. If, for Machado, race and its related issues were often subdued and muted, for his much younger but more militant younger contemporary, they were paramount. They were also aggressively presented, and in a way that would seem familiar to students and scholars accustomed to working with Black writing here in the United States. As Lamonte Aidoo and Daniel F. Silva put it, "Lima Barreto was particularly, if not unfairly, critical of" Machado, who as "a fellow mixed-race writer," in the judgment of Barreto, did not "overtly and consistently" address "issues of racial disenfranchisement in his fiction."[18] This conflict, too, may be not entirely unfamiliar to readers here in the United States. If we liken Lima Barreto to Richard Wright, then Machado reminds us of Ralph Ellison. But Machado is also like James Baldwin, who contended that racism and the myth of white supremacy hurt not only Black Americans but white ones as well. This is a point the Brazilian master makes in his 1904 novel *Esau and Jacob*. There, a character (the liberal Paulo), avers that "abolition is the dawn of liberty, we await the sun: the black emancipated, it remains to emancipate the white" (91). Machado's grand vision, one can reasonably conclude, is to free all of us from the desire to enslave and exploit others.

The last three decades have seen a serious reconsideration of Machado de Assis's relationship with slavery in particular and with Blackness more broadly. This current volume, born of the turmoil of the summer of 2020 and the global reckonings about race and colonization, is an addition to these conversations. In her 2002 article "Machado: três momentos negros," Gizêlda Melo do Nascimento examines the representation of the Afro-Brazilian characters in his novels *Iaiá Garcia* (1878), *Memórias póstumas de Brás Cubas* (1881), and *Dom Casmurro* (1899). Sidney Chalhoub analyzes the years Machado spends as a government official within the Ministry of Agriculture in his *Machado de Assis, Historiador* (2003). There, underscoring that this work was centered on the politics of slavery on the country's lands, specifically the application of the Law of the Free Womb of 1871, Chalhoub argues that we see glimpses of his official life in four of Machado's novels: those already previously mentioned, and *Helena* (1876).

Eduardo de Assis Duarte built on this research with his anthology *Machado de Assis Afrodescendente* (2007): there he gathers poems, crônicas, theater criticism, short stories, and excerpts from nine of Machado's novels, all of which reveal that Machado had been dealing with slavery in his work, for decades, in fact, only he was doing so in his particular manner (i.e., ironically), employing a voice that mimicked bourgeois ideals of the times.[19] 2007 also saw Duarte's ideas translated into English with his article "Machado de Assis's African Descent"; he has since continued to publish on this subject in English. The following year saw commemo-rations of the centennial of Machado's death; among the events that took place in 2008 was *Machado de Assis e a escravidão*, a colloquium at the University of Hamburg in Germany examining his relationship with slavery. Edited by Gustavo Bernardo, Joachim Michael, and Markus Schäffauer, the resulting volume includes essays such as "Machado de Assis e o século negro" ["Machado de Assis and the Black Century"]; "A desconstrução de estereótipos na obra de Machado de Assis: a questão da escravidão" ["The Deconstruction of Stereotypes in the Work of Machado de Assis: The Question of Slavery"]; and "A vida literaria de Machado de Assis e o negro em seu tempo" ["The Literary Life of Machado de Assis and the Black Man in His Time"]. Duarte continued this work of reconsidering Machado within the realm of Black literature in Brazil by coediting a four-volume critical anthology called *Literatura e afrodescendência no Brasil: antologia crítica* (2011) with Maria Nazareth Soares; in the first volume, they identify Machado de Assis as a precursor to a fuller Black consciousness of the twentieth and twenty-first centuries.

In 2012, G. Reginald Daniel published *Machado de Assis: Multiracial Identity and the Brazilian Novelist*; there he argues that Machado deals with a personal sense of racial ambiguity by attempting to universalize it in his literature. Lamonte Aidoo and Daniel F. Silva edited *Emerging Dialogues on Machado de Assis* (2016), which features essays by Sidney Chalhoub and G. Reginald Daniel. In 2018, New London Librarium published a bilingual edition of Machado's crônicas; written under the pseudonym of Bons Dias (Good Days), these chronicles appeared from April 5, 1888, until August 29, 1889, in the newspaper *Gazeta de Notícias*. Here we see the narrative voice's take on the abolition of enslavement and later the monarchy, as well as the establishment of the republic of Brazil. Our hope with this volume is to contribute to these reconsiderations of Machado by meaningfully expanding the conversation to include considerations about the reception of his work as a writer of African descent.

With "Machado De Assis in Brazil, the United States, and Greater America: A Writer, a Black Writer, Or . . . A Genius, Our Literary Pelé?," Earl E. Fitz offers an introduction to Machado de Assis's biography, to the nuanced strategies Machado employed in the works that most explicitly include references to the Afro-Brazilian population, and to the reception of his work particularly in the United States. Regina Castro McGowan lays bare how Machado's photographic image was manipulated through the years, facilitating a visual whitewashing of his appearance, in "Black, Then

White, Then Black Again: Brazil's Racial Politics and the Changing Face of Machado de Assis." Paulo Dutra focuses on one of the works featured in Fitz's essay in his " 'Father against Mother': Race and/in the Reception of the Works of Machado de Assis," presenting a comprehensive review of the short story itself so as to reveal the different interpretations possible when the protagonist is assigned a racial category.

Niyi Afolabi takes up this thread of Machado's ambiguous presentation and its legacies with his essay "Raimundo the Obscure: Enslavement, Abolition, and the Problematics of 'Uncle Tom' Agency in Machado's *Iaiá Garcia*." He also explores his own relationship with the work of Brazil's preeminent writer over the course of his career. In "Machado de Assis and the Color of Brazilian Literature in the United States," Benjamin Legg provides insight into the reception of Brazilian literature as a corpus within the US market and the US academy. Daniel F. Silva continues this thread with his essay, "Black Writer, White Letters?: Machado's Racialized Reception of Identity and Aesthetics." There he speaks to what he names as problematic Eurocentric paradigms of literary reception and analyzes how the processes of canonization and translation contribute to an inability to see, read, and assess Machado's work clearly. David Mittelman considers Machado's tenuous hold on both the periphery and the center of Brazilian letters by comparing other authors who also occupy seemingly precarious spaces in "Outsiders on the Inside and Insiders on the Outside: Narrating Race and Identity in Machado de Assis, Milton Hatoum, and Jeferson Tenório."

Finally, in the afterword, we (the coeditors of this collection) speak frankly about the genesis of this study, the historical context of its creation, the place Machado de Assis occupies in each of our lives, and our hopes for our work. For both of us, it is critical that our readers get a sense of the reasoning behind this scholarship: *Machado de Assis, Blackness, and the Americas* is in conversation with our own historical moment as well as with the realities of Black life in the Americas over the course of the last two centuries. Our study was conceived during the time of the COVID epidemic, the murder of George Floyd, the Black Lives Matter movement, and an ugly rise in anti-Black, anti-Asian, anti-gay, antisemitic, and anti-democracy sentiment in the United States. His texts can teach us a great deal about these fraught issues. But we also know that, in the long run, Machado's reception here in the United States, in the rest of the Americas, and in the world will depend, more than anything else, on his brilliance as a visionary writer, even as this brilliance is perceived through the lenses of translation and social consciousness.

Notes

1. Prior to the public embrace of miscegenation, Brazil, like other countries in South America, implemented a policy of *branqueamento* (whitening), which saw concerted efforts to increase the population with an influx of white European immigrants; see Skidmore (1990) and Andrews 117–51.

2. The recent fights against the instruction of critical race theory and the Advanced Placement courses in African American Studies in Florida, as well as the elimination of offices of Diversity, Equity, and Inclusion in public universities in Florida, North Carolina, South Dakota, Texas, and Tennessee, as of July 2023, are but the most recent manifestations of white supremacist resistance against the work of ethnic studies. For a stunning critique of the US penchant to distance itself from the "spectral weight of plantation sexual violence and miscegenation" (1), see Isfahani-Hammond. Interestingly enough, it was the affirmative action policies of the United States that inspired similar policies in Brazil, leading to greatly increased access to higher education by Afro-Brazilians; for more, see Johnson and Heringer.

3. For more on the complexities of interracial marriage in Brazil, see Telles and Esteve.

4. For more on the utilization of the name "Kiskeya" by Haitians and Dominicans both, see Saint Jean; for more on the Spanish exploration of these lands, see Landers and Sued-Badillo.

5. For more recent publications that recontextualize hemispheric American history and the contributions of Indigenous and African peoples, see Reséndez and Proenza-Coles; for more recent narratives emphasizing the contributions of these populations to US history, see Mays, Fischer, and Blackhawk.

6. For critiques of Freyre, see Isfahani-Hammond 35–49 and Afolabi (2021) 17–35.

7. Assis Duarte 16.

8. Within an African American context, it is the awareness of the necessity of this dissemblance that lies that at the heart of W. E. B. Du Bois's notion of double consciousness, as explained in his critical text, *The Souls of Black Folk* (1903). Houston A. Baker identifies the mask as a "space of habitation [. . .] for that deep-seated denial of the indisputable humanity of inhabitants of and descendants from the continent of Africa. And it is, first and foremost, the mastery of the minstrel mask by blacks that constitute a primary move in Afro-American discursive modernism" (17).

9. Schomburg 232.

10. Karasch xxi.

11. Castilho 89. In his accompanying note, Castilho writes: "For Rio, the estimate was 78,855 in 1849, and the ten US cities together were estimated at 76,944." He then cites Frank 47 and Goldin 52–53.

12. Lopes 98.

13. Chazkel 111.

14. Sidney Chalhoub notes: "Historians' traditional focus on ways of obtaining freedom in nineteenth-century Brazil must be balanced by further attention to the experience of freedom for this ever-growing contingent of ex-slaves and their descendants. In addition to the widespread practice of illegal enslavement, there existed several legally sanctioned situations—such as conditional manumissions and revocation of freedoms—that often made the boundaries between slavery and freedom uncertain" (409).

15. Chalhoub 116.

16. de la Fuente and Gross 5.

17. Alberto 85.

18. Aidoo and Silva 3.

19. *Machado de Assis Afrodescendente* has been republished twice more since 2007, with its most recent edition published in 2020.

Works Cited

Afolabi, Niyi. *Identities in Flux: Race, Migration, and Citizenship in Brazil.* SUNY Press, 2021.

Aidoo, Lamonte, and Daniel F. Silva, eds. *Emerging Dialogues on Machado de Assis.* Springer, 2016.

———. "Introduction." *Lima Barreto: New Critical Perspectives.* Lexington, 2014, 1–8.

Alberto, Paulina L. *Terms of Inclusion: Black Intellectuals in Twentieth-Century Brazil.* University of North Carolina Press, 2011.

Andrews, George Reid. *Afro-Latin America, 1800–2000.* Oxford University Press, 2004.

Baker, Calvin. " 'No Novel About Any Black Woman Could Ever Be the Same After This.' " *The Atlantic,* Sept. 2020, 90–98.

Baker, Houston A. *Modernism and the Harlem Renaissance.* University of Chicago Press, 1987.

Bernardo, Gustavo, Joachim Michael, and Markus Schäffauer, eds. *Machado de Assis e a escravidão / Machado de Assis und die sklaverei.* Annablume, 2010.

Blackhawk, Ned. *The Rediscovery of America: Native Peoples and the Unmaking of U.S. History.* Yale University Press, 2023.

Burns, E. Bradford. *A History of Brazil.* 2nd ed., Columbia University Press, 1980.

Castilho, Celso Thomas. "The Press and Brazilian Narratives of Uncle Tom's Cabin: Slavery and the Public Sphere in Rio de Janeiro, ca. 1855." *The Americas,* vol. 76, no. 1, 2019, 77–106.

Chalhoub, Sidney. "The Precariousness of Freedom in a Slave Society (Brazil in the Nineteenth Century." *International Review of Social History,* vol. 56, no. 3, 2011, 405–39.

———. *Machado de Assis, Historiador*. Companhia das Letras, 2003.

Chazkel, Amy. "Toward a History of Rights in the City at Night: Making and Breaking the Nightly Curfew in Nineteenth-Century Rio de Janeiro." *Comparative Studies in Society and History*, vol. 62, no. 1, 2020, 106–34.

Cuti. *Literatura Negro-Brasileira*. Selo Negro, 2010.

Daniel, G. Reginald. *Machado de Assis: Multiracial Identity and the Brazilian Novelist*. Penn State University Press, 2012.

de la Fuente, Alejandro, and Ariela J. Gross. *Becoming Free, Becoming Black: Race, Freedom, and Law in Cuba, Virginia, and Louisiana*. Cambridge University Press, 2020.

Duarte, Eduardo de Assis. "Memórias póstumas da Escravidão." *Machado de Assis e a escravidão / Machado de Assis und die sklaverei*, Gustavo Bernardo, Joachim Michael, and Markus Schäffauer, eds. Annablume, 2010, 11–26.

———. *Machado de Assis Afrodescendente*. 2007. 3rd ed, Malê, 2020.

———. "Machado de Assis's African Descent." Translated by Thomas Stovicek. *Lusophone African and Afro-Brazilian Literatures*, special issue of *Research in African Literatures*, vol. 38, no. 1, 2007, 134–51.

Duarte, Eduardo de Assis, and Maria Nazareth Soares. *Literatura e afrodescendência no Brasil: antologia crítica*. 4 vols. Belo Horizonte: Editora UFMG, 2011.

Du Bois, W. E. B. *The Souls of Black Folk*. 1903. *The Norton Anthology of African American Literature*, Henry Louis Gates Jr. and Nellie Y. McKay, eds. Norton, 1997, 613–740.

Fischer, David Hackett. *African Founders: How Enslaved People Expanded American Ideals*. Simon and Schuster, 2022.

Frank, Zephyr. *Dutra's World: Wealth and Family in Nineteenth-Century Rio de Janeiro*. University of New Mexico Press, 2004.

Freyre, Gilberto. *The Masters and the Slaves: A Study in the Development of Brazilian Civilization*. 2nd English-language ed., translated by Samuel Putnam, Alfred A. Knopf, 1971.

Goldin, Claudia. *Urban Slavery in the American South, 1820–1860: A Quantitative History*. University of Chicago Press, 1976.

Herring, Hubert. *A History of Latin America: From the Beginnings to the Present*. 2nd ed., rev., Alfred A. Knopf, 1961.

Howe, Irving. "Black Boys and Native Sons." *Dissent*, autumn 1963, 353–68.

Isfahani-Hammond, Alexandra. "Introduction: Who Were the Masters in the Americas?" *The Masters and the Slaves: Plantation Relations and Mestizaje in American Imaginaries*. Edited by Alexandra Isfahani-Hammond. Palgrave Macmillan, 2005, 1–17.

———. "Writing Brazilian Culture." *The Masters and the Slaves: Plantation Relations and Mestizaje in American Imaginaries*. Edited by Alexandra Isfahani-Hammond, Palgrave Macmillan, 2005, 35–49.

Johnson, Ollie, III, and Rosana Heringer, eds. *Race, Politics, and Education in Brazil: Affirmative Action in Higher Education*. Palgrave Macmillan, 2015.

Karasch, Mary C. *Slave Life in Rio de Janeiro, 1808–1850*. Princeton University Press, 1987.

Landers, Jane. *Black Society in Spanish Florida*. University of Illinois Press, 1999.

Lopes, Nei. *Dicionário Literário Afro-Brasileiro*. Pallas, 2007.

Machado de Assis, Joaquim Maria. *Esau and Jacob*. Translated and with an introduction by Helen Caldwell, University of California Press, 1966.

Mays, Kyle T. *An Afro-Indigenous History of the United States*. Beacon, 2021.

Nascimento, Gizêlda Melo de. "Machado: três momentos negros." *Terra Roxa e Outras Terras*, vol. 2, 2002.

Proenza-Coles, Christina. *American Founders: How People of African Descent Established Freedom in the New World*. NewSouth, 2019.

Reséndez, Andrés. *The Other Slavery: The Uncovered Story of Indian Enslavement in America*. Mariner, 2016.

Ribeiro, Darcy. *The Brazilian People: The Formation and Meaning of Brazil*. Translated by Gregory Rabassa, University Press of Florida, 2000.

Saint Jean, Albert. "Kiskeya Is a Term That Belongs to Both Dominicans and Haitians." *Remezcla*, 14 March 2018, https://remezcla.com/features/culture/kiskeya-for-short/.

Schomburg, Arturo A. "The Negro Digs Up His Past." 1925. *The New Negro*. Alain Locke, ed., Atheneum, 1992.

Seed, Patricia. *Ceremonies of Possession in Europe's Conquest of the New World, 1492–1640*. Cambridge University Press, 1995.

Skidmore, Thomas E. "The Essay: Architects of Brazilian National Identity." *Cambridge History of Latin American Literature*. Vol. 3, Roberto González Echevarría, ed., Cambridge University Press, 1996, 345–62.

———. "Racial Ideas and Social Policy in Brazil, 1870–1940." *The Idea of Race in Latin America, 1870–1940*. Richard Graham, ed., 1990. University of Texas Press, 2006, 7–36.

Sued-Badillo, Jalil, ed. *General History of the Caribbean*. Vol. 1, Autochthonous Societies, UNESCO Publishing / Macmillan, 2003.

Telles, Edward, and Albert Esteve. "Racial Intermarriage in the Americas." *Sociological Science*, vol. 6, 2019, 293–320.

Chapter One

Machado de Assis in Brazil, the United States, and Greater America

A Writer, a Black Writer, Or . . . A Genius, Our Literary Pelé?

EARL E. FITZ

In the United States, Brazilian literature is almost completely unknown. This is unfortunate since it ranks, arguably, as "the most independent, and perhaps most original, national literature in the New World" (González Echevarría, Pupo-Walker, and Haberly 1). Writing for himself a year later, and striking a more directly comparative stance, Roberto González Echevarría will argue that "Brazil's is, with that of the United States, the richest national literature in the New World" (*The Oxford Book* xii). Too often lost under the vague rubric of "Latin America," Brazil and its novelists, poets, and dramatists are largely ignored here in the States. This state of affairs is particularly egregious in the case of Machado de Assis, a singular figure who remains terra incognita to most US readers. Michael Wood, a professor of English and comparative literature at Princeton University and an admirer of Machado, sums up the problem when he observes, of the Brazilian writer, that "everyone who reads him thinks he is a master, but who reads him, and who has heard of him? When I talk to people about Borges, I often have to say the name carefully, but I don't always have to say who he is" (297).

So who is this Joaquim Maria Machado de Assis? The biographical facts of his life are well known. He "was born in 1839, in Rio de Janeiro. His father, a poor house painter, was the son of freed slaves. His mother was a servant from the Azores who worked in a wealthy household on the outskirts of the city. She died when her son was nine years old. Machado's father was remarried to a poor black woman, and then died a few years later. Machado de Assis, therefore, grew up a poor, mulatto orphan, the grandson of slaves in a country where slavery would continue officially to exist until he was fifty years old. He had no formal education and probably never attended school." (Sá Rego xviii–xix).

In spite of these daunting obstacles, Machado "acquired French and English"—the former, it is said, by working in a neighborhood French bakery and the latter by studying Shakespeare—and "read voraciously in several languages," including Italian and German (Sá Rego xix). In addition to well over two hundred short stories, many of which are brilliant and often in the manner of Chekhov at his best, Machado also "wrote nine novels, a few plays and volumes of poetry, some literary criticism, many journalistic columns, and also published a few excellent translations from French and English" (Sá Rego xix).

We can conclude from all this that Machado was a Black writer by virtue of his biological background—his father was Black—but we can also see that he was a writer who came of age in a society that was itself profoundly Black and racially mixed, much more so, in fact, than the United States was then or is today. This question of long-term miscegenation, then, understood both as a matter of blood and of culture, is crucial to properly evaluating Machado as a Black writer in Brazil, in the United States, and in the Americas generally (see Fitz 2002). Praising Machado as "the premier nineteenth-century Latin American writer and one of the best of all time anywhere," González Echevarría adopts an inter-American perspective when he first favorably compares the Brazilian to Melville, Hawthorne, and Poe and then, looking to our southern hemisphere, to Borges (*The Oxford Book* 95). The Yale professor of Spanish and comparative literature further opines that Machado "anticipates and equals Borges's penchant for ironic detachment and authorial self-effacement, but his skepticism was less corrosive and more compassionate" (95).

Interestingly, Machado liked to refer to himself as a "Carioca[1] *enragé*," an appellation that suggests a strong sense of social awareness on his part, but there is no doubt that he also saw himself as a literary artist, one for whom "art was all" (Caldwell, *Machado de Assis*, 124). Because the one does not exclude the other, however, there is no reason we cannot conclude that the question of Machado's Blackness, his status as a Black writer, or as a Black literary artist in a society where slavery still exists, is considerably more complex than it might at first appear to be.

In Brazil, Machado is celebrated even today as that nation's greatest writer. Because of his capacious vision and because these two European writers were major influences on his development, we can envision Machado as the Brazilian Shakespeare and the Brazilian Dante rolled into one. He is of that stature. As David Jackson has pointed out, Machado is unquestionably one of the greatest writers ever produced in the Americas—one, moreover, who cultivated "a constant dialogue between the national and the universal" (6; see also Passos 218). David Haberly is of the same opinion, noting that Machado "is the greatest nineteenth-century novelist of Latin America and one of the most remarkable literary talents to appear in the Americas as a whole" (xi). Writing in 1948, Samuel Putnam, an early enthusiast, compares Machado with his US contemporary, Henry James, and finds that, for all their similarities, the Brazilian possesses greater depth, a keener sense of the human condition, in all its pathos and bathos (184). James, for all his excellence, Putnam concludes, "doesn't have the *sabedoria*, the great, deep life wisdom of Machado" (169). And then there are Machado's experiments with self-conscious and unreliable narrator/ protagonists, his systematic involvement of the reader, his cultivation of ambiguity, and his new, pre-Saussure theory of narrative (Fitz 2019). As a final fillip, Machado, possessed of a wry sense of humor, makes us laugh—something James rarely does. For those who know his work, it is no surprise that today Machado is regarded "as one of the fundamental authors of world literature" (Jackson 7). His recognition by the literary establishment in the United States is long overdue.

It is important for the US reader to know, however, that for the past several years a controversy has been raging in Brazil over the question of what we might term Machado's "racial"[2] identity, to wit: Is he a Black writer, or a black writer who has been literally whitened by his pictorial representations and, more subtly, by a Brazilian elite that has historically been dominated by white people anxious to portray at least artistic and intellectual Brazil as a white culture? It is also important for readers in the United States to realize that of all the several Latin American nations, it is Brazil in particular that can boast a long history of producing outstanding Black writers. As González Echevarría, Pupo-Walker, and Haberly argue, for example, Brazil's João da Cruz e Sousa "is perhaps the greatest black poet of Latin America," and the one possessed of one of the "most powerful and unique voices" of all New World literature (7). The anger at racial discrimination that surges forth from Cruz e Sousa's late nineteenth- and early twentieth-century poetry recalls the anger Richard Wright expresses in *Native Son* (1940). Wright's Black protagonist, Bigger Thomas, would, one feels, immediately understand Cruz e Sousa's bitterness and his searing indictment of racism.

Brazil's history of Black writers and writing go back even further. Before Cruz e Sousa, there were the late eighteenth-century poets Manuel Inácio da Silva Alvarenga (1749–1814), José da Natividade Saldanha (1796–1830), and Domingos Caldas Barbosa (1740–1800), the latter of whom made his Blackness a key part of his work. Something similar could be said of Antônio de Castro Alves (1847–1871), celebrated in Brazil as "the poet of the slaves" and a writer who used lyricism to drive home his political arguments. The same argument applies to any number of other Brazilian writers, including Jorge de Lima (1893–1953), Luís Gonzaga de Pinto Gama (1830–1871), and Machado de Assis. While virtually everyone agrees that Machado de Assis is a great writer, some even in Brazil have fretted that his greatness would be diminished in the eyes of the world if he were seen to be a Black man or even a mulatto. But times have changed, and today Machado is being proudly promoted in Brazil as a Black writer and as a Black man who writes and who does so at a level that commands respect and admiration around the world. Still, it is difficult for some people to accept this—and there lies the problem.

While no one would ever mistake the "racial" history of Brazil, where mixing has long been the norm, and the United States, where until 1967 and the Loving vs. Virginia Supreme Court decision the "one-drop rule" made marriage between people of two different races a legal impossibility, these two giant American cultures do not differ on this question (the worth of a Black writer versus the worth of a white writer) as much as one might think. In the post–World War II US, Black writers, along with Jewish writers and Southern writers, began to challenge the established hierarchy, the one in which northeastern WASPs (men, primarily, who were white, Anglo-Saxon, and Protestant) ruled the roost. Racial segregation was still the law of the land, an insidious antisemitism discriminated against Jews, and the South was thought of as barbarous and backward. It was into this period of transition and turmoil that Machado, as a novelist, was first thrust. In 1952, the same year that Ralph Ellison's landmark *Invisible Man* appeared and a year before Richard Wright's *The Outsider* was published, Machado's landmark work, the *Memórias Póstumas de Brás Cubas*, appeared in its first English translation, by William L. Grossman, as *Epitaph of a Small Winner*. In the United States, the concept of being a Black writer dates, then, from the late 1940s, the 1950s, and the 1960s, when Black writing finally gained its rightful place in the academy and in the public's mind. But, even today, there are still some who refuse to accept it as being something of value, and this is where the question of Machado de Assis's reception in the United States of 2022 is most apt. How will he be regarded?

The question is complex. On the one hand, we have the famous comment from Harold Bloom that Machado de Assis is "the supreme black literary artist to date" (674). On the other hand, we have this determination from scholar Maria Luisa Nunes: Machado "did not wish perhaps to be known as a black, white, or mulatto artist but as an artist" (x). In the first case, we do not know in what context, if any, Bloom intended his comment to be considered. Does he mean in Latin America, in hemispheric America (and therefore including the United States, the Caribbean, and Canada), or even in the world? He does not say. In the second case, that "perhaps" calls our attention to the fact that we just do not know for certain how Machado saw himself, though the assertion of Nunes that Machado considered himself an artist, first, last, and always, is well founded (see Caldwell, *Machado de Assis*, 228n2). Helen Caldwell, too, tends toward this position, arguing that Machado was loath to have his work evaluated in terms of his life and that, for him, "his writing was paramount" (12, also 3).

On this point, whether Machado should be read as an artist, as a craftsman of the novel form, or as an advocate for racial justice, his case recalls that of Ralph Ellison, whose 1952 novel *Invisible Man* was hotly debated in the 1960s United States and for strikingly similar reasons. In *A World More Attractive* (1963), the white and politically engaged critic Irving Howe charged that while it had many virtues, imagination and linguistic virtuosity being paramount among them, *Invisible Man* was nevertheless "marred" by the "ideological delusions" of the late 1940s and early 1950s (114). Although Howe admired Ellison's novel, it failed, he finally determined, because it had not "changed forever," as Richard Wright had succeeded in doing in 1940 with *Native Son*, the ways we would envision US culture (Howe 100). In sum, Ellison was derelict in his duties as a "Negro writer" because he did not write more overtly "protest" novels, as Wright had done twelve years earlier (99, 100)—and as the times, the racially charged 1960s, seemed to demand.

This same period, when, in the United States, the nature and purpose of literature was being scrutinized, coincides with what is commonly thought of by Latin Americanists as "the Boom": that stretch of some ten to fifteen years when Latin American literature (which, in truth, meant only Spanish American literature) began to establish itself in the US Brazilian literature, including that of Machado de Assis, was lost in the tidal wave of what was, in truth, a series of brilliant Spanish American writers, beginning with Jorge Luis Borges but also featuring such poets and narrativists as Julio Cortázar, Carlos Fuentes, Pablo Neruda, César Vallejo, Octavio Paz, Mario Vargas Llosa, and Gabriel García Márquez, among others. Unfortunately, critics and scholars in the United States even today tend to elide Brazil when seeking to speak of "Latin American" literature.[3]

As a student at the University of Iowa during those tumultuous days who read US writers like Wright, Ellison, John Barth, and others and who studied both Spanish and Portuguese, I can attest to how deeply the Cuban Revolution of 1959–1960 affected the consciousness of the US public. Cuba was the catalyst. To the extent that it existed at all, American awareness of Latin American history and culture was almost entirely a matter of political concerns. It was the changes wrought by Fidel Castro and the charismatic Ernesto "Ché" Guevara that provided the context, both pro and con, for the reception of "Latin American" (again, read Spanish American) literature in the United States of the 1960s. Cuba was the touchstone, and then, by extension, all of Spanish America. Though covered extensively in the press, the US intervention in Brazil's 1964 coup did not, oddly, generate much interest in Brazil's writers, several of whom—Clarice Lispector, João Guimarães Rosa, and Machado de Assis—were available in good English translations.

The political power of "Latin American" literature, however, was clear and obvious, though it did not appeal to everyone. Karl Shapiro, for example, writing in *The American Scholar* and in reference to a host of Spanish American poets (including Neruda), lambasted what for him was the pernicious influence of "Marxist" "Latin American" poets who, via "garish translations," were infecting the pristine corpus of US poetry with "large doses of angst, warmed-over surrealism, anti-American hatred, and Latino blood, sweat, and tears" (210).

What was not so obvious, and what was therefore paid scant attention to, was Brazil, both its political trends and its literature. Brazilian letters did not just get short shrift, they barely got shrift at all. For the great majority of the US public (though not for the US State Department, which regarded

Brazil as of immense importance, more so than even Cuba), Brazil, like Ellison's invisible man, was simply not seen; with one exception, it did not much register on anyone's cultural radar screen. The lone exception was John Barth, whose first novel, *The Floating Opera* (1956), was deeply influenced by his discovery of Machado (see Fitz 1986; Barbosa; and Barth 44–45, 165–67, 290). In the intervening years, I have often thought about how much a better knowledge of Brazil, and specifically its racial history, could have helped the US deal with its own racial conflicts. But it did not happen—not even with Machado de Assis, who was, during the 1960s, slowly becoming more widely available to English-speaking readers. Perhaps now, at long last, it finally will.

While we may not be in a position to know what Machado thought about the relationship between his identity as a Brazilian and his art, what we do have are his many and varied works. And what these consistently show is a writer who, though never obvious about it, is fully aware of what it means to be Black or mulatto in Brazil. And, again without ever being overt, links being nonwhite to marginality. And to slavery. In *The Posthumous Memoirs of Brás Cubas*, the 1880[4] novel, or anti-novel, that kicks off Machado's late and most brilliant period and that appeared eight years before slavery was abolished in Brazil, the blight of slavery appears in a telling yet artfully oblique fashion.

In chapter eleven, as Brás Cubas, our affable if ultimately unreliable narrator/protagonist, is telling us a story from his childhood, one in which he, a white "Devil Child," would amuse himself by abusing the Black house servants, sometimes violently (24). In the episode recounted here, Brás, now six years of age, would make the slave boy, Prudêncio, get down on the floor so that Brás could ride him like a horse. "I would whip him, make him do a thousand turns, left and right, and he would obey—sometimes moaning—but he would obey without saying a word or, at most, an—'Ouch, little master!'—to which I would retort, 'Shut your mouth, animal!'" (25). It requires no procrustean wrenching of the text to read this scene as a metaphor for how Brazilian society of the time worked—how its white upper classes, into which Brás was born, rode Black Brazil like a beast of burden.

Powerful and telling as it stands here, this scene is essentially repeated later on (in chapter sixty-eight) when, after many years have passed, an older (but no wiser!) Brás Cubas, out walking in Valongo, which in colonial times was the site of Rio's main slave market, happens upon a Black man beating another Black man in the street. Curious, Brás stops to inquire about what is going on, at which point he discovers that the man doing the beating is none other than Prudêncio his former slave, now an adult. Having gained his manumission, Prudêncio has now become a slave owner himself. And he is doing to his slave exactly what Brás had done to him years earlier. He is even addressing his slave with the same dehumanizing language Brás had directed at him. Here, as in chapter eleven, Machado is leading his reader to see the pernicious effects slavery has on a society, and most especially on one that wants to be a democratic Republic, as Brazil did in 1880–1881 and as the United States still seeks to be today.

History, as the saying goes, repeats itself (a point already broached in chapter seven of Brás's novel). The question Machado leads us to consider is: Why? Why do we insist on continuing to exploit and abuse each other? Machado never answers this question for us. He is not that crude. But, as attentive readers and citizens, it is the question he and his art lead us to ask ourselves.

On this point, Machado, ever the politically aware writer, gives us something extra to contemplate: he suggests to us that the desire to enslave someone else may well be not merely a problem of light-colored skin oppressing people of Black or dark skin but part of our nature; it is part of who we are as human beings. This sobering thought sounds a note of even greater tragedy to what is already a lacerating narrative about slavery in yet another American culture, Brazil. Like most Brazilians, Machado had watched in horror as, only a few years earlier, the United States had very nearly torn itself to pieces with its Civil War, which, as Brazilians clearly understood, was fought over the question of slavery. They saw how the lofty ideals of a great civilization could be undermined by human folly and the desire to enslave others. Even in the United States, an American culture founded on the principles of justice and liberty for all, the ideal could be debased by human conduct of the most ignoble kind. The kind of engaged reader Machado wanted can easily extrapolate all of this from his texts.

Machado, through his unreliable narrator, Brás Cubas, utilizes the same sort of outside/inside structuring to advance his argument. "On the outside," Brás tells us, "the Valongo episode," which the Brazilian reader of the time would have interpreted not merely as what a now-free Prudêncio is doing to his own Black slave but as Brazil's entire experience with slavery, "was dreadful but only on the outside. As soon as I stuck the knife of rationality deeper into it I found it to have a happy, delicate, and even profound marrow" (109). If one substitutes "rationalization" for the word Brás selects, "rationality," then it becomes clear that Machado is showing his reader that what Brás is doing here is using the process of rationalization to spin an odious, despicable fact—the practice of slavery—to make it seem a "happy" thing, one that seems to be perfectly reasonable and therefore justifiable. The very end of this chapter, in fact, shows Brás, whose values represent those of Brazil's ruling class, praising Prudêncio for what we might otherwise think were deplorable actions on his part. History repeats itself, Machado suggests, because we human beings are better at rationalizing cruel, violent, and oppressive behavior than we are at comporting ourselves at a higher, more enlightened level.

Although this conflict between how things appear on the outside and how they really are on the inside is a motif of this novel, it comes up for a third time, and very forcefully, in chapter 123, which allows us to see the true nature of one of Machado's most vile characters, a well-to-do and upper-class man named Cotrim. Seen from the outside, Cotrim "possessed an extremely honorable character" (170). Proud of presenting himself as a pious conservative, he is the epitome of people who, in today's United States, promote themselves as righteous "family values" types but who are anything but. True to form, Cotrim, on the inside, is a repugnant hypocrite. An unrepentant slave trader, even as Brazil, in its protracted struggle to abolish slavery, has in 1850 and the Queirós Law made it illegal to import slaves from abroad, Cotrim is infamous even among his peers for sending slaves "to the dungeon, from where they would emerge dripping blood. But," Brás again rationalizes, "alongside the fact that he only sent recalcitrants and runaways, it so happens that, having been long involved in the smuggling of slaves, he'd become accustomed to a certain way of dealing that was a bit harsher than the business required, and one can't honestly attribute to the original nature of a man what is simply the effect of his social relations" (170). Thus does Brás excuse Cotrim's crimes. Because he works assiduously at gulling people into thinking of him as a paragon of virtue and a pillar of society, the loathsome Cotrim gets a free pass from the ruling class; he can do whatever he wants. If, for readers in the United States, this sounds like the society we are living in today, it should.

Machado's concern with being Black continues in his next novel, *Quincas Borba*, which appeared in 1891. Whereas in *The Posthumous Memoirs of Brás Cubas* the connection between making money and slavery was more implicit, in *Quincas Borba* it is much more explicit. In the later narrative, the protagonist, a good but naïve man named Rubião, has unexpectedly inherited a fortune and, though he is not aware of it, is now being slyly manipulated by a swindler, one Cristiano Palha (whose conduct belies the Christian ethics implied in his name). Rubião is being advised by Palha to embrace capitalism on the argument that doing so will make him even wealthier than he already is. What poor Rubião does not see is that the parasitical Palha is going to use Rubião's fortune to make himself rich and leave his host penniless. Seduced by this appeal to greed and social status, and not fully realizing what is happening, Rubião acquiesces to Palha's exhortations.

Although Rubião does not want to replace his Brazilian compatriots (his loyal "blacks from Minas Gerais"), his false friend, Cristiano Palha, insists that as he is now a man of wealth and substance, Rubião must now employ only "white servants" in his house (*Quincas Borba* 6). Black and mulatto people will have to be dismissed or demoted. The dissection of this same problem, the yoking of Blackness and unemployment, or underemployment, continues as Rubião ponders the situation of "his good manservant, whom he wished to keep in the parlor as a touch of the provinces" but who, he now realized, "couldn't even stay in the kitchen, where a" presumably white "Frenchman, Jean, reigned. The slave was downgraded to other duties" (6). "While Rubião takes Cristiano Palha's advice and hires European servants, hidden behind the kitchen door is Rubião's black slave—symbolic of the hundreds of thousands of black slaves who served imperial Brazil until the abolition of slavery in 1888" (Haberly xiii).

In *Esau and Jacob*, a novel published in 1904 (one year after James's *The Ambassadors* and the same year as *The Golden Bowl*), one of Machado's characters, a liberal political leader, celebrates the official end of slavery in Brazil but then enunciates a penetrating insight about race relations, one that resonates even more in today's United States than in 1888 Brazil. While Pedro, his conservative twin brother, correctly finds the emancipation of the slaves to be "an act of justice," Paulo, his liberal sibling, pronounces it to be all of that but also "the beginning of a revolution," one which, if successful, would liberate not only Black slaves but white people as well (91). The word (verbal sign) "emancipation" is too often limited in our thinking to issues of freedom, equality, and skin color, whereas in fact, Machado implies, its meaning (based here on slavery) also applies to a wide range of possible applications, including women's rights and gay rights. We have to emancipate ourselves from our desire to force others into a state of lesser status. Neither he nor the (again, unreliable) narrator elaborates further on this enigmatic statement, though the attentive reader understands that Machado here employs the local Brazilian scene of 1888 to comment on the human condition, specifically our enthusiasm for abusing and exploiting others. In the United States of 2024, a culture still shamed by racism and the stubborn cults of white nationalism and white supremacy, this message should be easily understood.

Machado did not limit his concern with Blackness to his novels, however. The same preoccupation is a common feature of his stories as well. In the late tale "Father Versus Mother" (1905), for example, the issues of slavery, race, gender, and poverty are deftly intertwined so as to produce one of the most powerful texts Machado ever wrote. A basic conflict stems from how a lack of gainful employment can lead otherwise decent people to pursue professions that abuse the rights of others. If a father and mother cannot find work that allows them to put food on their family's table and to secure a clean, safe place to live, then they will be forced to seek socially undesirable sources of income. Significantly, Machado selects a woman, Aunt Monica,[5] and not a male character to see what is wrong and to enunciate what needs to be done.

But Machado is no starry-eyed romantic; on the story's final page, he shows us that women, too, are susceptible to the corrupting lure of monetary gain. Poverty makes us do things we should not be doing. Still, Aunt Monica was right, and we know it. She speaks for the gimlet-eyed realist, the person who sees things as they are. For US readers, this deeply affecting story has an additional lagniappe in that it will inspire comparative commentaries concerning our own Fugitive Slave Laws and their effect on our society. And while the racial lines in "Father Versus Mother" are, as befits a Brazilian text, more blurred than they are in today's United States,[6] Machado's story will also invite discussions that involve the issues raised in our Black Lives Matter movement.

In his final novel, *Counselor Ayres' Memorial*, published the year of his death in 1908, Machado continues with this promotion of women as the key players in Brazil's future as a democratic Republic (see Fitz, 2015, 4–5, 181 et al). Just as its slaves had been liberated, so too do Brazil's women have to be liberated. Written as a diary, the author of which is a retired Brazilian diplomat who seems very much to be Machado himself, this slim, early twentieth-century Brazilian and American narrative focuses on a series of decisions made by a determined young woman, Fidelia. The daughter of a plantation owner, the Baron of Santa-Pia who represents the past, Fidelia represents the future of the new Brazil. She is smart, strong-willed, progressive, and kind, but as our narrator, the old diplomat, Ayres, also understands, she is the product of a patriarchal and slave-owning society. And both will have to be overcome if Brazil is to move ahead and take its rightful place in the global community of nations. When, not long after slavery is abolished in Brazil (the entry for 13 May 1888), her father, the Baron, dies and Fidelia inherits the plantation and all its former slaves, most of whom remain there as they contemplate their futures as free men and women. As the new owner of the land but not the people, Fidelia must make some decisions. She could decide to live there and pay the former slaves to work for her. As an independent young woman who has other plans about where and how she wished to live out her life, this option does not appeal to her. She could sell the property and its buildings to a bank or to a private buyer and let the former slaves fend for themselves in the labor market. This outcome would be financially beneficial to her, but it would be bad for the newly-emancipated, none of whom possess the education or training necessary to compete successfully in a newly capitalistic market structure. Or, she finally determines, she could simply give the plantation to the freed laborers and allow them to own and run it themselves, which they already know how to do. And this is indeed what Fidelia does.

As the entries for 13 May, 15 April, and 28 April show, while Ayres secretly applauds this progressive decision on Fidelia's part, he also worries that, without proper preparation and lacking not the skills necessary to run a plantation but the experience in how one makes the many decisions about animal husbandry, agricultural science, and changing market conditions that have to be made, these newly free women and men may well find themselves unable to survive. The reader who knows Brazilian history and Machado de Assis also knows that Ayres's concern here with the future of the newly-freed owners of the Santa-Pia plantation can be taken as a metaphor of what Machado feared could happen to Brazil and its newly reborn status as a republic.

In the preceding pages, I have tried to show how and why, as Machado's fame spreads around the world, he can most accurately be read simultaneously as a Black writer and as a brilliant literary artist. Machado was acutely aware of what it meant to be a nonwhite Brazilian, but as a writer he was also committed to his craft. And while he refused to subordinate the latter to the former, his outrage at injustice is always there, hidden behind the door, so to speak, like Rubião's "good manservant." We can conclude with some measure of confidence, therefore, that while "Machado's view of the world in which he lived . . . was conditioned by the rage he must have felt, as a descendent of African slaves on his father's side, at the continuation and omnipresence of slavery in Brazil," he was driven even more by his desire to demonstrate what I believe was a revolutionary theory of what literary Realism[7] had to be like (Haberly xix; Fitz 2019).

Like Henry James, Machado sought to elevate the novel form to new levels of sophistication, and as discerning US readers like John Barth, Susan Sontag, and, most recently, Dave Eggers, have discovered, he succeeded in doing so. And so, slowly but surely, he is beginning to get the global recognition he deserves. Though we are cheered by this bit of international literary justice, our satisfaction is tempered by our knowledge that Machado has too long been ignored by students and scholars outside the ken of Luso-Brazilian letters. The great Brazilian writer expanded how we think about narrative, its relationship to reality, and its status as art, and he did it in ways that made us both laugh and cry. From now on, however, when we think of the history of the novel in the Americas and the world, we must include Machado de Assis in the conversation.

As to whether he should be read as a Black writer or simply as a writer, I suspect Machado would want us to think of him, first and foremost, as a writer, albeit an iconoclastic one and one devoted to narrative as art and not merely a story told. But there can be no doubt at all that he was also keenly aware of being a man of African descent who wrote both before and after Brazil abolished slavery and who knew what injustice was. He would want to be recognized as both, I think: as a Black man and as a literary artist. So why not read him as both? Or in even more ways, as a feminist, for example? Looking ahead to our collective American future, why limit ourselves to an either/or choice on this question?

I propose something else. Let's think of Machado de Assis, in Brazil and in the United States,[8] as a genius, a literary giant who transcends all labels and limiting categorizations.[9] What would be wrong with reading Machado as an Afro-Brazilian man who was a surpassing literary talent? What if that were our starting point for responding to him and to his work? To think of Machado de Assis as a genius is not naïve, nor does it hearken back, nostalgically, to some earlier time when we supposedly read literature as if it had no social context; rather, the term refers to the level of Machado's excellence. No one thinks of Pelé as a great Black player, only as a great player—a footballing genius, in fact. So let's read Machado as our New World[10] Pelé, the truly exceptional player who, upon getting a killer pass from his teammate, Garrincha (whom we can think of here as the enlightened reader), is set free to score yet another fabulous goal. Maybe, by proceeding in this fashion, we could all free ourselves from parochial and prejudiced thinking. That would be a step forward. We're justified in thinking of Machado as an American genius. And we should. Period.

Notes

1. A "Carioca" is a resident of the city of Rio de Janeiro. The play on words present in *enragé* shows Machado seeking to lure the reader into thinking of him as a "Carioca" who is politically conscious and who is not satisfied with how things are. Machado's use of the term should be taken to mean something akin to what Sartre meant with his term *engagée* many years later, but with an added dollop of geographic specificity.

2. I use the term "racial" here guardedly and in the full knowledge that, as geneticists have proven, there is only one "race" of people on our planet: the human race. There are, genetically speaking, as many differences within our supposed "racial" groups as there are between them, which means that what we have for so long thought of as "race" is an entirely spurious conception. In Machado's time, this knowledge did not exist, however, and the best science of the day posited that people like the mixed-race Brazilian master were doomed, by biology, to inferior status and unable to achieve anything of excellence. For Brazilians—a racially mixed people—this idea was devastating.

3. In his very useful book *Conquest of the New Word*, Johnny Payne writes of the impact modern Latin American literature has had on writers and critics in the United States. The problem is that his examples of "Latin American" texts are all from Spanish America. Brazil is neither mentioned nor discussed. It is as if it and its writers did not exist.

4. The novel was first published in 1880 via installments in a popular journal of the time, the "Revista Brasileira," and as a book the following year, 1881.

5. We can be sure that Machado's use of this name was not an idle choice. It references Saint Monica, whose importance to an earlier Machado work, the novel *Dom Casmurro* (1899), has already been noted. For more information on this issue, see Caldwell, *The Brazilian Othello of Machado de Assis*, 156–58.

6. In Brazil, where racial and cultural mixing involving Indigenous peoples, Africans, Europeans, and immigrants from all over the globe has been the rule since its beginning in 1500, it is impossible to say of any single work, as Howe

does of Wright's 1940 novel *Native Son* and its impact in the United States, that it "changed forever" the ways its citizens would think of their culture (Howe 100).

7. For Machado, literary Realism had to reflect the symbolic nature of language and how it generates meaning. It could not be merely a mode of writing; to mean anything, Realism had to reflect what language, its raw material, was and how it worked. As early as 1879, Machado had written that "a realidade é boa, o realismo é que não presta para nada"/"reality is good; it's Realism that isn't worth anything" (translation mine; "A Nova Geração"/"The New Generation," Obra Completa III, 830). For the new kind of writing Machado was committed to realizing, the traditional Realism of the past was no longer adequate and would have to be jettisoned. This decision led directly to the birth of Machado's own, quite distinctive "new narrative," the first in Latin America, the first in the Americas, and, arguably, the first in Western literature.

8. In writing this novel, the question of Brazil's long relationship with the United States is clearly on Machado's mind. We know this because in the diary entry for 19 April 1888, when Brazil is on the cusp of declaring its own emancipation proclamation, Ayres, his protagonist, invokes Abraham Lincoln and quotes him, approvingly, as another great American nation that has abolished this shameful human institution.

9. Machado's countrywoman, Clarice Lispector, preferred being termed "a writer" rather than "a woman writer."

10. In employing this term, I am fully aware that, thanks to its hemispheric Indigenous traditions, our so-called New World is, in truth, an ancient world, one that lives on in our many, varied, and still vital pre-Columbian cultures.

Works Cited

Assis, Joaquim Maria Machado de. *The Posthumous Memoirs of Brás Cubas*. Translated by Flora Thomson-DeVeaux, with an introduction by Dave Eggers, Penguin Classics, 2020.

———. *The Posthumous Memoirs of Brás Cubas*. Translated by Gregory Rabassa, Oxford University Press, 1997.

———. *Esau and Jacob*. Translated and with an introduction by Helen Caldwell, University of California Press, 1966.

———. *Quincas Borba*. Translated by Gregory Rabassa, Oxford University Press, 1998.

———. *Obra Completa*. Afrânio Coutinho, organizador, vol. III., Rio de Janeiro: Editôra José Aguilar, 1962.

Barbosa, Maria José. "Life as an Opera: *Dom Casmurro* and John Barth's *The Floating Opera*." *Comparative Literature Studies*, vol. 29, no. 3, 1992, 223–37.

Barth, John. *Further Fridays: Essays, Lectures, and Other Non-Fiction, 1984–94.* Little, Brown, and Company, 1995.

Bloom, Harold. *Genius: A Mosaic of One Hundred Exemplary Creative Minds.* Warner Books, 2002.

Caldwell, Helen. *The Brazilian Othello of Machado de Assis: A Study of Dom Casmurro.* University of California Press, 1960.

———. *Machado de Assis: The Brazilian Master and His Novels.* University of California Press, 1970.

Eggers, Dave. "Rediscovering One of the Wittiest Books Ever Written." *The New Yorker,* 2 June 2020, https://www.newyorker.com/books/second-read/rediscovering-one-of-the-wittiest-books-ever-written.

Fitz, Earl E. "From Blood to Culture: Miscegenation as Metaphor for the Americas." *Mixing Race, Mixing Culture: Inter-American Literary Dialogues,* edited by Monika Kaup and Debra J. Rosenthal, University of Texas Press, 2002, 243–72.

———. "The Influence of Machado de Assis on John Barth's The Floating Opera." *The Comparatist,* vol. 10, 1986, 56–66.

———. *Machado de Assis and Female Characterization.* Bucknell University Press, 2015.

———. *Machado de Assis and Narrative Theory: Language, Imitation, Art, and Verisimilitude in the Last Six Novels.* Bucknell University Press, 2019.

———. "The Reception of Machado de Assis in the United States During the 1950s and 1960s." *Luso-Brazilian Review,* vol. 46, no. 1 (2009), special issue, "Edição Comemorativa do Centenário da Morte de Machado de Assis," Pedro M. Monteiro, guest editor, 16–35.

González Echevarría, Roberto. "Preface." *The Oxford Book of Latin American Short Stories,* edited by Roberto González Echevarría, Oxford University Press, 1997, xi–xiv.

González Echevarría, Roberto, Enrique Pupo-Walker, and David Haberly. "Introduction to Volume 3." *The Cambridge History of Latin American Literature,* 3 vols., edited by Roberto González Echevarría and Enrique Pupo-Walker, Cambridge University Press, 1996, 1–10.

Haberly, David T. "Introduction." *Quincas Borba,* translated by Gregory Rabassa, Oxford University Press, 1998, xi–xxvi.

Howe, Irving. *A World More Attractive: A View of Modern Literature and Politics.* Horizon Books, 1963.

Jackson, K. David. *Machado de Assis: A Literary Life.* Yale University Press, 2015.

Nunes, Maria Luisa. *The Craft of an Absolute Winner: Characterization and Narratology in the Novels of Machado de Assis.* Greenwood Press, 1983.

Passos, Gilberto Pinheiro. "Cosmopolitan Strategies in *The Posthumous Memoirs of Brás Cubas,*" translated by Barbara Jamison, and the afterword to *The Posthumous Memoirs of Brás Cubas,* translated by Gregory Rabassa, Oxford University Press, 1997, 206–19.

Payne, Johnny. *The Conquest of the New Word: Experimental Fiction and Translation in the Americas.* University of Texas Press, 1993.

Putnam, Samuel. *Marvelous Journey: Four Centuries of Brazilian Literature.* Alfred A. Knopf, 1948.

Sá Rego, Enylton de. "Warning: Deadly Humor at Work," the preface to *The Posthumous Memoirs of Brás Cubas*, translated by Gregory Rabassa, Oxford University Press, 1997, xi–xix.

Shapiro, Karl. "The Critic Outside." *The American Scholar* 50, spring 1981, 197–210.

Sontag, Susan. "Afterlives: The Case of Machado de Assis. *The New Yorker*, 7 May 1990, 102–8.

Wood, Michael. "Master Among the Ruins." *The Author as Plagiarist—The Case of Machado de Assis*, João de Castro Rocha, guest editor. *The Journal of Portuguese Literary & Cultural Studies*, nos. 13/14, fall 2004/spring 2005, the Center for Portuguese Studies and Culture, University of Massachusetts Dartmouth, 2006, 293–303.

Chapter Two

Black, Then White, Then Black Again

Brazil's Racial Politics and the Changing Face of Machado de Assis

Regina Castro McGowan

This essay is a historiographic analysis of the representation and reception in Brazil's media of Machado de Assis and his work, starting in the 1870s. The digital archives of Brazil's National Library include the first published photo of Machado de Assis, which appeared in a literary journal in Rio de Janeiro in 1873. In this photo, Machado de Assis is clearly seen as a person of African descent. However, the succession of pictures that appeared in Brazilian books, literary journals, and newspapers from the early twentieth century on show Machado de Assis as whiter over the years, while often not hiding the fact that he was of mixed race. Acknowledging that Assis's father was Black while still promoting the writer as white was emblematic of a systematic racist culture that in the 1930s created Brazil's ideology of racial democracy[1].The ideology, with the mulatto as its national symbol, can be found in Gilberto Freyre's early work and in his later *lusotropicalismo* theory.[2] The narrative around Brazil's so-called racial democracy created a culture that praised the mulatto's whiteness while negating his Blackness. It is not surprising, then, that it was precisely around the 1930s that editions of Machado de Assis's books and his innumerous portraits in the media showing him with light skin would become the writer's prevailing image (as fig. 2.1 shows) until the 2019 photo rendition by Grey Brasil for the *Faculdade Zumbi dos Palmares* (see fig. 2.2).

33

Figures 2.1 and 2.2. On the left (fig. 2.1), cover of *Dom Casmurro*. Edições Santo António, 2018. On the right (fig. 2.2), Project *Machado de Assis Real*, Faculdade Zumbi dos Palmares, 2019.

The portrait of writer Machado de Assis familiar to most Brazilians in the twentieth century has at long last been replaced by a more real representation of the man himself, thanks to the 2019 work commissioned by Faculdade Zumbi dos Palmares (FAZP) to Grey Brasil, a São Paulo publicity firm.[3] The new rendition of the iconic photograph of the bearded old white man presented a Machado de Assis with distinct African features. The change resonated loud and clear in Brazil, making a statement on the author's ethnicity while celebrating him as both a Black man and one of the world's most revered writers. The effect of FAZP's photographic rendition was felt almost immediately. On 7 May 2019, the Academia Brasileira de Letras (ABL) convened a ceremony in which Marco Lucchesi, ABL's president, received the framed photograph of "*Machado de Assis negro*" ("Machado de Assis Black") from FAZP student Alex André.[4] The ABL's immediate recognition of its illustrious founding member as a Black writer prompted the country's publishing industry to include the new face of Machado de Assis in their books. The first book showing Machado de Assis as Black came out just one month after FAZP's public announcement.[5] Brazil's media, some of whom who had until very recently been reluctant to accept Machado as Black, swiftly followed suit.

Literary history in Brazil shows that for the last three quarters of the twentieth century, many editions of Machado's books, as well as many books written about him, would have the writer's image on their cover and/or some of his biographical data on the inside jacket, introduction, or back cover: "Nascido em 1839 no Morro do Livramento, Rio de Janeiro, Machado de Assis era filho de um pintor mulato e de uma lavadeira açoriana. Órfão de ambos muito cedo, foi criado por sua madrasta, Maria Inês."[6] Not all editions would include a mention of Machado's African blood, though. Many would simply omit it altogether: "Romancista, contista, poeta e crítico. Considerado um dos grandes nomes da literatura brasileira, fez apenas o primário, tornando-se autodidata. Aos 16 anos, publicou seu primeiro poema na revista *Marmota Fluminense*."[7] While some editions' succinct biography would only superficially inform the reader that the writer's father was mulatto, the presence of a very light-skinned (if not Caucasian) Machado de Assis on school boards, textbooks, and in the media would only serve to cement the narrative that Machado de Assis was, in fact, white.

Machado's famous character Brás Cubas in the preface to his eponymous *Memórias Póstumas* says "A obra em si mesma é tudo" ("The work itself is everything"). Whereas the statement aptly applies to Machado de Assis's voluminous literary production, the private life of the Bruxo do Cosme Velho (the Wizard of the Cosme Velho neighborhood, as Brazilian critics have for decades called Machado de Assis) has long been surrounded by mystery and speculation.[8] How much of that wall around the man he erected himself and how much went up by the media has been the subject of more than one publication. Unambiguous, however, had been the carefully crafted, racially manipulated image of the author, articulated in writing and visually promoted by Brazil's mainstream media, which for several decades purposely denied Machado de Assis of his Black identity, even long after his passing.

In 2018, an article published in Brazil's newspaper *O Globo* discusses the controversy surrounding a photograph of Machado de Assis, uncovered in the 1908 Argentinean journal *Caras y Caretas* (see figs. 2.3 and 2.4). The controversy was in the fact that the photograph showed a much darker Machado de Assis than people in Brazil had grown up with. In the article, *O Globo* asks the curator of Brazil's *Biblioteca Nacional*'s portal *Brasilianas Fotográfica* to analyze the photograph. Just one year before

Figures 2.3 and 2.4. Machado at two different moments: in an 1893 photo attributed to Juan Gutiérrez (left, fig. 2.3) and in a photo found in a 1908 edition of the Argentinean journal *Caras y Caretas* (right, fig. 2.4). Source: *O Globo*.

FAZP's photo rendition of *Machado de Assis Real*, *O Globo* still seemed to cast doubt as to what an increasing number of scholars, in Brazil and abroad, saw as a fact:

> A pedido do Globo, Joaquim Marçal, historiador da fotografia e curador do portal Brasilianas Fotográfica da Biblioteca Nacional, analisou a foto da Caras y Caretas. Para ele, as variações de luz e sombra prejudicam a avaliação da cor da pele (a mão direita do autor, por exemplo, está muito mais clara do que o seu rosto). Por outro lado, ele defende que as feições do rosto indicam um homem muito mais negro do que o dos retratos feitos por Pacheco: "A maior diferença está no nariz: largo no primeiro, afinado no segundo. O que não significa, necessariamente, que tenha havido algum retoque. Usando a luz, tudo é possível para um fotógrafo, inclusive afinar um nariz. O retoque pode ter até acontecido, inclusive como um acordo tácito entre Machado e Pacheco, mas não há como saber ao certo."[9]

Interviewed for the same article about the photo discovery, Eduardo de Assis Duarte, of Universidade Federal de Minas Gerais and editor of the 2007 anthology *Machado de Assis Afro-descendente*, says that in that picture,

Machado de Assis can be seen "[c]om traços nitidamente negros, muito mais do que na maioria de seus retratos. Não há texto ou registro algum de Machado em que ele diz ser branco. Ainda assim, por causa do nosso racismo institucional, a elite sempre fez de tudo para apresentá-lo como tal. Esse é um debate que ainda vai durar por muitas gerações, e por isso fotos como essa são importantes para desmontar o embranquecimento do escritor."[10]

From the nineteenth century to the twenty-first century, Machado de Assis's face goes from Black, to white, to Black again. In an 1873 cover of *Archivo Contemporâneo Periódico Illustrado*, a photo of Machado appears alongside that of Brazilian Romantic writer José de Alencar (see fig. 2.5). The picture undeniably shows that Machado de Assis is a person of African descent.

Figure 2.5. *Archivo Contemporâneo Periódico Illustrado* 30 January 1873. *Source*: Biblioteca Nacional Digital.

In 1880, a portrait of Machado de Assis on the cover of the literary journal *Penna e Lápis* further confirms his Black ethnicity (see fig. 2.6). The sketch portrait appears to be reproduced from an 1880 photograph of Machado by Insley Pacheco (as fig. 2.7 shows). Machado de Assis was then forty years old.

Figure 2.6. Cover of *Penna e Lápis*, vol. 2, 1880. *Source*: Biblioteca Nacional Digital.

Figure 2.7. Machado de Assis by Insley Pacheco (1880) *Source*: Felipe Rissato in ABL *Revista Brasileira*, December 2016.

literary genius, calling him the most talented Brazilian writer of his day. The periodical, however, would conveniently excuse itself from disclosing Machado's full biographical information ("A sua biographia ainda não está escripta, e provavelmente não o será nunca" / "His biography is not yet written, and probably never will be"), which would naturally include that Machado's father was mulatto. For the absence of biographical data, the journal cites the author's own modesty: "Machado de Assis é hoje, incontestavelmente, o primeiro litterato nacional. . . . A sua biographia ainda não está escripta, e provavelmente não o será nunca; porque neste particular a modéstida de Machado é, não direi só excessiva e infundada, mas feroz."[11]

Artur Barreiros (1856–1885), the same journalist who in 1880 had written an article that included a photograph of Machado for *Penna e Lápis*, would publish in 1884 an edition of the *Galeria Contemporânea do Brazil* entirely dedicated to Machado de Assis. In this edition, Barreiros expanded on the brief information initially contained in his article for *Penna e Lápis*. The accompanying picture to the biography (see fig. 2.8)

Figure 2.8. From *Galeria Contemporânea do Brazil*, 1884 impression in platinotype by Marc Ferrez, from a glass-plate negative by Joaquim Insley Pacheco. *Source*: Biblioteca Nacional Digital.

shows a young and dark-skinned Machado de Assis. The edition, however, avoids any mention of race, focusing instead on meritocracy:

> Joaquim Maria Machado de Assis nasceu no Rio de Janeiro, a 21 de Junho de 1839, e é filho legítimo de Francisco José de Assis e D. Maria Leopoldina Machado de Assis.
>
> Sendo ambos pobres, o pai operário, os estudos que teve foram muito irregulares, e, na maior parte, obtidos por seu esforço incalculável e tenaz.
>
> À volta do seu berço não lhe sorriram as boas fadas da lenda, que lhe outorgassem bens transitórios e de sua natureza injustos; o Talento e o Trabalho, em compensação, estenderam-lhe as mãos e da humildade do seu nascimento o trouxeram ao homérico o combate da vida e o armaram cavaleiro, certos de que os seus triumphos seriam sem conto e as victorias gloriosas.[12]

Barreiros's talk of class rather than race ("a humildade do seu nascimento" / "his humble birth"), emphasizing the merits of "o Talento e o Trabalho" ("Talent and Work"), exposes a meritocratic ideology, which to this day, by employing the colorblind myth, serves only to negate the historical impact of slavery and racism on the lives of African descendants in the diaspora. By rewriting Machado de Assis's biography, and tacitly omitting any reference to the obvious fact that Machado was of African descent—in spite of the photo that accompanied the text—Barreiros was at once stripping Machado of his own Black identity and labeling him an exception to the rule, or in Gilberto Freyre's terms, "a sociologically white mulatto."[13]

In the section *"Livros a ler"* ("Books to read") from the periodical *Revista Illustrada*, also published in 1884, one finds a reference to that same photograph of Machado that Artur Barreiros included in his edition of *Galeria Contemporânea* (see previous transcription and photograph). Here is the transcription from *"Livros a ler"*:

> Temos à vista o primeiro número da Galeria Contemporânea do Brazil, publicação quinzenal, política, literária, artística, agrícola e industrial dos Srs. Lombaerts & C., photographo o Sr. Marc Ferrez. Estrea com o Sr. Machado de Assis, de quem nos dá o retrato, um fac-simile e a biographia. A biographia foi escripta pelo Sr. Artur Barreiros; o fac-simile é, se não me engano, um capítulo das Memórias de Braz Cubas; e o

retrato . . . O retrato é difícil dizer por quem foi feito. Na capa se diz: Marc Ferrez, photógrafo; dentro porém, no baixo do retrato, está escripto d'um lado: "Photographia inalterável, Marc Ferrez"; do outro lado: "Cliché, Insley Pacheco." Ora, em primeiro lugar, a photographia não é tal inalterável; em segundo, como é que sendo o cliché do Sr. Insley Pacheco, o photógrafo é o Sr. Marc Ferrez? A empresa que resolva o caso.[14]

The anonymous author of the above "*Livros a ler*" could not have been more correct: "Ora, em primeiro lugar, a photographia não é tal inalterável" ("Well, first, the photograph is not at all unalterable"). Pictures of Machado de Assis would soon turn out to be not so unchangeable after all. By 1939, one of Machado de Assis's most circulated pictures had surely been altered; the following is a sketch portrait of Machado de Assis found in a 1939 publication for *Centro Carioca* (see fig. 2.9). Machado's hair texture, facial features, and skin color present the reader with a Caucasian version of the writer.

Figure 2.9. Homage by *Centro Carioca* on the centennial of Machado's birth, 31 June 1939. *Source*: Biblioteca Nacional Digital.

Photographic reproductions, portraits, sketches, and drawings of Machado de Assis, especially those showing him in his later years, would from the 1930s on show an increasingly white person. A commemorative book published by Brazil's Biblioteca Nacional in remembrance of the sixtieth anniversary of the writer's death includes reproductions of the following pictures (see figs. 2.10, 2.11, and 2.12), originally taken in 1891, 1892, and 1905.[15]

Originally taken in 1905, therefore three years before Machado's death, the third photograph in Biblioteca Nacional's 1968 commemorative edition would unambiguously present a man whose literary peers, political elites, and the public in Brazil had already, for about sixty years, been imagining and publicizing as white. The previous three photos show just how much, in the six-decade period from his death, change was made to effectively turn Machado de Assis into a white person. The careful photo selection for the Biblioteca Nacional's commemorative volume is undoubtedly a testament to that transition, as the pictures, taken at different periods, show the steady racial erasure of Machado's African heritage with each passing decade.

By the 1960s, the ideology of racial democracy would become deeply rooted in Brazil's collective unconscious. Yet, the 1965 publication of Florestan Fernandes's *A Integração do negro na sociedade de classes* (published in the US in 1969 as *The Negro in Brazilian Society*) would help to initiate the slow process of deconstructing Brazil's myth of racial democracy. Notable in Fernandes's book is the almost complete absence of any direct mention of Gilberto Freyre, whom many consider the ideologue of a racially harmonious Brazil. According to Fernandes, "[a]s long as the 'racial democracy' myth cannot be openly used by Negroes and mulattoes as an instrument to control

Figures 2.10, 2.11, 2.12. Machado de Assis in 1891 (fig. 2.10), 1892 (fig. 2.11), and 1905 (fig. 2.12)—photos from a commemorative edition of the sixty years of Machado's death. *Source*: Biblioteca Nacional Digital.

their desire for social classification and upward mobility, it will be innocuous in terms of the very democratization of the prevailing social order."[16]

During his lifetime, and certainly more so after his passing, Machado de Assis would not have Black agency. Sadly, Machado would die without being acknowledged as the nineteenth-century Black literary master he was. Just twenty days after his death, on 19 October 19 1908, the state would decide that Machado was not "preto" or "pardo" (the latter a term used in Brazil's birth and death records of people of mixed race) but that he was, unabashedly, "branco." On that day, Brazil officially invented the image of twentieth-century Machado de Assis: a talented, respected—and white—writer (as fig. 2.13 shows). According to Simone da Conceição

Figure 2.13. Machado de Assis's death certificate, 1908. *Source*: Arquivo Nacional.

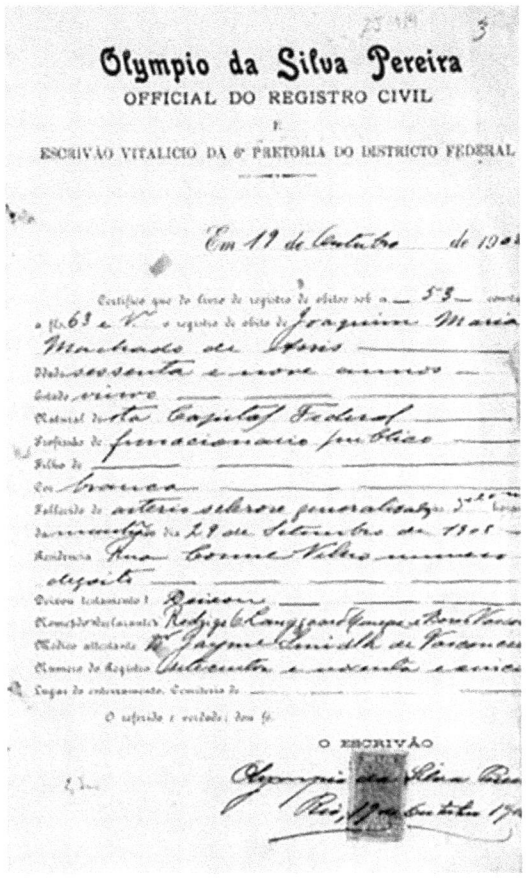

Silva, the intentionality behind adding skin color to Machado de Assis's Atestado de Óbito (death certificate) certainly would have been deliberate. Machado was already an acclaimed writer, but the country's ruling elite, subscribing to the racial theories of the time, would see it as imperative for future generations that Machado not be recognized as a man of African descent, as it would directly contradict the eugenics and racist theories in vogue, which did not attribute to Black people the same intellectual abilities as white people. As Silva notes, until it became law in 1973, it was not necessary nor praxis in Brazil to add skin color to death certificates.[17]

The news of Machado de Assis's passing in the early hours of 29 September 29 1908 was received and reported by Brazil's press on the same day and caused national commotion. The following is the first page of *Gazeta de Notícias*, at the time one of Rio de Janeiro's (then the capital of Brazil) most influential newspapers (see fig. 2.14).

The following day, an editorial on page two of *Gazeta* by one going by the nom de plume TIC-TAC pays tribute to Machado de Assis. TIC-TAC would end his eulogy saying that no further biography of the man was needed; that Machado's literary triumph was already a biography in itself: "Machado de Assis, o 'Machadinho,' era uma destas individualidades de difficílimo estudo. A sua organização physica só nao affectava as suas potentes e extraordinárias qualidades de talento, de observação e de estudo. Ferreira de Araújo disse que Machado de Assis conquistara as posições que occupava, subindo sem acotovelar, nem arrestar ninguém do seu caminho. Não está ahí a biographya completa de um homem de carácter e de trabalho?"[18]

Figure 2.14. News of Machado's death, *Gazeta de Notícias*, 29 September 1908. *Source*: Biblioteca Nacional Digital.

In the following days, Joaquim Nabuco, in writing about Machado de Assis to fellow writer José Veríssimo, would privately comment that Machado was indeed mulatto, but that in his (Nabuco's) mind, Machado had become a white man: "Mulato, ele foi, de fato, um grego da melhor época. Eu não teria chamado Machado de Assis de mulato e penso que lhe doeria mais do que essa síntese. A palavra não é literária e é pejorativa. Basta ver-lhe a etmologia. O Machado para mim era um branco, e creio que por tal se tornava; quando houvesse sangue estranho isso nada alterava sua perfeita caracterização caucásica. Eu pelo menos só vi nele o grego."[19] On the recognition of Machado de Assis's literary talent vis-à-vis the physical representations of him in the media (not to mention the deliberate change of his real ethnicity by the state), one could again think of Florestan Fernandes's analysis of the acceptance of rising Black individuals in Brazilian society: "It is clear that acceptance of the Negro and mulatto is governed by images and appraisals constructed by whites. Although there is considerable conflict between these images and appraisals on the one hand and the probable form of real behavior on the other—the former is expressed as if they were open and the latter tends to be very limited—taken together they define alternatives of personal and group behavior that in practice take a social form."[20] Even the times when Machado de Assis's Afro-descent entered the foreword to his books, the constructed light-skinned face that had become Machado was already embedded in Brazil's collective imaginary. To Fernandes, this contradiction is at the core of the country's ideology of racial democracy: "First, certain standardizations encourage the opinion that the Black man's social prestige is a function of his socioeconomic situation. . . . 'You are worth what you have; if you have nothing you are worth nothing.' Those whites most identified with the ideology of racial democracy go as far as those quoting the proverb above, declaring: 'Every time the Negro succeeds, he becomes whiter, as Gilberto Freyre says.' "[21]

A few decades earlier, Getúlio Vargas's *Estado Novo* had begun using Freyre's ideas on miscegenation from his book *Casa-grande & Senzala* for ideologically crafting a Brazilian national identity that purposely omitted the country's history of slavery in favor of presenting the country as a miscegenated and racism-free society of ever historically harmonious race relations: "Todo brasileiro, mesmo o alvo, de cabelo louro, traz na alma, quando não na alma e no corpo . . . a sombra, ou pelo menos a pinta, do indígena ou do negro."[22]

Freyre's later concept of lusotropicalism develops from his work on *Casa-grande & Senzala*. In the preface to the first edition of the book, he writes: "E dos problemas brasileiros, nenhum que me inquietasse tanto como o da miscigenação. . . . A miscigenação que se praticou aqui corrigiu a distância social que de outro modo se teria conservado enorme entre a casa-grande a a mata tropical, entre a casa-grande e a senzala."[23]

Afonso Henriques de Lima Barreto, a Black Brazilian writer of a generation later than Machado de Assis, would have one of his books (*Diário Íntimo*) posthumously prefaced by Gilberto Freyre. In the 1954 preface, Freyre writes that Lima Barreto was "poor and obligated, by his economic condition, to be, in large part, sociologically a man of color, with no chance of transforming himself into a sociologically white mulatto."[24] Lima Barreto, whose short life was afflicted by poverty, alcoholism, and mental health problems, was considered a controversial figure in his lifetime for his unabashed denunciation of what he saw and personally felt as Brazil's racial injustices. If with lusotropicalism Gilberto Freyre praises miscegenation (the figure of the mulatto as Portugal's colonizing gift to the tropics), the political articulation of his thought, the ideology of racial democracy reveals an assimilationist discourse that values the mulatto's whiteness, while structurally and systemically working to suppress the mulatto's right to his own unequivocal Black identity.

In the decades after Machado's death, there were not many (if any) public references to the author's Blackness. In 1933, however, an article for *Gazeta de Notícias* by Brazilian writer Humberto de Campos openly addresses Machado's skin color: "Era miúdo de figura, mulato de sangue, escuro de pele e usava uma barba curta e de tonalidade confusa, que dava ares de antigo escravo brasileiro. [. . .] e tornara-se pelo estudo e pelo trabalho o mais belo nome, a glória pura e mais legítima, das letras nacionais."[25] As with Barreiros decades earlier, one may notice that Humberto de Campos places emphasis on "pelo estudo e pelo trabalho" ("through his own study and work") while not omitting Machado's African origins. It is important to understand that, beginning in 1930, Getúlio Vargas's nationalist project (ideologically aligned with European fascism) would not have ignored that, demographically, Brazil was for the most part composed of descendants of slaves, Black people, and mulattoes. Conducive to expanding his base and advancing his nationalist project, Vargas attempted to forge a sense of national identity built upon Brazil's Black and mulatto culture, albeit a whitened version; one that would please the masses, yet not anger the elites.[26] The image of the "cordial"[27] mulatto, who through his own personal hardworking effort would become white by means of integration and assimilation to a white society, would naturally find an emblematic representation in Machado de Assis.

Unchallenged in the media that had helped shape the country's public perception of race and race relations, the myth of racial democracy in Brazil would continue into the 1990s. Unsurprisingly, the decades-long systematic whitening of one of Brazil's most important writers (and the appropriation of his image by the state) would in 1987 bring Machado de Assis's face to the one thousand Cruzados bill (turned into one Cruzado Novo two years later) (see fig. 2.15).

It is important to reflect that the man on the 1987 Mil Cruzados is not the real Machado de Assis; it is a decades-long and carefully articulated representation of what the country's political and intellectual elites had wanted Brazilians to see. As poignant as the appropriation and manipulation by the state of Machado's image is, it would however be the reproduction of the following 1892 photo of the author in its various forms—touched up, in sketch or painted, in fewer or many shades lighter (but never completely dark)—that would become the ever so iconic image of Machado de Assis for the last three quarters of the last century (see fig 2.16).

In the twenty-first century, internet searches for images of Machado de Assis will invariably turn out numerous versions of his iconic photograph. One more recent Brazilian webpage dedicated to information on the writer and last updated in 2014 includes, for example, various

Figure 2.15. One thousand Cruzados bill with Machado de Assis's face printed on it. *Source*: Wikimedia Commons.

Figure 2.16. Machado de Assis by Juan Gutiérrez (1892). *Source*: Felipe Rissato in ABL *Revista Brasileira*, Dezembro 2016.

sketches of Machado de Assis.[28] Figure 2.17 provides a sample of just a few of the many drawings found on the site appearing to represent a Caucasian Machado.

Out of the twenty drawings of Machado de Assis that one can find on the aforementioned website, only the following four will show Machado as a person of African descent. Notably, five years before Faculdade Zumbi dos Palmares forever changed Machado's picture back to show the real man, there were already artists who took it upon themselves to represent the author as he was, and there were media outlets willing to present them. These four pictures from elfikurten.com.br represent a dark-skinned Machado de Assis and a Machado with more definite African features (see fig. 2.18a–d).

The pictures and excerpts discussed in this work are by no means intended to be exhaustive on the iconography, bibliography, literary historiography, or any study of Machado de Assis. The information provided here is intended to encapsulate instances in which, for over a century, Machado de Assis's image appears manipulated by the media to favor the elites and the state in their pushing of the racial democracy narrative. As this work has purported to show, the nineteenth-century Brazilian press's early published pictures of the rising young literary star show him as he was—a man of African descent. Yet, in writing, Machado de Assis was rarely described as such. Beginning with his death, concerted efforts appear to have been made to rewrite Machado as a white man.

Figures 2.17a–f. Six contemporary black-and-white drawings of Machado de Assis from 2014, all depicting him as a white man. The illustrations show a variation of his iconic image, but in all the drawings he is wearing glasses, a shirt, a suit, and tie. Credits: 2.17a (top left) by Toni; 2.17b (top center) by unknown artist; 2.17c (top right) by Constança Lucas; 2.17d (bottom left) by Renato Mota; 2.17e (bottom center) by André Brown; and 2.17f (bottom right) by Hugo Enio Braz. *Source*: http://www.elfikurten.com.br/2014/07/machado-de-assis-o-bruxo-do-cosme-velho.html.

In the decades after his death, the media's, publishing industry's, and state's reproductions of Machado's iconic photo would become many shades lighter, and his features more Caucasian. Oftentimes, a biographical note would still talk about his mulatto father, but it would never directly say that

Figures 2.18a–d. Four contemporary illustrations of Machado de Assis's photographs from 2014, showing him as a Black man. Credits: 2.18a (top left) by Fernando Campos; 2.18b (top right) by Kácio; 2.18c (bottom left) by Fraga; 2.18d (bottom right) by CVM. *Source*: http://www.elfikurten.com.br/2014/07/machado-de-assis-o-bruxo-do-cosme-velho.html.

Machado de Assis, por Fernando Campos

Machado de Assis, por Kácio

Machado de Assis, por Fraga

Machado de Assis, ilustração CVM

Machado himself was also mulatto. That narrative and perception lasted until very recently: in the eyes of the elite and to the public, Machado de Assis had become usefully, a white writer. But in 2019, thanks to Faculdade Zumbi dos Palmares's irrevocable challenge to that historically false representation, Machado would at long last become "*Machado de Assis Real*" (as fig. 2.19 shows) the Brazilian Afro-descendant who created a national Realist literature, founded the Academia Brasileira de Letras, and became one of the country's most important authors.

Notes

1. In *Casa-Grande & Senzala* (*Masters and Slaves*), published in 1933 in Brazil, Gilberto Freyre proposes the narrative that interactions between the white colonizer and the enslaved people in Brazil resulted in a miscegenated society free of racial discrimination. Freyre's romanticizing of the country's master/slave relations would help to create the myth of Brazil as a racial democracy. During the regime of Getúlio Vargas (1937–1945), the term *democracia racial* was adopted and turned into an ideology aimed to promote a Brazilian national identity. See Freyre, *Casa-Grande & Senzala: Formação da Família Brasileira sob o Regime da Economia Patriarcal*, 48th ed. (Recife: Global Editora, 2003).

Figure 2.19. Project *Machado de Assis Real*, Faculdade Zumbi dos Palmares, 2019.

2. Freyre coined the term *lusotropicalismo* in his later works about the Portuguese presence in the tropics. He argues that in comparison to English or Spanish colonialism, Portuguese colonialism in Africa and South America was rather benign and resulted in the formation of a new race. See Freyre, *Integração Portuguesa nos Trópicos* (Lisboa: Junta de Investigações do Ultramar, 1958); *Interpretação do Brasil: Aspetos da Formação Social Brasileira como Processo de Amalgamento de Raças e Culturas* (Rio de Janeiro: José Olympio, 1947); "*O Luso e o Trópico*" (Lisboa: Comissão Executiva do V Centenário da Morte do Infante D. Henrique, 1961); and *O Mundo Que o Português Criou* (Rio de Janeiro: José Olympio, 1940).

3. FAZP is a mostly Black college named after Zumbi dos Palmares, the seventeenth-century hero in the resistance against slavery and colonialism in Brazil.

4. "*Presidente da ABL, Marco Lucchesi, recebe foto de Machado de Assis negro,*" Academia Brasileira de Letras, https://www.academia.org.br/noticias/presidente-da-abl-marco-lucchesi-recebe-foto-de-machado-de-assis-negro.html.

5. Lauro Jardim, "*Machado de Assis negro já aparece em capa de livro,*" *O Globo*, 14 May 2019, https://blogs.oglobo.globo.com/lauro-jardim/post/o-machado-de-assis-negro-ja-aparece-em-capa-de-livro.html.

6. "Born in Rio de Janeiro's hillside community of Livramento in 1839, Machado de Assis was the son of a mulatto wall painter and a washer woman from the Portuguese Azores. Orphan of both parents at a young age, Machado was raised by his stepmother, Maria Inês." Joaquim Maria Machado de Assis, *Dom Casmurro*, "*O autor e sua obra*" (São Paulo: Círculo do Livro, 1969), 249; unless stated otherwise, all translations are mine.

7. "Novelist, author of short stories, poet and literary critic. Considered one of the greatest names in Brazilian literature, Machado completed just grammar school, and was self-taught afterwards. At the age of 16, he published his first poem in the literary journal *Marmota Fluminense*." Machado de Assis, *Quincas Borba* (São Paulo: Editora Record, 2007), back cover.

8. For a contemporaneous criticism of Machado de Assis's lack of direct participation in the abolitionist movement as well as accusations of internalized racism, see José do Patrocínio in Luiz Murat, "*Machado de Assis e Joaquim Nabuco,*" *Revista da Academia Brasileira de Letras*, vol. 21, June 1926.

9. "At the request of *O Globo*, Joaquim Marçal, a photo historian and curator to Brazil's National Library's portal *Brasilianas Fotográfica*, analyzed the photograph in *Caras y Caretas*. According to him, the variations in light and shade make it difficult to evaluate the skin color (the author's right hand, for example, appears much lighter than his face). Otherwise, he defends that the facial features indicate a much darker man than the one in Pacheco's photographs: 'The major difference is in the nose: large in the former, thinner in the latter. This does not necessarily mean that there was any touch-up. Using light, anything is possible for a photographer, including making the nose thinner. The touch-up could have

happened, perhaps with a tacit agreement between Machado and Pacheco, but there is no way of knowing it for sure.' " Bolívar Torres, "*Foto inédita de Machado de Assis reaquece polêmica sobre embranquecimento do autor*," *O Globo*, 6 July 2018, https://oglobo.globo.com/cultura/livros/foto-inedita-de-machado-de-assis-reaquece-polemica-sobre-embranquecimento-do-autor-22860398.html.

10. "With Afrocentric facial features, more so than in most of his other photographs. There are no texts of records by Machado in which he says he is white. Nevertheless, because of our institutional racism, the elite has always done everything to present him as such. This debate will last many generations, and that is why photographs like this one are important to deconstruct the whitening of the author." Torres, *O Globo*, 6 July 2018, https://oglobo.globo.com/cultura/livros/foto-inedita-de-machado-de-assis-reaquece-polemica-sobre-embranquecimento-do-autor-22860398.html.

11. "Machado de Assis is today, uncontestably, the nation's number one *litterato*. . . . His biography is not yet written, and probably never will be, because on this particular aspect Machado's modesty is, I will say not only excessive and unfounded, but fierce" (*A Estação*, vol. 12, 30 June 1880, 128). *Biblioteca Nacional Digital*, https://bndigital.bn.gov.br/hemeroteca-digital/.

12. "Joaquim Maria Machado de Assis was born in Rio de Janeiro on June 21, 1839. He is the legitimate son of Francisco José de Assis and D. Maria Leopoldina Machado de Assis. Since both of them were poor, his father a salaried worker, [Machado's] studies were very irregular, and, for the most part achieved through his own unmeasurable and tenacious effort. There were no mythical fairies around his crib to award him with any transitory and by nature unfair wealth; Talent and Work, in recompense extended their hands to him and from his humble birth they carried him to life's Homeric battle and armored him as a knight, certain that his triumphs would be countless and his victories glorious." *Galeria Contemporânea do Brazil*, 1884, *Biblioteca Nacional Digital*, https://bndigital.bn.gov.br/hemeroteca-digital/.

13. See Gilberto Freyre in Afonso Henriques de Lima Barreto, *Diário Íntimo* (São Paulo: Brasiliense, 1954), preface.

14. "We have the first issue of *Galeria Contemporânea do Brazil*, a biweekly political, literary, artistic, agricultural and industrial publication by Messrs. Lombaerts and Co., the photographer, Mr. Marc Ferrez. The first issue starts with Mr. Machado de Assis, of whom we are given a photograph, a fac-simile and a biography. Mr. Artur Barreiros wrote the biography. The fac-simile is, if I am not mistaken, a chapter from *As Memórias de Braz Cubas*; and the photograph . . . [i]t is difficult to say who took the photograph. On the cover it says Marc Ferrez, photographer; inside however, below the photograph, there is an inscription on one side that says: 'Inalterable photograph, Marc Ferrez'; on the other side, it says 'Cliché, Insley Pacheco.' Well, first, the photograph is not at all inalterable; secondly, how is it that being the cliché by Mr. Insley Pacheco, the photographer is

Mr. Marc Ferrez? Let the company solve the case." *Revista Illustrada*, ed. 00389.1, 1884, 6, *Biblioteca Nacional Digital*, https://bndigital.bn.gov.br/hemeroteca-digital/.

15. *Exposição Comemorativa do Sexagésimo Aniversário do Falecimento de Joaquim Maria Machado de Assis* (Rio de Janeiro: Biblioteca Nacional, 1968). *Biblioteca Nacional Digital*. https://bndigital.bn.gov.br/acervodigital/

16. Florestan Fernandes, *The Negro in Brazilian Society*, ed. Phyllis B. Eveleth, trans. Jacqueline D. Skiles, A. Brunel, and Arthur Rothwell (New York: Columbia University Press, 1969), 145.

17. Simone da Conceição da Silva, "*O Preto e Branco do Escritor Brasileiro: Machado de Assis, no Plural ou no Singular,*" 2000, Universidade Federal Fluminense, PhD dissertation.

18. "Machado de Assis, 'Machadinho,' was one of those individuals of difficult study. His physical condition would not affect his potent and extraordinary qualities of talent, observation and erudition. Ferreira de Araújo said that Machado de Assis achieved all the positions that he did without elbowing or opposing anyone on his way up. Isn't this the complete biography of a man of character and work?" *Gazeta de Notícias*, September 30, 1908, 2, *Biblioteca Nacional Digital*, https://bndigital.bn.gov.br/hemeroteca-digital/.

19. "Mulatto, he, in fact, was, a Greek of the best times. I would not have called Machado mulatto and I think it would have hurt him more than this summary. The word is not literary, and it is derogatory. One needs only see the etymology. Machado to me was white, and I believe that he did become so; whether there was any strange blood it did not at all alter his perfect Caucasian characterization. I, at least, only saw the Greek in him." Joaquim Nabuco in Hélio de Seixas Guimarães and Ieda Lebensztain, *Escritor por Escritor: Machado de Assis segundo Seus Pares: 1908–1939* (Imprensa Oficial do Estado de São Paulo, 2020).

20. Fernandes 337–38.

21. Fernandes 347–48.

22. "Every Brazilian, even the white, blond one, carries in his soul, if not in his soul and body . . . the shadow, or at least the taint, of the indigenous and the Black." Freyre, *Casa-Grande & Senzala: Formação da Família Brasileira sob o Regime da Economia Patriarcal*, 367.

23. "And out of Brazil's problems, there was not one that worried me as much as that of miscegenation. . . . The miscegenation that was practiced here corrected a social distance that otherwise would have remained enormous between the masters' house and the tropical forest, between the masters' house and the slaves' quarters." Freyre, *Casa-grande & Senzala*, 31.

24. Afonso Henriques de Lima Barreto, *Diário Íntimo*, preface.

25. "He was short in stature, a mulatto by blood, dark skinned, and had a short beard of indistinct color, which gave him airs of an old Brazilian slave. [. . .] [A]nd he became through his own study and work, the most beautiful name, the purest and most legitimate glory of our national literature." *Gazeta de*

Notícias, 30 September 1933, *Biblioteca Nacional Digital*, https://bndigital.bn.gov. br/hemeroteca-digital/.

26. In his discussion of Vargas's nationalism and the appropriation of samba for those purposes, see Magno Bissoli Siqueira, "*Caixa Preta: Samba e Identidade Nacional na Era Vargas—Impacto do Samba na Formação da Identidade e na Sociedade Industrial 1916–1945*," 2004, Universidade de São Paulo, PhD dissertation.

27. In his book *Raízes do Brasil* (*Roots of Brazil*), published in 1936, Sérgio Buarque de Holanda proposes the concept of *homem cordial* ("the cordial man") to understand the formation of Brazil's cultural identity as socially and historically constructed from rural patriarchal relationships that extended beyond into public spheres. The "cordial man," according to Holanda, acts from the heart and develops relationships through interpersonal cordiality. See Buarque de Holanda, *Raízes do Brasil*, 26th ed. (São Paulo: Companhia das Letras, 1995).

28. Elfi Kürten Fenske, *Templo Cultural Delfos*, http://www.elfikurten.com. br/2014/07/machado-de-assis-o-bruxo-do-cosme-velho.html.

Works Cited

A Estação. Vol. 12, 30 June 1880, *Biblioteca Nacional Digital*, https://bndigital. bn.gov.br/hemeroteca-digital/.

Academia Brasileira de Letras, https://www.academia.org.br/noticias/presidente-da-abl-marco-lucchesi-recebe-foto-de-machado-de-assis-negro.

Archivo Contemporâneo Periódico Illustrado. 30 January 1873, *Biblioteca Nacional Digital*, https://bndigital.bn.gov.br/hemeroteca-digital/.

Buarque de Holanda, Sérgio. *Raízes do Brasil*. 26th ed., São Paulo: Companhia das Letras, 1995.

Certidão de Óbito de Machado de Assis. "Página do Inventário do Escritor Machado de Assis, 1908." Arquivo Nacional, https://sian.an.gov.br.

Exposição Comemorativa do Sexagésimo Aniversário do Falecimento de Joaquim Maria Machado de Assis. Rio de Janeiro: Biblioteca Nacional, 1968. *Biblioteca Nacional Digital*, https://bndigital.bn.gov.br/acervodigital/.

Fenske, Elfi Kürten. *Templo Cultural Delfos*, http://www.elfikurten.com.br/2014/07/machado-de-assis-o-bruxo-do-cosme-velho.html.

Fernandes, Florestan. *The Negro in Brazilian Society*. Edited by Phyllis B. Eveleth and translated Jacqueline D. Skiles, A. Brunel, and Arthur Rothwell, Columbia University Press, 1969.

Freyre, Gilberto. *Casa-rande & Senzala: Formação da Família Brasileira sob o Regime da Economia Patriarcal*. 48th ed., Recife: Global Editora, 2003.

———. "*O Luso e o Trópico*." Lisboa: Comissão Executiva do V Centenário da Morte do Infante D. Henrique, 1961.

———. *Integração Portuguesa nos Trópicos.* Lisboa: Junta de Investigações do Ultramar, 1958.

———. *Um brasileiro em Terras Portuguesas.* Rio de Janeiro: José Olympio, 1953.

———. *Interpretação do Brasil: Aspetos da Formação Social Brasileira como Processo de Amalgamento de Raças e Culturas.* Rio de Janeiro: José Olympio, 1947.

———. *O Mundo Que o Português Criou.* Rio de Janeiro: José Olympio, 1940.

Galeria Contemporânea do Brazil. 1884. *Biblioteca Nacional Digital,* https://bndigital. bn.gov.br/hemeroteca-digital/.

Gazeta de Notícias. 29 September 1908, *Biblioteca Nacional Digital,* https://bndigital. bn.gov.br/hemeroteca-digital/.

Gazeta de Notícias. 30 September 1908, *Biblioteca Nacional Digital,* https://bndigital. bn.gov.br/hemeroteca-digital/.

Guimarães, Hélio de Seixas, and Ieda Lebensztain. *Escritor por Escritor: Machado de Assis segundo Seus Pares: 1908–1939.* Imprensa Oficial do Estado de São Paulo, 2020.

Jardim, Lauro. "*Machado de Assis Negro Já Aparece em Capa de Livro.*" *O Globo,* 14 May 2019, https://blogs.oglobo.globo.com/lauro-jardim/post/o-machado-de-assis-negro-ja-aparece-em-capa-de-livro.html

Lima Barreto, Afonso Henriques de. *Diário Íntimo.* São Paulo: Brasiliense, 1954.

Machado de Assis Afro-descendente: Escritos de Caramujo. Edited by Eduardo de Assis Duarte, Rio de Janeiro: Pallas, 2007.

Machado de Assis, Joaquim Maria. *Dom Casmurro.* 1899. São Paulo: Edições Santo Antônio, 2018.

———. *Dom Casmurro.* 1899. São Paulo: Círculo do Livro, 1969.

———. *Quincas Borba.* 1891. São Paulo: Editora Record, 2007.

Machado de Assis: Homenagem do Centro Carioca no Centenário do Seu Nascimento. Centro Carioca, 31 June 1939, *Biblioteca Nacional Digital,* https:// bndigital.bn.gov.br/acervodigital/.

Murat, Luiz. "*Machado de Assis e Joaquim Nabuco.*" *Revista da Academia Brasileira de Letras,* vol. 21, June 1926.

Penna e Lápis. Vol. 2, 1880, *Biblioteca Nacional Digital,* https://bndigital.bn.gov. br/hemeroteca-digital/.

"*Presidente da ABL, Marco Lucchesi, Recebe Foto de Machado de Assis Negro.*" Academia Brasileira de Letras, https://www.academia.org.br/noticias/presidente-da-abl-marco-lucchesi-recebe-foto-de-machado-de-assis-negro.

Revista Illustrada, ed. 00389. 1884, *Biblioteca Nacional Digital,* https://bndigital. bn.gov.br/hemeroteca-digital/.

Rissato, Felipe Pereira. "*Iconografia fotográfica de Machado de Assis.*" *Revista Brasileira,* vol. 89, Academia Brasileira de Letras, 2016.

Silva, Simone da Conceição. "*O Preto e Branco do Escritor Brasileiro: Machado de Assis, no Plural ou no Singular.*" 2000. Universidade Federal Fluminense, PhD dissertation.

Siqueira, Magno Bissoli. "*Caixa Preta: Samba e Identidade Nacional na Era Vargas—Impacto do Samba na Formação da Identidade e na Sociedade Industrial 1916–1945.*" 2004. Universidade de São Paulo, PhD Dissertation.

Torres, Bolívar. "*Foto Inédita de Machado de Assis Reaquece Polêmica sobre Embranquecimento do Autor.*" *O Globo*, 6 July 2018, https://oglobo.globo.com/cultura/livros/foto-inedita-de-machado-de-assis-reaquece-polemica-sobre-embranquecimento-do-autor-22860398.html.

Chapter Three

"Father against Mother"

Race and/in the Reception of the Works of Machado de Assis

Paulo Dutra

The ambiguous racial identity of its protagonist grants central status to "Father against Mother"[1] within the ongoing project to reconsider the works of Machado de Assis as a man of African descent. Some readers and scholars make a claim that Neves is a white character. Others affirm that he is Black. Both claims are founded on disputable axioms and assumptions—developed in the aftermath of the rise of (and debates around) the myth of racial democracy—regarding the place of Black people and white people in nineteenth-century Brazil. Such a disparity among approaches not only represents the perplexed reception of Machado de Assis's works in general but also unveils, again, the renowned richness of his oeuvre and the prospects offered by reading race as a topic that is vital to his work.

Originally published in 1906, barely eighteen years after slavery was officially abolished, "Father against Mother" is among his most intriguing and challenging texts. One of the several works in which the most celebrated Brazilian author addressed slavery and its lingering legacies more explicitly, the short story recounts through a retrospective angle urban uses and mores that comprised racial relations under the legality of the slave regime. Readings that assign a specific race to Neves a priori find no grounding in textual evidence: such readings overlook or stretch crucial points in the text, even as they contribute to scholarship in other ways. Using Toni Morrison's ambiguous short story "Recitatif" as a starting point, I present a reading of Neves that explores and promotes the ambiguity of his racial identification, and I examine how Machado dealt with race and how literary criticism has approached his work.

Scholars who have approached the short story have either tacitly assumed (Wood, Vital, Fantini) or made considered claims (Duarte) that the main character is a white man, or they have argued that, most likely, he is not a white man (Rocha). The diametrically opposed positions are only possible because, throughout the twentieth century, the erasure of the memory of slavery and of the promotion of symbolic whitening took precedent over an examination of the complex consequences that the centuries of slavery and constant devaluation of people of African descent had in the formation and development of Brazilian society. As a result, whiteness and Blackness became categories associated with specific characteristics. In what follows, I contribute to this discussion by analyzing the representations of Cândido Neves's race and its implications. I show that none of the claims has a textual basis. I briefly discuss some of the features to which scholars resort in order to support their conclusions regarding Neves's race; in doing so, I reexamine the construction of Neves's race.

The Issue of Machado de Assis's Racial Identification

Until twenty years ago, we were accustomed to understanding Machado de Assis and his works as summarized in David Brookshaw's conclusion: Machado was "the classic example of the mulatto who devoted his life to being accepted above the comportment line, and therefore studiously avoided any reference to his origin" (180), and his works were "totally divorced from his racial origin" (179). Brookshaw comes to the conclusion that ethnicity is not central to "Father against Mother." He does so by applying the first of three literary attitudes that C. L. Inness says are left to colonized intellectuals:[2] "The writer could conceal his identity and take pride in his ability to write so skillfully that no critic could guess his origins; he could write 'as a native,' using the stock dialect forms and 'the two main stops, humour and pathos' . . . ; or he could openly protest against the economic and political oppression of his people, using the literary language and form that had long been sanctioned by the European tradition" (13–14). If one accepts Brookshaw's proposal, one might argue that Machado de Assis used all three of Innes's literary attitudes at some point in his career, except that Brookshaw's reasoning is misplaced and is based on forced analogies. Strictly speaking, none of Innes's literary attitudes fits Brazilian writers of the nineteenth century. Critics never had to guess Machado's origin, which was well known, until his image was transformed into that of a white man in the twentieth century.[3] In regard to the second attitude, Machado did not write "as a native" because he was a "native" in his society, and even if we assume that Innes refers to "native" as primitive or primitivist discourse, it would not apply to Machado. Finally, in terms of the third attitude, the oppression that people of African descent experienced was not political or economic, though these factors undoubtedly played an important role.

Brookshaw's vision is shared by Domício Proença Filho, who affirms that "Machado's literature is indifferent to the problem of blacks and black descendants, like him" (172).[4] Proença Filho maintains this position because he fails to see that not all the main characters in Machado de Assis are necessarily white and also because, according to him, Machado never focuses on the ethnic question even when the text, such as "Father against Mother," explicitly involves slaves (172). However, the ambiguity of Neves's racial identity, unseen by Proença Filho, negates the possibility that the ethnic question would not be a central topic in the short story. Proença Filho tacitly endorses Brookshaw's conclusion.

Today, scholarship challenges the allegation that slavery[5] and the lives of people of African descent are absent in Machado de Assis; this newer scholarship pierces the mindset of mainstream approaches that have rendered racial issues in Machado's work invisible. Although most scholars agree and accurately point out that "Father against Mother" is an attack on what was an ongoing process to erase the memory of slavery, scholars who scrutinize race and slavery in Machado de Assis and in his works diverge in their consideration of this short story. The discrepancy lies in the racial identification of the main character. The question is not simply to determine whether Neves is a white man, but rather to examine what the assumptions regarding his race reveal about twentieth-century Brazilian society, the reception of Machado's work, and Machado's keen eye to nineteenth-century Brazilian society's make-up and customs.

The White Candinho

Although it is a quixotic task to determine when the convention of reading Neves as a white man started, several moments in the criticism are easily spotted, after which such a habit became a scholarly tradition. On the one hand, Raymundo Faoro (1976)[6] does not mention race or skin color but only the fact that Arminda is enslaved and Neves is not (320–25). Carmelo Virgillo's commentary (1966) contrasts the life of a "little mulatto" to that of Candinho's offspring, suggesting an assumption of a white Neves (783). On the other hand, Alfredo Bosi (1982) straightforwardly asserts that "Cândido Neves, poor but very white even in his name, marries Clara and, in order to survive, 'yields to poverty' by becoming a captor of blacks, who leads them back for a good reward" (455). More recently, Eduardo de Assis Duarte (2007) has made a similar assertion.

Duarte is probably one of the first scholars to challenge more sharply the criticism that denounces Machado for his alleged lack of concern for slavery and his personal dissociation with his mixed-race origin. Although Duarte's approach to "Father against Mother" presents the same strong argument in favor of reclaiming Machado's place within Afro-Brazilian literary production, Duarte's interpretation of the main character relies on rather questionable elements. Commenting on the characters' names, Duarte argues that they "indicate the insertion of the characters into a status quo marked by the slaveowner's hegemonic discourse" (261). Oddly, Duarte turns a blind eye to the narrator's own comments on the main characters' names–"Even their bright, snow-white names—Clara, Neves, Cândido—were the subject of jokes" (844). Like Bosi, although for different reasons, Duarte unequivocally claims that "Cândido Neves assumes the figure of the white man, constituted by a manner of thought that demeans and devalues work" (261). Duarte is seconded by Leda Marana Bim (2010), who also assumes that Cândido "is the symbol of the poor white man, reduced to an insensitive being, one who needed the suffering of black people in order to provide for his family" (122).

Marli Fantini's (2011) approach to "Father against Mother" resembles Duarte's both in her presentation of Machado as a writer concerned with slavery and the living conditions that people of African descent faced, and in her interpretation of Neves as a white man. Fantini develops her reasoning by intensifying the dichotomy between a cruel social system on the one hand and those who are butchered by "white masters" on the other. She reserves for the narrator and for Neves a very specific position because of the "intestinal cruelty" she attributes to them (155–56). For Fantini, though both Arminda and Neves navigate the same marginalized space, the crucial difference in their skin color is what gives the latter alternatives. Therefore, like Bosi, Fantini reads Neves literally as a cruel, poor white man.

Selma Vital (2012) seems to agree with Fantini regarding the contrasting conditions of Neves and Arminda: "although his misery is comparable to that of slaves, Candinho has guaranteed his superiority because he is a white man, and therefore, 'free' " (109). Vital, who makes the timely claim that not all of Machado's characters should be read as white, nonetheless promptly assumes that Candinho and Clara are, based solely on their names, "as if they needed to claim their whiteness to differentiate them from the mass of slaves in the city" (110). When it comes to the landlord, Vital exercises more caution than she does in Neves's case; she notices that the narrator does not provide a physical description of him but mentions that "to look at him, you would never think he was a landlord" (847). This leads Vital to speculate on his race, which she does not consider doing for Neves.

Sidney Chalhoub (2016) also reads Neves as a white man because he believes that his and Clara's names "highlight their whiteness to the point of caricature" (66). In a previous essay (2018), I acknowledge that Flynn et al. accurately remind us that all the signs in the narrative "far from prov[e] that the characters are white" (17); however, I deliberately choose to read Neves as a white man, explaining that such a choice is not based on the historical whitening of Machado and his work. Rather, I argue, the grounds for reading Neves as a white man lie "in a comparison of the role Machado assigned to male characters in the female character's denouement in 'Pai contra mãe,' 'O caso da vara,' and 'Noite de almirante' " (127). Offering no explanation for his remarks, Marcus Wood (2019) states directly that the central character is "a thirty-year-old poor white man" (93); so, too, do Debora Gutierrez and Vitor Cei (2020) state twice without evidence that the main character is a white man (20–22). In sum, scholars who read Neves a priori as a white man mainly base their conclusions on either an allegedly inherent or socially acquired wickedness of white men or the names Machado decided to give his character.[7]

The "Nonwhite" Candinho

Categorically rejecting the possibility of a white Neves, Fernando Souza de Rocha sees "Father against Mother" as a story that portrays a community of free, freed, and enslaved Africans and people of African descent (91).

Rocha reiterates this firm posture more explicitly when he describes his reasoning on the issue of Candido's race: "Although Assis's text never explicitly states Candinho's race, it is suggested that both Candinho and his wife Clara are not white. Pointing out the couple's propensity to laughter, the narrator says that 'the newlyweds laughed at everything' and 'even their names were the objects of puns: Clara (bright), Neves (snow), Candido (white) (104)'. Their names were laughable precisely because they were paradoxical given the true color of their complexions" (97). There are two important conclusions to be drawn from Rocha's interpretation. The first is that he acknowledges that Machado never makes Neves's race explicit, which is a fact. The second is that after building his argument around the notion of a micro-community of Africans and Afro-descendants, Rocha relies on the question of their names in order to support the claim that Candido is not white. Let us not forget that several scholars also refer to their names in order to affirm that he is a white man. Another point to consider is that usually scholars assume that Candido and Clara share the same racial identification. Nevertheless, as I have shown elsewhere ("Interracial Love"), Machado did depict interracial couples; hence, another layer of irony and ambiguity surrounds their names and their laughter at these names: they themselves may be an interracial couple. The only conclusion that can safely be reached at this point regarding the names is that the narrator's reference to them only increases the ambiguity of the characters' racial identification.

Assuming that Neves is a Capitão do Mato, Giulia Ricco states, without providing a source, that Capitães do Mato were former slaves and poor whites (240). Debret and Rugendas have described slave catchers as being Black. However, Silvia Lara's chapter on Capitães do Mato leaves a small window for other possibilities. In Table 6, Lara provides the official register of the Jail of the Village of São Salvador (318). Here, there is a list of the kind of runaways taken to this facility and the identity of those who caught them. Nineteen runaways were caught by Capitães do Mato, five by auxiliary soldiers, sixteen by probational officers, three by slaves, none by foremen/overseers (feitores), one by owners, two by Indians, eight by "unknown," and, most interestingly, nineteen (the same number of those caught by Capitães do Mato) by a category listed as outros ("others," or none of the above). The categories of "unknown" and "other" are both vague. "Unknown" could mean that the person who arrested the runaway was simply not registered in the books, and "other" most likely means that at least nineteen runaways were not caught by Capitães do Mato, police, probational officers, owners, slaves, overseers, or Indians.[8] Although we cannot unquestionably affirm that every slave was promptly perceived as Black, aside from the Indians, that is the only racial category explicitly given, since even slave owners were sometimes freed blacks, as Prudêncio, Brás Cubas's former houseboy, attests. As the table shows, not every slave catcher was indeed African or of African descendant. Moreover, we cannot affirm that Candinho was indeed African or of African descent, as Rocha wants to believe, because not every slave catcher was a Capitão do Mato. More importantly and more explicitly, let us not forget either that Machado de Assis never refers to Neves as Capitão do Mato. It is worth noting that, as Lara pointed out, Capitão do Mato was a documented and government-regulated occupation; therefore, Neves cannot be a Capitão do Mato, and the possibility of his belonging to one of the other categories ("other," "unknown," or even Indian) cannot be promptly dismissed.

The Ambiguous Candinho

Alex Flynn, Elena Calvo-González, and Marcelo Mendes de Souza ("Whiter Shades of Pale") may be the first scholars to notice the impossibility of assigning a race to the characters and to question the widely accepted assumption of a white Candinho. They examine the short story in order to demonstrate the naturalization of whiteness, which, in the twentieth century, became a fixed category with assumed specific features. As for the device with which Machado addresses race, their argument goes as follows: "Machado employs a playful irony, inviting the reader to "color in" the characters, something he never explicitly does himself. Machado's text is not prescriptive; the author's intention is rather to invite the reader into what amounts to a common misreading and thereby demonstrate that the solidity of whiteness, which many take for granted, is in fact negotiable and socially constructed" (5).

Unquestionably, Machado did not "color in" the characters. However, the reason that Flynn et al. propose for why he did not seems anachronistic: it disregards the fact that the solidity of whiteness as a category may be a twentieth-century construction that did not quite exist in the time the plot of the tale is set or had not yet became fixed when Machado was writing.[9] This construction has become fixed in contemporary Brazil, as the readings of a white Candinho quickly demonstrate. Christopher T. Lewis (98) interprets the abovementioned passage quoted from Flynn et al. as a suggestion that the difference between Neves and Arminda is legal and not racial. Other commentators such as Rocha, Faoro, and Mattos have called attention to the nineteenth-century categories of free and slave as a clear-cut opposition. Whiteness as a fixed idea seems to be posterior to the time that the plot of the narrative is set, and thus it is hard to agree with Flynn et al. that Machado would have invited "the reader into what amounts to a common misreading": what led readers to misread Neves and Clara as white is the twentieth-century process of symbolic whitening and the myth of racial democracy.

Although he recognizes that Candinho's racial ambiguity is due to the fact that Machado never made the characters' race explicit, Lewis explains why Machado constructed his characters' race ambiguously by making recourse to Brookshaw's questionable interpretation of Machado's personality and literary attitude, mentioned above. Flynn et al., on the contrary, trust the notion of the unreliable Machadian narrator and argue that the ambiguity of the characters' race is achieved through vague narration. Without dismissing such an approach, I want to argue that the moments when the narration is ambiguous are not enough to support the claim of it being the main source of Neves's racial ambiguity; its combination with the codes that Machado scattered in the text should demonstrate a more complete picture. Lewis points out one of these codes when he reminds us that Clara is a seamstress, which was an occupation that would place her in "social and racial categories not very far removed from slavery" (99). Lewis, however, does not elaborate on the reason why Machado chose to make Clara a seamstress. As a consequence, the truly central question—the real (even if unattainable) reason why Candinho's and Clara's race is not explicitly given—remains unanswered. In what follows, I provide possible answers for such a crucial question.

Machado's Récitatif

The reactions that "Father against Mother" elicited in scholars who chose to assign a race to the characters is not a unique phenomenon. In 1983, award-winning author Toni Morrison published a short story that generated similar reactions from readers.[10] "Recitatif" is the story of Roberta Fisk and Twila, who, following their first encounter in an orphanage, keep running into one another throughout their lives. As Elizabeth Abel has pointed out "this is a story about a black woman and a white woman;

but which is which?" (471). From the beginning, the narrator states that one girl is white and the other is Black, but she (Twila is the narrator) never states who is the white girl and who is the Black girl. The central question of racial identity in the short story is systematically intensified because of "the racial ambiguity so deftly installed at the narrative's origin through codes that function symmetrically for black women and for white women" (471).

According to Morrison, the short story is intentionally crafted to make it impossible for the reader to racially identify Twila or Roberta because " 'Recitatif' was an experiment in the removal of all racial codes from a narrative about two characters of different races for whom racial identity is crucial" (*Playing in the Dark* xi). In "Father against Mother," because of the whitening process that both he and Brazilian society as a whole underwent in the twentieth century, it is impossible to ascertain whether Machado intentionally resorted to the same strategy. There are at least three possibilities regarding Candinho's case: (a) Machado de Assis simply created a character and a situation that for his contemporary readers would have been immediately explicit, and which only became ambiguous due to the later historical whitening process; (b) Machado created a character and a situation in which race was unimportant; or (c) just like Morrison, Machado created the ambiguity with intention. Bearing in mind Machado's craftsmanship and keen eye to his society, the latter is not only more appealing, but it is also the most likely of the possibilities.

In "Recitatif," the racial ambiguity only exists because Morrison plays with stereotypes, which Abel calls codes "that function symmetrically for black women and for white women" (471). For example, at the beginning of the story, Twila remembers a conversation with her mother on one of the occasions she came to visit her at the shelter: "Mary, that's my mother, she was right . . . she said that they never washed their hair and they smelled funny. Roberta sure did. Smell funny" (243). Another good example of how Morrison played with stereotypes relates to alimentary habits: "I sneaked a look at Roberta. Her mother had brought chicken legs and ham sandwiches and oranges and a whole box of chocolate-covered grahams. . . . The wrong food is always with the wrong people. . . . Roberta just let those chicken legs sit there" (248). It goes without saying that in American culture, often derogatively, the consumption of chicken is associated with African Americans. Such use of stereotypes intensifies throughout the narrative. They range from olfactory sensations to culturally embedded practices and social context and position.

I will not list every occurrence of a code that can be racialized, but it is important to point out two more. At one point in their lives, Twila and Roberta meet in a Howard Johnson's restaurant, a restaurant chain involved in debates over segregation and desegregation; there, Twila waits tables and Roberta is having dinner with friends while talking about Jimmy Hendrix. Later in their lives, they meet again on the opposite sides of demonstrations for and against bussing, which was aimed at desegregating schools. In short, a stereotypical background, which can be racialized, is present every time they meet, where several codes are employed that can function for both Black women and white women.

In order to analyze how Machado scatters codes throughout "Father against Mother," I undertake a close reading in which I highlight and examine these codes. Perhaps the best way to start is with the characters' names, as referred to previously. Abel reminds us that Twila's and Roberta's names are also a topic for commentary. The former can be easily associated with the white dancer Twila Tharp, while the latter's last name, Fisk, is the name of one of the most renowned Black universities in the United States (Abel 476). Morrison's narrator, Twila, never comments on the characters' names; however, Machado's does make an observation on how his characters react to their names: "Joy was common to all three. The couple would laugh at anything. Even their names—Clara, Neves, Cândido—were the subject of puns" (13, my translation). Remarkably, this passage has been read as an indicator of their whiteness, but it has also been read as an indicator of their Blackness. A literal reading claims that Machado clearly identified their race by naming them in such a manner, while a reading that takes into account the possibility of irony would show that they are not white because they laugh at their own names, which contrast with their skin color. Both readings are possible, but there is a deeper level of irony that is usually overlooked. There is a third element that complicates the matter: "Aunt Monica."

There is no consensus on the meaning and origin of the name Monica. The *Dicionário de nomes próprios* dismisses the Latin meaning of the name as "advisor" and favors the Greek etymology that would refer to "one," "alone/lonely," and "widow"; the *Dicionário* provides no further explanation. The *Dicionário etimológico Nova Fronteira* provides the medieval Latin meaning or "solitária" (lonely), related to the word "monja" (nun). In the *Dicionário de sinônimos*, Antenor Nascentes refers to both the Greek and the Latin meanings, including "advisor." Although Aunt Monica carries the name of the Catholic Saint known as the patron saint of married women, she is not married. Wilberth Salgueiro, who has explored naming in Machado, has shown how Machado would diligently and ironically play with such a resource as onomastics; therefore, all the nuances of the name Monica must be included in the discussion.

As the third member of Cândido and Clara's household, Aunt Monica's equally ambiguous racial identification—like Maggie's in "Recitatif"[11]—serves as a counterpoint. She is a character who does not always fulfill her own onomastic possibilities, so why should readers assume that Neves and Clara would? In spite of the more immediate association with the Latin and Greek meanings, Monica is a name that may have come from Numidia, North Africa, where Saint Monica was born. She may bear the name of the saint of African origin; therefore, Machado brings together elements of the Western tradition with a not-so-clear mention to Africa. Although it is usually overlooked, it is a fact that Machado manages to allude to Africa—directly or indirectly—quite often. Ironically, Aunt Monica could be a white woman who bears the name of a saint born in Africa, or, of course, not a white woman at all. It is worth noting that the character is not named just Monica, but Aunt Monica because the addition of such an epithet furthers the ambiguity of the character. In Brazil, aunt can mean several different things, ranging from an actual aunt to any middle-aged woman who never married, an adult who is friends with the family, just someone whose name is unknown, or even a "procurer." Therefore, in addition to furthering the possibilities for ambiguities, even racial ones, the mysterious Aunt Monica serves as a counterpoint that should also be considered in the attempts at interpreting Neves's and Clara's names as fixed racial markers. Rocha is not far from the truth when he affirms that "it is *suggested* that both Candinho and his wife Clara are not white" (emphasis added): that is how the issue of their names should be read, as a suggestion and not as proof. The character's names increase the ambiguity rather than providing "clarification."

I mentioned Twila's contempt in relation to Roberta leaving food untouched. In "Father against Mother," food also invites speculation about racial identity. Neves reminds Aunt Monica that in spite of their dreary situation, they never wanted for bacalhau (salted codfish). Providing no source for his remarks, Marcus Wood (4) mentions that salted codfish was a type of food associated with Afro-Brazilians. I have found no evidence to support such a claim. Thaina Karls (14) points out that at least one nineteenth-century restaurant (Restaurante Ypiranga) had bacalhau on the menu.[12] The famous nineteenth-century recipe book *Cozinheiro imperial* (*Imperial Cook*) lists several recipes for bacalhau. The website www.bacalhau.com.br claims that bacalhau indeed used to be cheap and was often present in Brazilians' everyday meals until the first half of the twentieth century. The website also mentions a newspaper note that proclaims that Machado de Assis habitually gathered with friends on Sundays at downtown Rio de Janeiro's restaurants in order to enjoy a conversation over a meal of bacalhau. Despite the fact that today salted codfish is not an inexpensive means of nutrition and it is more readily found in the dietary choices of the affluent in Brazil, it seems that in the nineteenth century bacalhau was a popular dish not restricted to enslaved people. The only food Machado chooses to associate with his characters' diet does not make Neves's racial identification less ambiguous, but it does tempt the reader to invest energy in making assumptions.[13]

Another sign that has led readers to claim Neves's whiteness is an alleged intrinsic evilness of white people that is inscribed to him. Once again, such an assertion finds no grounds in the text. It is understandable that readers tend to associate wickedness with the slave catcher because the story's denouement displays a horrifying predicament for Arminda. Nevertheless, the way the narrator constructs Neves's personality throughout the tale and the way the narrator constructs the practice of slave catching as a socially accepted and even necessary custom—"Human and social order cannot always be achieved without the grotesque or, indeed, without occasional acts of cruelty" (841)—should suffice to prevent this single-minded conclusion. The short story does not dwell on an evil versus good dichotomy. Commenting on mild means of punishment unleashed upon enslaved people for having escaped, the narrator mentions that one of the reasons for not resorting to violence was that "the owner wasn't necessarily a bad man" (842). Reading the short story from an ahistorical perspective leads to approaches that overlook the actual social organization surrounding slavery and its place in society at the time. As the narrator states, after almost casually introducing the disturbing instruments of torture that would be on display at shop entrances, "pursuing fugitive slaves was one of the trades of the time. It might not have been a very noble profession, but since it involved helping the forces who defend the law and private property, it had a different sort of nobility" (842). Slave catching was perfectly legal; thus, blaming Candinho for a societal organization he was born into does not seem to be an optimal way of interpreting what Machado de Assis was doing. Furthermore, "no one took up that trade in the pursuit of entertainment or education" (842), so the character is literally doing society's "dirty work."

Affirming Neves's cruelty based on the last lines[14] of the short story, when that emphatical demeanor that the narrator steadily helps to build erodes completely, is also a misconception. As mentioned above, Bim interprets Neves at the end as "reduced to an insensible being, who needed black people's suffering in order to provide for his family" (122). Bim seems to overlook the narrator's account of how Neves sheds genuine tears once reunited with his own son and family, and his account of Neves' personality. According to the narrator, Neves had but one grave fault: "an inability to hold down any job or trade" (842). Clara's friends "did not deny that her husband was a decent enough fellow . . . that he had certain other virtues" (843). When pushed by Aunt Monica, "he went to see the aunt, not in anger, but nonetheless rather *less meekly than usual*" (845, emphasis added). We need to remember that the narrator states that the story is about one episode of an escape in which Neves is somehow caught up: "Cândido Neves . . . is the person to whom *the story of an escape* is linked" (12, my translation, emphasis added). Arminda's story is never told: only the terrible fragment when the miscarriage occurs is presented to the reader. The plot gradually builds the situation of despair on the part of Candinho, while Arminda only shows up at the end with no other background than the "runaway" mark.

The enslaved woman Arminda is reduced to a synecdoche while Neves is a more complex character. The irony of the narrator's choice of words ("the story of an escape," not of a runaway/a person) may go unnoticed because the escape itself is never narrated. With this phrase, the narrator seems to point in one direction but then moves in another and becomes lost in Neves's heartbreaking story, forgetting to tell the story of the escape. When it comes to Arminda, what he tells is not the escape but, ironically, only the catching. Neves's ambiguous nature should suffice to demonstrate that he is not a synecdoche of either white or Black men, while Arminda, whose story is lacking, does function as a representative of the obliterated humanity of enslaved people, which the narrator starts building at the beginning of the short story.

Neves is definitely depicted as a "decent enough fellow" who is caught up in a dreadful personal situation until he becomes the agent of even more dreadful suffering. Commenting on Aunt Monica's advice that Candinho should give up his child, the narrator seems to pity him as he faces this terrible dilemma: "a piece of advice I find painful even to write down, although not as painful as it was for Candinho to hear" (846). Arminda, on the other hand, does lose her child, through a miscarriage: this loss is due to the struggle and fear of her owner's punishment, which she says will be violent. Neves did play an active role in Arminda's terrible fate, but those who condemn him or conclude that he can only be an insensible, cruel, poor white man ignore the social context in which "[a]nyone passing by or standing in a shop doorway would have realized what was going on and would, *naturally*, have done nothing to help" (850, emphasis added). Anyone in this case really means anyone, Black or white, free or enslaved. Therefore, the rather disturbing reading of an intrinsic and inexorable wickedness of white men has no grounds in the text because Neves is neither evil nor white; he is, fascinatingly (and "Morrisonly"), ambiguous.

There are many other signs or codes that can be examined but suffice it for now to introduce only one more. The last potential racial code I address here, which has been interpreted as such, is the characterization of Neves as someone unable to keep a steady job. Duarte makes the claim that Neves represents a white man who is "constituted by the thought that demeans and devalues work" (261). Flynn et al. remind us that "Cândido's indolence, debts, and inability to hold down employment therefore identify him squarely with the prejudices regarding slaves, freed slaves, and indigenous peoples that the contemporary readership would have held" (14). To agree with Duarte would mean to accept that Neves, as an individual, devalues work, rather than see him as defying a social organization that leads people to settle for underpaid and underappreciated jobs. Let us not forget that, according to the narrator, slave catching only became an unlucrative activity for Neves when competition arose; in other words, the "trade" attracted many others who may have been in a similar position in society, as the chart from Lara's chapter shows.

To agree, on the contrary, with Flynn et al., which is more defensible, would mean to acknowledge Machado's powerful technique of crafting irony. On the one hand, a white Candinho—who bears traits that could have been perceived by contemporary readers as negative and associated to Black people—could function as a commentary on the prejudices regarding work relations already being inscribed upon people of African descent. On the other hand, a Black Candinho who ostensibly shows negative traits, while at the same time is a "decent enough fellow" and is forced to consider abandoning his child, would function as a fierce commentary on the actual lack of opportunities for people of African descent outside more affluent circles. None of these possibilities can be discarded. Neither can they be fully embraced. Not being able or willing to hold employment is not a fixed characteristic of either white or Black people, even for contemporary readers. Black and white are, indeed, perceived differently, but this difference is because a white man will be seen as many things (socially unfit, a visionary, a rebel, etc.) but never as a lazy person, while a Black man will be perceived simply as lazy. The issue furthers the ambiguity of both Cândido and of Machado's text. Although there is no way to affirm Neves's race based on his inability to hold a steady job, the societal development does allow for racialized readings. Machado's sharp eye to his ambiguous and mixed-race society is once more revealed.

Conclusion

"Father against Mother" allows for different readings. In addition, "by replacing the conventional signifiers of racial difference . . . with radically relativistic ones and by substituting for the racialized body a series of disaggregated cultural parts" (Abel 471–72), the short story does indeed render "race a contested terrain variously mapped from diverse positions in the social landscape" (Abel 471–72). Although Bosi could not see through his white-tinted glasses or exercise his own theoretical propositions about Machado's works, he is entirely right in stating that Machado's work, "as a whole, contains the ambiguity of seeing the world now on one side and now on the other; and even more, to see one side through the other" (450). That is why scholars might read Cândido as a white man or as a Black man without fully invalidating their conclusions; after all, Neves can only be a nineteenth-century Brazilian male within the racial parameters such a society offered to Machado de Assis. Both readings are possible: one does not necessarily annul the other. More importantly, these two readings reveal the way we accustom ourselves to understanding the late nineteenth century. Bearing in mind Bosi's aforementioned assessment relentlessly would enable us to reconstruct a different understanding of both Machado's texts and the nineteenth century he depicted.

Notes

1. Because I make reference to both a translation of the short story and to the original, I will indicate when the translation is mine.

2. Brookshaw also trusts Joaquim Nabuco's opinion expressed in his famous letter to José Veríssimo: "Our poor friend was so sensitive that he would have preferred anonymity to fame at the expense of having his origins made the subject of public inquiry." Letter from Nabuco to José Veríssimo on the death of Machado, published in *Revista da Academia Brasileira de Letras*, vol. 22, no. 115, July 1931, 387.

3. Brazilian bank Caixa Econômica Federal's 2011 TV commercial is the most striking example. In addition, the same letter Nabuco wrote complaining that the word "mulato" had been employed to refer to Machado de Assis attests that his origins were well known.

4. All the translations of scholarly worked cited in this chapter are my responsibility.

5. Such allegations remain present as Krista Brune (2020, 184) tangential commentary on Machado de Assis attests: "Machado, a self-taught bureaucrat, addressed slavery only briefly in his work." Brune trusts G. Reginald Daniel's conclusion from his well-documented 2012 book *Machado de Assis: Multiracial Identity and the Brazilian Novelist*, which, according to her, "foregrounds his identity as both black and white, yet neither, as key to his aesthetics sensibilities and sociopolitical affinities" (227). However, the conceptualization of a multiracial identity in the context of Brazilian nineteenth-century society seems to point to a precursory notion of the myth of the racial democracy. Furthermore, as the newly found pictures of him testify, Machado de Assis was unmistakably a Black man.

6. In this section, I provide the dates in order to better illustrate a chronology.

7. As demonstrated above, the reading of Candinho as a white man ranges from 1982 to 2020.

8. The person labeled "other" could also have lied or asked to not have their names on record. However, it would make more sense to have such a person entered under the category of "unknown."

9. The chronology of the readings of a white Candinho corroborates this idea, and so does Flynn's interpretation of Jerry Dávila's proposition: "Dávila (2003) describes how from the turn of the nineteenth century, state actors in Brazil implemented policies that had at their heart a belief in whiteness as a naturalized state identified with strength, health, and virtue. This racial category was gradually shaped in opposition to 'blackness,' a status that carried an explicit cargo of laziness, primitive and childlike nature, and an inherently antimodern gaze to the past" (4).

10. According to Elizabeth Abel: "I was introduced to 'Recitatif' by a black feminist critic, Lula Fragd. Lula was certain that Twyla was black; I was equally convinced that she was white; most of the readers we summoned to resolve the dispute divided similarly along racial lines" (471).

11. At the end of the short story Twila and Roberta argue over Maggie's racial identification.

12. Karls speculates on the matter of Portuguese cuisine: "It is also a possibility to assume that Portuguese cuisine was the daily food of the less wealthy population in the city and was part of more popular establishments. However, we can only dwell in the field of assumptions for these issues" (13, my translation).

13. I mention the issue of bacalhau because a former student—probably unaware of the fact that bacalhau used to be an inexpensive dish—made the claim that Neves must be white because he eats bacalhau. This, together with Wood's mention of exactly the opposite, represents an ambiguity that may have not existed in the text for Machado's contemporaries, who may have immediately known whether the consumption of salted codfish could work as a racialized code. Since the narrators calls attention to instruments of torture in the opening lines of the short story, it is worth mentioning that bacalhau is also a common nickname for the azorrague (a kind of whip), which is an instrument of torture used on enslaved people in Brazil.

14. "Kissing his son and shedding genuine tears, Cândido Neves, on the other hand, blessed the fugitive and gave barely a thought to her dead child. 'Not all children make it,' his heart told him" (851).

Works Cited

Abel, Elizabeth. "Black Writing, White Reading: Race and the Politics of Feminist Interpretation." *Critical Inquiry*, vol. 19, no. 3, 1993, 470–98.

Bim, Leda Marana. "Amor e morte: uma comparação dos contos 'Pai contra mãe' e 'Mariana.'" *Machado de Assis e a escravidão*, edited by por Gustavo Bernardo et al., Annablume, 2010, 115–24.

Bosi, Alfredo. "A máscara e a fenda." *Machado de Assis*, edited by Alfredo Bosi et al., Editora Atica, 1982, 437–57.

Brookshaw, David. *Race and Color in Brazilian Literature*. The Scarecrow Press, 1986.

Brune, Krista. *Creative Transformations: Travels and Translations of Brazil in the Americas*. SUNY Press, 2020.

Chalhoub, Sidney. "The Legacy of Slavery: Tales of Gender and Racial Violence in Machado de Assis." *Emerging Dialogues on Machado de Assis*, edited by Lamonte Aidoo et al., Palgrave, 2016, 55–69.

Cunha, Geraldo Antônio da. *Dicionário etimológico Nova Fronteira*. 2nd ed., Editora Nova Fronteira, 1986.

Daniel, G. Reginald. *Machado de Assis: Multiracial Identity and the Brazilian Novelist*. Pennsylvania State University University Press, 2012.

Dicionário de nomes próprios, www.dicionariodenomesproprios.com.br.

Duarte, Eduardo de Assis. *Machado de Assis afro-descendente: escritos de caramujo (antologia)*. Pallas/Crisálida, 2007.

Dutra, Paulo. " 'Noite de almirante': Interracial Love in Machado de Assis's Nineteenth Century." *Aletria*, vol. 28, no. 4, 2018, 119–36.

Fantini, Marli. "Machado de Assis." *Literatura e afrodescendência no Brasil: Antologia crítica*, edited by Eduardo de Assis Duarte, Editora UFMG, 2011, 143–71.

Faoro, Raymundo. *Machado de Assis: a pirâmide e o trapézio*. 2nd ed., Companhia Editora Nacional, 1976.

Flynn, Alex, et al. "Whiter Shades of Pale: 'Coloring in' Machado de Assis and Race in Contemporary Brazil." *Latin American Research Review*, vol. 48, no 3, 2013, 3–24.

Gutierrez, Debora Priscila Arrevalo, and Vitor Cei. "A reificação do negro em Machado de Assis e Rubem Fonseca: estudo comparado dos contos 'Pai contra mãe' e 'Placebo.' " *Revista Lampejo*, vol. 8, no. 2, 2020, 19–32.

Innes, C. L. "Through the Looking Glass: African and Irish Nationalist Writing." *African Literature Today*, vol. 9, 1978, 10–24.

Jull Costa, Margaret, and Robin Patterson, trans. *The Collected Stories of Machado de Assis*. Liveright, 2018.

Karls, Thaina. "O Rio de Janeiro à mesa: A alimentação nos restaurantes e confeitarias do século XIX (1854–1890)." *Revista de História (São Paulo)*, no. 178, Sept. 2019, 1–28, https://doi.org/10.11606/issn.2316-9141.rh.2019.142528.

Lara, Silvia Hunold. *Campos da violência: Escravos e senhores na Capitania do Rio de Janeiro 1750–1808*. Paz e Terra, 1988.

Lewis, Christopher T. "To Beat or to Abet in Machado de Assis's 'Pai Contra Mãe': The Text in Superposition." *Machado de Assis em Linha*, vol. 11, no. 24, Aug. 2018, 94–115, https://doi.org/10.1590/1983-6821201811247

Machado de Assis, Joaquim Mari. "Pai contra mãe." *Machado de Assis: contos e crônicas*, Malê, 2019, 11–22.

Mattos, Hebe Maria. *Escravidão e cidadania no Brasil monárquico*. 2nd ed., Jorge Zahar, 1999.

Morrison, Toni. *Playing in the Dark: Whiteness and the Literary Imagination*. Harvard University Press, 1992.

———. "Recitatif." *Confirmation*, edited by Amiri Baraka and Amina Baraka, William Morrow and C, 1983, 323–62.

Nascentes, Antenor. *Dicionário de sinônimos*. 3rd ed., Editora Nova Fronteira, 1981.

Proença Filho, Domício. "A trajetória do negro na literatura brasileira." *Estudos Avançados*, vol. 18, no. 50, 2004, 161–93.

R.CM. et al. *Cozinheiro imperial ou nova arte do cozinheiro e do copeiro*. 10th ed., Laemmert & C, 1887.

Ricco, Giulia. "Framing Violence: Narrator and Reader in 'Pai contra mãe.' " *Emerging Dialogues on Machado de Assis*, edited by Lamonte Aidoo et al., Palgrave, 2016, 239–49.

Rocha, Fernando Souza de. 2016. " 'Father versus Mother': Slavery and Its Appa-ratuses." *Emerging Dialogues on Machado de Assis*, edited by Lamonte Aidoo et al., Palgrave, 2016, 91–103.

Salgueiro, Wilberth. "Nomes não mentem (quase nunca): 'Noite de almirante,' de Machado de Assis, à luz da onomástica." *Prosa sobre prosa: Machado de Assis, Guimarães Rosa, Reinaldo Santos Neves e outras ficções*, edited by Wilberth Salgueiro, EDUFES, 2013, 31–42.

Virgillo, Carmelo. "Love and the 'Causa Secreta' in the Tales of Machado de Assis." *Hispania*, vol. 49, no. 4, Dec. 1966, 778–86.

Vital, Selma. *Quase brancos, quase pretos: Representação étnico-racial no conto machadiano*. Intermeios, 2012.

Wood, Marcus. *The Black Butterfly: Brazilian Slavery and the Literary Imagination*. West Virginia University Press, 2019.

Chapter Four

Raimundo the Obscure

Enslavement, Abolition, and the Problematics of
"Uncle Tom" Agency in Machado's *Iaiá Garcia*

Niyi Afolabi

Machado de Assis Was of African Descent?

In an era of strategic political campaigns like "Black Lives Matter"[1]—be it in
the context of now recurrent police brutalities that flash through breaking
news reporting, arrogant racism of right-wing militia groups, and sheer
"disposability" of Black lives when faced with the spur-of-the-moment
judgment call (or lack of it) by some conscienceless police officers who
are quick to discharge a lethal weapon on Black and Brown bodies—the
revisionist mission of the edited volume to which I have been called to
contribute is highly timely. The call to action in reexamining Machado de
Assis in the twenty-first century, as a preeminent Brazilian Black writer of
the nineteenth century, comes with some trepidation, anguish, an enduring
sense of betrayal, and an inner burden of critical responsibility. A part of
me went through a series of painful emotions: (1) Was Machado indeed a
Black writer who was masked as a white or mestizo writer for many generations? (2) To what do we attribute this egregious disservice to humanity
and gross miscarriage of justice (other than racism in a whitening social
disposition of the era of enslavement) for both Machado and his "gullible"

readers? (3) What will be the major impact of this revisionist project beyond publishing another book on Machado, who is likely to remain obscure despite the celebration of his Black ingenuity and identity two centuries after he lived? (4) As an African who has been in the field for about three decades, and yet whose critical approach has been to theorize the ambiguity of purpose in Machado's works, what does this rediscovery mean for the angered self, our collective jeopardized curriculum due to this perplexing whitening of Machado, and the fate of the generation after us regarding how Machado is understood, reengaged, and analyzed?[2] (5) Regardless of the rippling effects of such a laudable project, the damage has been done already and the Caixa Econômica's rendition of Machado as a white man in the twenty-first century strikes a provocative chord on the long road still ahead in terms of necessary corrective action on the mind, the spirit, and the soul of Machado's critical reception.[3]

Against the foregoing state of mind, I consider this essay more as a critical reflection on the possibilities and impacts of being "bamboozled"[4] for many decades as an African critic who always thought Machado was at least a biracial and, possibly, even a "white" writer (given the Europeanized "features" of the images made available to us at the time), rather than a fully convinced subscriber to the urgently needed *new* Black agency that seems so wishful, superfluous, debatable, and even idealistic at the same time, given the odds of creating a formidable critical corpus that will undo the woeful damage of the miscegenation thesis to date à la Gilberto Freyre. It was not the intellectual capacity of Machado as a Black man that was in question during my own first navigation of the world of Machado as a graduate student in the 1990s, but the absence of any expected sentimentality toward the plight of the Black characters he created. Machado was at best ambiguous in his portrayal of Black characters, naively hoping that the reader will read between the lines. It is arguable indeed that by focusing on mostly the colonial elite characters as well as their shortcomings and absurdities, he may have seen his potential success more in their collateral privileges as opposed to the negative stereotypes of his own Blackness, especially since whiteness was more desirable than Blackness under enslavement. Conceivably, the identitarian crisis of consciousness was real for Machado. He had to be strategic in order to survive and ultimately succeed as a writer. Yet, at what cost? Even if he had openly assumed his Black identity, I seriously doubt his works would have survived as they have today. Afro-Brazilian contemporaries of Machado such as Cruz e Souza and Lima Barreto do not command the same high reputation as Machado does in Brazilian literary historiography, despite the obscurity of Machado's Black characters. Coloniality (à la Aníbal Quijano) committed an egregious crime by whitening Machado to the rest of the world; undoing that racial injustice is a compelling though daunting task that goes beyond academically recoloring him into his due Blackness.

A dialectical reading of Machado and Stowe à la Frantz Fanon may offer a potential escape from the nagging dilemma faced by Machado on the one hand and the criticism of opportunism leveled at Stowe on the other. In psychoanalyzing the motives of Machado in not openly embracing his Blackness or naively accepting the imposed "whiteness" of the colonial Other, one may conjecture that the writer subscribed to Fanon's notion that alienation has lasting psychological effects on the alienated self, and the process of de-alienating himself meant that he had to "seek the response elsewhere than in Europe"[5] by exposing the frailties of colonialism and imperialism through what seems to be a complicit disregard for Black characters and their total humanity; but, in actual fact, Machado's strategy was an effort to push the colonizer or enslaver to see their own complicity with systemic violence against the colonized or the enslaved. Stowe, in her own right, seeks to humanize Uncle Tom despite his weakened agency in the colonial context. Given the complexity faced by both Machado and Stowe in humanizing the enslaved African, their representations call for multivalent critical approaches that coalesce in the metaphors of masking and subversion as manifest in the tropes of the veil, double consciousness, and capoeira. Through the metaphoric act of *ginga* (swinging rhythm of the body in order to deceive potential adversaries), both Machado's Raimundo and Stowe's Uncle Tom were compelled to negotiate their survival while not completely negating their humanity. Though the two texts could not openly challenge the oppression of the enslaved African subjects due to the censorship of Black people in the colonial era, as opposed to contemporary activist street marches and denunciation of Black pain and social death, both do protest in strategic ways the marginality and commonality of oppression that define their relative status quo regardless of the time period in which they lived. It is conceivable that with the current attack on CRT (critical race theories), writers and critics may be compelled to use the same survival strategy of veiled anti-racism by either avoiding racial problematics or at least by creating new engagements through neologisms and inevitable protest activism.

In the context of critical race studies, less attention has been paid to *Iaiá Garcia*, which was not only part of his romantic phase but also represented the most significant Black character in Machado studies. By privileging the psychological-realist phase of Machado, most critics have missed the significance of the transition phase between Machado's Romanticism and Realism—a moment in which the character of Luiz Garcia embodies the virtues and vices of impeding abolition of slavery in 1888. When it comes to the reception of Machado in Brazil and in the United States, especially in the context of race relations, the critical engagement has been relatively dismal, even though it is gradually emerging. Drawing on scholarship from both critical race studies and Machado de Assis studies, this essay compares Machado's *Iaiá Garcia* (1878) with Harriet Stowe's *Uncle Tom's Cabin* (1852).[6] In comparing these two impactful novels, this study highlights Machado's sensitivity to the plight of the enslaved African, Raimundo, who may well be qualified as the most compelling of Machado's Black characters. Raymond Sayers indeed aptly refers to Raimundo as "Machado's tribute to the Negro."[7] If Machado was comfortable with his Blackness in nineteenth-century Brazil, would he really have considered portraying Raimundo as a potential alter ego, despite the demeaning characteristics of such a character? When juxtaposed with Stowe's Uncle Tom's impact on the American expansive abolitionist and post-abolitionist psyche, Machado's portrayal of the same Black character was more cryptic, passive, and subtle than direct.

Raimundo, the freed slave in *Iaiá Garcia*, was not oblivious to his need to be obedient to the yearnings of his enslaver, but he was also skillful in complicating the plot by not delivering the vital letter to a suitor he felt was not appropriate for *Iaiá Garcia*. In sum, Raimundo's Black agency[8] is at least liberating and empowering. While not completely fulfilling, it is perhaps the point of departure to some semblance of Black redemption and regeneration in the context of struggling to move beyond mental enslavement.

In his genuine questioning of white appropriation of a Black genius such as Machado, Eduardo de Assis Duarte has painstakingly spent a large portion of his academic career to rescue Machado from Eurocentric representation and reception of his works. In defense of Machado, he ruminates on his racial dilemma quite conceptually:

> In analyzing Machado's treatment of Afrodescendants with regard to the exigent racial relations imposed by slavery, one must not lose sight of one's horizon of reception that has been

basically forged by the privileged dominant class. Thus, by surrendering the power of criticism to the elite, albeit through transverse means; Machado nonetheless raises the question by *touching* on the origins of the huge social hurt of his era. This questioning eye runs through his entire creative works, even if they apparently address themes of love, jealousy, or betrayal.[9]

While Duarte's decolonial contribution to the process of reconfiguring Machado's literary and racial legacy is commendable, the question remains for this critic: Is celebrating the Black identity of Machado enough? Of what ideological or practical significance is this perpetual struggle to help the racist establishment see itself in the mirror? To return to the Caixa Econômica's offensive commercial as a quick illustration of crafty elusiveness on the part of the Brazilian bank and broader Brazilian official governmental position on racism (whether acknowledged, apologized for, or not), it is not as if the management of such a popular Brazilian bank is suffering from amnesia or totally oblivious to the reality of racial relations and the exigency of equality as well as political correctness; it is more of the arrogant racism that can only be satisfied by creatively transforming that which is genuinely Black into white in order to feel better and still be in control despite the end of enslavement. Duarte's painstaking editorial and critical work to rescue Machado from his imposed whiteness is only beginning to scratch the surface of this misplaced categorization of a Black or biracial man as white. Undoubtedly a compelling labor of love for future students and scholars—with an anthology comprising of three poems, twenty-one chronicles, two critical pieces on theater, six short stories, nine novels (all by Machado), and six essays by Duarte on the "poetics of dissimulation"—Duarte has compellingly invigorated the debate, especially since he has taught a course on the same subject of "African Descent Machado de Assis." However, it may not be enough for conscientious scholars to change the colonial image or identity of Machado; we must also change the colonial mentality of the Other, whose inventive appropriation of the "whiteness" of Machado in the context of the Caixa Econômica's commercial is offensive, but who has no reason to give up that same power of appropriation as long as they are permanently in control of the modes of production—whether literary, cultural, critical, political, or economical. In other words, the revisionist mission is at best symbolic, political, and transformative, but it has yet to have any significant economic impact on the lives of millions of Black people all over the world who continue to wallow in tragic heroism, sacrifice, obscurity, and poverty. I must content myself with this initial effort at revisionism even if I have chosen to process Machado's racial dilemma from a comparative prism with Harriet Stowe, who faced a different dilemma as a white writer and abolitionist in the United States in the nineteenth century. Both writers must contend with the challenge of "uncletomism" (the ambivalent double bind of being seen as both a hero and a traitor) while celebrating their symbolic contributions to abolition.[10]

Problematizing the "Uncle Tom" Paradigm in Machado

Acclaimed as the greatest Brazilian writer of all times, Machado de Assis remains an embodied enigma, especially when it comes to how his Blackness, which he consciously obscured, may have impacted his legacy and reputation, as well as his ability to openly challenge the horrors of Brazilian enslavement in his creative and journalistic works. Nevertheless, the global critical reception of Machado has been remarkable, placing him in the ranks of William Shakespeare, Marcel Proust, Thomas Mann, Thomas Hardy, Emily Dickinson, and Herman Melville (Fitz 1989, 2005, 2009); Henry James (Passos 2007); James Joyce (Marcus Wood 2019); Edgar Allan Poe (Bellin 2005); Stendhal (the pseudonym of Marie-Henri Beyle), Gustave Flaubert, and Guy de Maupassant (Fitz 1989); and Fedor Dostoyevski and Anton Chekov (Earl Fitz 1989; Marcus Wood 2019), among other major Western writers. It is indeed arguable that had he been a white Brazilian writer and not a victim of the ideologies constructed about mixed-race identity, particularly those of the twentieth century, which strategically obscured his Blackness, Machado may well have been better received in the Western critical imagination. While this steady comparative analogy with major canonical writers is commendable, Machado's critical reception is limited to his mature phase and creative nationalistic treatise, privileging such works as *Memórias Póstumas de Bras Cubas* (Posthumous Memoirs of Brás Cubas), *Dom Casmurro, Quincas Borba, Esau e Jacó* (Esau and Jacob), and *Memorial de Aires* (Memorial of Aires).

Capoeiragem, or Theorizing the Uncle Tom Agency in Machado

By invoking capoeira, a fighting technique that originated in Angola but was disguised as a dance[11] by Afro-Brazilian slaves in the seventeenth century as a way to survive plantation oppression and strategize on whether to fight for freedom or run away into the mountains as self-emancipated maroons, I am drawing an analogy between the Uncle Tom attitude and enslaved Africans in Brazil. Despite my theorizing being specific to Brazilian culture, evidence of this attitude, whether for Machado or his Black characters, can only be a matter of discursive interpretation and is not to be found in statements from the writer himself. Nonetheless, in *Playing in the Dark* (1992), Toni Morrison concludes her engagement with darkness within the white literary imagination when she scolds: "All of us, readers and writers, are bereft when criticism remains too polite or too fearful to notice disrupting darkness before its eyes."[12] The cunningness of the capoeira game allows for deliberate masking, which Morrison captures in her notion of "playing in the dark," and allows for many ambiguities. In the capoeira game, "playing in the dark" refers to the first of three stages of professionalization or initiation. The second refers to "playing on water" or taking risks, and the third refers to "playing in the light" or being masterly. Morrison warns that her project is "to avert the critical gaze from the racial object to the racial subject."[13] Machado's gaze is more on the white elites as subjects, while the Black subject was treated as an object. In other words, by focusing on "the white elites as subjects," Machado allows us to see something about the abolitionist project that we would otherwise not be able to see if we were to solely focus on the objectification of Black subjects in his novels. Morrison's critique is also betrayed by her reference to the figure of Uncle Tom: "Certainly no American text of the sort I am discussing was ever written *for* black people—no more than *Uncle Tom's Cabin* was written for Uncle Tom to read or be persuaded by."[14] In other words, despite Stowe's good intentions when she depicts Uncle Tom as a faithful yet tragic enslaved African, only Uncle Tom, if he had a chance to do so, could have depicted himself as truly human. Yet, because he is characterized as the Other, his humanity is left to the discretion of the writer and the text's imagined readers, including enslavers. In contextualizing Machado within the capoeira dynamics, Eduardo de Assis Duarte suggests that, just like capoeira, "concealment is also the path chosen by Machado de Assis, especially with regard to the critical tendency that runs through his texts, both in chronicle and in fiction."[15] In order to evade the censorship of the era, Machado metaphorically deploys the deceptive[16] art of capoeira to ensure that his literary production not only survives but also would be able to provide him with economic sustenance in the course of his brilliant career.

Beyond the deceptive consciousness of capoeira, or what W. E. B. Du Bois termed "double consciousness" to describe the experience of negotiating the split personality of being both American and African, a number of scholars of American and Brazilian literature have also engaged with the ways Machado deals with his double racialization, which kept him from being overtly judgmental on the brutalities of enslavement. In *The Souls of Black Folk*, Du Bois theorizes the "warring ideals" of double consciousness: "It is a peculiar sensation, this double-consciousness, this sense of always looking at one's self through the eyes of others, of measuring one's soul by the tape of a world that looks on in amused contempt and pity. One ever feels his two-ness—an American, a Negro; two souls, two thoughts, two unreconciled strivings; two warring ideals in one dark body."[17] Machado was, of course, more inclined to embrace racial ambivalence than the revolutionary ideal that would privilege his African "soul" that he was more or less obliged to suppress in the convenient choice of pragmatic economic survival. By deciding not to threaten the white establishment, Machado succeeds in preserving his own literary legacy for posterity, even if the stigma of "uncletomism" may never be overcome.

Of all the critical efforts (Sayers 1956; Marcus Wood 2019; Daniel 2012) to theorize Machado's relationship to race, slavery, and the crisis of consciousness, G. Reginald Daniel's study of Machado's multiracial identity is the most compelling and authoritative, given its multicultural lens. In these studies, there are echoes of inherent, deceptive dispositions in the shifting survival strategies of enslaved Africans, from the acts of Uncle Toms during enslavement, to revolutionary runaway escapades for freedom, through coping mechanisms of the "cool pose" posture when faced with social inequalities in the post-emancipation era. What these attitudes have in common is they are all survival instincts. The enslaved must envision the actions and reactions of the aggressor/oppressor in order to better prepare his counteraction, like cunningness in capoeira, which is geared toward flooring the opponent, possibly with a humorous vindication. In an assessment of the characters of Damião in "O Caso da Vara" (The Flogging Affair), Prudêncio in *Memórias Póstumas de Brás Cubas* (Posthumous Memoirs of Braz Cubas), and Raimundo in *Iaiá Garcia*, Sayers (1956) acknowledges Machado's contribution to the treatment of Black characters in pre-abolition Brazilian literature. Yet, all of these characters are mostly flat characters who do not develop much beyond stereotypical images of Blackness: Damião remains unsympathetic in the face of another maltreated and pregnant slave; Prudêncio grows up to be a freed slave who subjugates other slaves; and Raimundo, who even after being set free still behaves and acts like a slave by virtue of his docility. Sayers also recognizes the limitations of Machado: though the writer "disapproved of slavery," he is wanting in terms of producing "works of propaganda" or an "anti-slavery campaign."[18]

Meanwhile, Wood argues that Machado was more or less a victim of the "whitening" society in which he was living. Through his penetrating analysis of Machado works in relation to slavery and the responses they have garnered from critics, especially through the prism of Roberto Schwarz's *A Master on the Periphery of Capitalism: Machado de Assis* (2001), Wood argues that all Machado had to work with was a plot in which "the body of the domestic slave hovers around the bourgeois and erotic concerns of his white, socially paralyzed and morally vapid Carioca cast of characters."[19] In other words, Machado was apt at having slave bodies enact the frames of mind of the white characters even through the actions and nonactions of such silenced characters who indirectly challenge their subservient treatment by the oppressive other.

Yet, it is in Daniel's *Machado de Assis: Multiracial Identity and the Brazilian Novelist* (2012) that Machado's work is majestically situated within the complex reality of Brazilian race relations and that celebrates the ambiguous and camouflaging nature of Machado's own multicultural identity. If capoeira offers justifications for cunningness, parody, satire, and survival, Machado may well be recognized metaphorically as a literary capoeira master, even though he was too epileptic to have physically practiced the combative, cultural, and artistic expression.

In that problematic in-between space, between the negative stereotype of "Uncle Tom" and the positive qualities of the ideological enslaved African who resists the pressure to betray his own people, Machado de Assis defies any singular or simple explanation. Daniel's argument is a philosophical explanation, and he theorizes that Machado is fascinated with "subject-object duality and ambiguity." According to Daniel, these Romantic values are juxtaposed in order to expose the contradictions and paradoxes of the modernist period. The stylistic strategies deployed by the author allow him to play his capoeira between "fantasy and reality, beauty and ugliness, the tragic and the comic, the human and the ludicrous," creating all at once a "blend of anxiety and superiority, repulsion and fascination, disgust and pity, horror and amusement."[20] When this *capoeiragem* is extended transnationally, it can also be analogous to the trappings of the Uncle Tom agency, as well as the "cool pose" phenomenon in the contemporary African American experience. In *Uncle Tom Mania: Slavery, Minstrelsy, and Transatlantic Culture in the 1850s* (2005), Sarah Meer provides the reader with a lasting synthesis of the controversy surrounding the Uncle Tom character and the distorted charge of "race traitor." Meanwhile, in *Uncle Tom: From Martyr to Traitor* (2018), Adena Spingarn conjectures that when the cultural power of theater is deployed to transform Uncle Tom from the heroic Christian martyr intended by Stowe into a submissive race traitor, the complex dynamics inherent in the politics of race and slavery are at work, which allows minstrel shows to exploit the new image of Uncle Tom to counter Stowe's antislavery message. Yet, it is in Majors and Billson's *Cool Pose* (1993) that Black masculinity takes on a new meaning. According to Majors and Billson, the Black gangsta figure rejects the agency of "Uncle Tom," replacing it with a more defiant, visible, and blunt image that is ready and willing to make sacrifices in order to negotiate equal opportunity within the racist establishment. Capoeira here takes on a whole new meaning. The playful agent of "coolness" could also be violent if challenged, provoked, or humiliated. Rather than subject young Black males to risky and counterproductive criminal behavior, Majors and Billson propose manhood training programs as a measure to equip Black youths with effective negotiation skills when they find themselves in awkward situations in indifferent and hostile environments. Machado's works, which address enslavement ambiguously, offer no such recipe for coping with racism, except through the passive, survivalist agency to which his era was conditioned.

Raimundo's Agency

In this essay, I argue for the primacy of Raimundo's passive agency in *Iaiá Garcia*, while also contending that the sociopolitical context of enslavement in Brazil did not provide much leverage for the enslaved to be overtly articulate, combative, or confrontational when compared to the Uncle Tom personage, who was portrayed as a faithful slave and, yet, who suffered the same dehumanization as the freed slave. The temporal gap between the dates of abolition in the United States and Brazil (1865 and 1888, respectively) partly explains the prevailing political contexts in which both writers wrote. Against all odds, Raimundo, an Afro-Brazilian character in the nineteenth century during which slavery was still thriving, while obscure and apparently powerless, embodies a humanist agency even in the midst of the moral turpitude in which the major characters in *Iaiá Garcia* were entangled. In this regard, Machado humanizes the weak while ridiculing the strong in order to critique the capitalist theory of the survival of the fittest (*humanitismo*). Machado may be having it both ways with his many readers by playing with ambiguity. This creative strategy, where moral absurdity that is essentially deceptive, especially through psychological dramas and tensions, is couched within the passionate, romantic, and existential conditions that characterize most of his works. Ultimately, behind the veil of Machado's ambiguity lies his moral sensitivity, regardless of the spectrum of race with which he is associated. In this essay, I argue that, though he was from a mixed-race background, Machado was proud of his Blackness, as much as he was able to be within the racially polemical period of slavery, the context with which he had to contend as an emerging man of letters in the nineteenth century. It hurts deeply to see the same past atrocities being relived, as a matter of routine and captured on American television, under the different mask of police brutality—a reality that has led to the "Black Lives Matter" movement to call attention to endless violations of human rights in the twenty-first century.

Raimundo and Uncle Tom, the two protagonists who constitute this comparative case study, are situated within different, although similar, colonial settings, especially relative to slavery and the subsequent agitations for emancipation. Consequently, the mutual oppressive and patriarchal realities that both the American and the Brazilian contexts share call for a sociology of the historical moments that define the controversial texts and the ensuing challenges they faced from ambivalent critical reception. As a mixed-race Brazilian writer emerging in the mid-1800s, when Brazilian abolition only took place in 1888, Machado faced the challenge of not quite being ready to openly confront[21] the heated political issues of the era, especially concerning slavery and its explicit violence and oppression. Conversely, Harriet Stowe—a privileged yet sympathetic white abolitionist and writer, who sought to use her serialized novel to appeal to the national conscience of the white establishment, which controlled the slavery machine and was responsible for the dehumanization of enslaved Africans—faced a different upheaval in terms of her true intentions. Stowe's book was an instant success and is often considered to be a catalyst for abolitionist agitations in the United States and, subsequently, the American Civil War. As an African trying to situate the significance of Machado de Assis by reading about the atrocities of slavery in the US and Brazil, I am struck by the verities of enslavement and its burdens, past and present. I cannot but be humbled that human beings went through such unbelievably evil atrocities just because of the color of their skin.

While it is tempting to question Machado's lack of political courage for his adoption of an Uncle Tom agency[22] in order to survive the challenges of rising to become the foremost Brazilian writer, especially in the unsettling racial context of the nineteenth century, the reality remains that most of his works, which we celebrate or critique in our research and teaching today, might not have otherwise seen the light of day, whether due to censorship or rejection, which would have frustrated the writer even more acutely. Though the phrase "Uncle Tom" is nowadays considered an insult and even a racial slur, I understand this passive yet survivalist attitude as that in which the subject masks their true feelings of disgust by acting to be content, harmonious, and cooperative in relations with whites in order to protect assumed but token privileges. I do not go as far as reading "Uncle Tom Agency" in Machado's constrained context of creating docile or ambivalent Black characters during slavery as being a traitor of his race but as a Christlike, sacrificially, politically, and psychologically conditioned state of submissive consciousness that was beyond his control.

In his seminal essay "Instinto de Nacionalidade" (Instinct of Nationality) (1873), Machado responds to his critics regarding his ambivalent attitude toward enslavement: "What we should expect from the writer above all is a certain intimate feeling that renders him a man of his time and space."[23] Machado seeks to point the nation toward a broader universal concern about the human condition. To become a popular writer for his generation and beyond meant that he was limited in his ability to openly condemn the very establishment that supported his creative efforts, whether through the civil service positions he held, as a well-revered founder and the first president of the Brazilian Academy of Letters, or through the access he was given to publishing outlets. In other words, he could not have openly engaged with abolitionists who openly criticized the injustices of enslavement and racial discrimination. Yet, despite masking most of his works under the pretexts of romantic love, Machado was apt to reveal the frailties and falsities of humankind, as the major white characters in his novels are unveiled as amoral, compromised, egotistical, and even pathological. By dealing ambiguously with the brutalities and violence of the rich, white oligarchs against enslaved Africans in Brazil, Machado may have subscribed to the subtle and subconscious manifestation of the Uncle Tom syndrome, which is defined as "a ritualized, accommodating, sycophantic style of behavior in African Americans toward Caucasians" and which compels the victim to "act in a docile, nonassertive manner to appear nonthreatening to European Americans."[24] While we can only speculate on Machado's survival strategy in the hostile world of Brazilian slavery in which he was living and writing in the mid-1800s, ample evidence from his creative corpus reveals that when he creates Afro-Brazilian characters, they are secondary, docile, and subservient to their masters, which is to be expected within the colonial context. By exposing the human frames of mind of such "enslaved" characters, Machado moves the reader to be appalled at the injustices of slavery and to be compelled to desire social change. Despite his enduring efforts to theorize the universal aspects of the local Brazilian culture, Machado, as Earl Fitz notes, was himself, ironically, a "victim of isolation and neglect."[25]

Harriet Stowe, on the other hand, has been accused by critics since the mid-1800s of not being a genuine abolitionist who sought to humanize the enslaved Africans but rather an opportunist. Within four years of publication, her novel *Uncle Tom's Cabin* had sold two million copies. Most African Americans felt that the depiction of Uncle Tom by Stowe was nothing short of an exploitative, patronizing, and offensive gesture.[26] As a matter of fact, the abolitionist position of Stowe was distorted by commercial stage shows of the era because they realized that the American audience was less interested in the heroism of Uncle Tom, who refused to betray the two Black women who had run away from the plantation and who knew that by not revealing their whereabouts, he was risking being beaten to death. Instead of celebrating Uncle Tom's tragic heroism as intended by Stowe, who wanted to appeal to the moral conscience of whites and turn them against the brutality of slavery, stage adaptations unfortunately manipulated and distorted the character of Uncle Tom into a propagandist figure of servility and self-hate.

Stowe wrote *Uncle Tom's Cabin* in response to the Fugitive Slave Act of 1850,[27] which she found reprehensible because it required northerners protecting Blacks through the Underground Railroad to return them to slavery in the South. Stowe's novel was actually based on a real slave in Maryland, Josiah Henson, whom she had researched through slave narratives that documented those who had escaped into freedom through the Underground Railroad. Despite the odds against Uncle Tom, Stowe endows him with Christlike qualities. In the novel's tragic ending, he is beaten to death without betraying his people, a self-sacrifice for a greater communal good. It is remarkable that, at the end of the narrative, Uncle Tom, despite so much pain and hurt and about to give up the ghost due to repeated beatings, manages to plead with his enslaver and murderer,

Legree, to save his life. Yet, to no avail. Unrepentant and resolved to "take every drop of blood he has" (Stowe 377), Legree orders Sambo to keep beating Uncle Tom to death. The victim not only preaches to his murderers as they kill him, but he also forgives them in a dramatic moment reminiscent of the crucifixion of Jesus:

> Tom opened his eyes and looked upon his master. "Ye poor miserable critter!" he said, "there an't no more ye can do! I forgive ye, with all my soul!" . . .
> "I forgive ye, with all my heart!" said Tom, faintly. . . .
> They wept,—both the two savage men. . . .
> "Poor critters!" said Tom, "I'd be willing to bar' all I have, if it'll only bring ye to Christ! O, Lord! Give me these two more souls. I pray!
> That prayer was answered![28]

That the oppressed and enslaved could find it in his heart to forgive his oppressor and enslaver is remarkable and Christlike, but it is neither natural nor human. It requires something of a divine grace to forgive. The human penchant, a notable logic of the novel, would be to seek revenge or invoke retributive justice. In this sense, Uncle Tom is indeed a hero and not a villain or a sellout, as popular culture has managed to recharacterize him. In contrast to this tragic ending, Raimundo's dilemma of obscurity and passivity in *Iaiá Garcia* pales significantly. Regardless of their divergences and convergences, both novels display abolitionist agitations (whether blatant or subtle), which signals an effort to humanize the enslaved and appeal to the human conscience of the enslavers toward the dignity of freedom and humanity.

Critical Reception of Machado's *Iaiá Garcia* in the United States and Brazil

In defense of Machado's seeming indifference toward the plight of enslaved Africans in his works, Raymond Sayers, one of the foremost critics of Afro-Brazilian literature in the United States, speculates on the many possible reasons for Machado's cryptic position: his co-optation within the Brazilian bureaucracy given his literary fame, which he did not want to compromise; his marriage to an aristocratic Portuguese woman, Carolina;

his epilepsy, which forced him to avoid conflict or stressful situations, such as social activism; his desire to be accepted by the aristocratic society, which would not be approved should he have decided to take a strong position in favor of abolition; or his complete resignation to human misery and his use of satire as a coping strategy, a strategy he found to be less effective in the case of his Black characters, with whom he would rather not be seen to sympathize. Machado's rationale need not be so far-fetched or ambiguous. After reviewing such works as "O Caso da Varra" (The Flogging Affair), "Pai contra Mãe" ("Father versus Mother"), *Memórias Póstumas de Brás Cubas* (Posthumous Memoirs of Brás Cubas), and *Iaiá Garcia*, Sayers postulates that Machado "sympathized with the Negroes [sic] and hated all injustice. However, his sympathies for the Negroes [sic] did not cause him to take any part in the struggle against slavery."[29] As much as one tries to understand the dilemma Machado faced as a mixed-race writer who desired social ascension and was keen not to lose his privileges, one cannot help but feel that his cryptic efforts to symbolically expose the injustices of enslavement portray him to be a crafty writer of ambiguities. When it comes specifically to *Iaiá Garcia*, Sayers commends Machado for portraying Raimundo as "the healthy, beneficent influence that the freed Negro [sic] could exercise in a white family, perhaps in white society."[30] I find Sayers's critical position somewhat troubling; he is at once praising Machado for not being openly anti-racist and yet justifying his co-optation by the white establishment by suggesting that both the enslaved Africans and the white enslavers were circumstantial victims of history. In other words, Sayers may be inclined to see a permanent situation in which enslaved Africans never gained their freedom. One wonders what kind of society we would be living in if a segment of the human race had been consistently subjected to enslavement. In retrospect, I could not agree more with Saidiya Hartman, who compellingly argues in *Lose Your Mother* (2007), based on her two-month spiritual sojourn in Ghana, that both Africans and African descendants are living in the shadows of enslavement: "Ghana was a good place as any other to think about the afterlife of slavery and the future of the ex-slave. Secretly I hoped that it wasn't too late to believe in freedom dreams."[31] While I understand that Sayers was trying to balance his criticism with encomium, I contend that it does more disservice to the overall legacy of Machado to excuse Machado's crafty silence for temporary and survivalist gains.

In his brief discussion of *Iaiá Garcia*, Eduardo de Assis Duarte argues that the character of Raimundo is more of an "allegory of empowerment" for the historic moment of crisis for slave labor, not necessarily for the ex-slave but rather for women, principally. According to Duarte, this allegory dislocates the enslaver's power without completely eliminating it, as the same paternal discourse is still betrayed through tensions between the inheritors of the enslaver's oppressive enterprise and the "alterity of the non-submissive Other," a tension with which Machado copes through his "agonistic relations" with his narratives.[32] If Machado was indeed critiquing Brazilian paternalism of the enslavement era, just ten years before its abolition, the "death of the master" (19) can only be read in symbolic terms.[33] In contrast to the enslaver, Luís Garcia, and the inheritor of the enslavement machine, Iaiá Garcia, Raimundo, who even when he is a free man is still a domesticated personage in his actions and nonactions, within the elite "familial" relations of which he is more or less an obscured and re-enslaved outsider, is nothing short of a dependent object. He is not an independent subject operating within his own political will or agency. Rather, Raimundo is only "empowered" in symbolic terms without any palpable agency of freedom.

While trying to deconstruct Machado's stereotypification of Black characters, another critic, Eduardo de Faria Coutinho, suggests that the author is very apt at deploying humor as a strategy of protest.[34] But he goes even further to argue that the average reader, who finds slavery repulsive, may also find it difficult to accept the "well-placed position" in which Machado found himself, and of which he perhaps took advantage without feeling the need to apologize: "Machado's humor is the great weapon with which he executes his denunciation; and, he is the same one who is present, with total force, in the famous scene of *Posthumous Memoirs of Brás Cubas* in which the protagonist's former slave, now serves as his slave."[35] In each instance, both Raimundo in *Iaiá Garcia* and Prudêncio in *Memórias Póstumas* are victims of the same oppressive system, which either silences them or forces them to transfer their enraging hurts to another, regardless of whether that "other" is Black or white. It is arguable that Machado nonetheless translates his desire to denounce the social forces that disempower Raimundo. Indeed, Machado's decision to highlight Raimundo's "passive agency" may be read as his ploy to denounce the violence of enslavement as well as the negative impacts of racial segregation, without necessarily presenting the reader with compelling acts of social change. Neither Raimundo nor Prudêncio captures vividly the agency of indignation at having to behave like a double personality, one who cannot freely articulate his pain or forcefully express his anguish in the face of oppression. Instead, one is submissive and the other transforms his anger into a violent action onto another slave.

While scholarship on Machado from both sides of the Americas largely concerns his politics of identity, narrative form, influences, complexities, ambiguities, tragicomedy of the human condition, nationalism, universalism, deceptive strategies, depiction of female passions within triangulated romantic love, and overall penchant for the satiric, Machado craftily distances himself from the corrupting forces of the powerful while also expressing his perplexity in the melancholic face of the human condition. Moreover, scholarship on slavery and abolition, issues that continue to attract increasing interests throughout the Americas, often conflates Machado's multicultural identity with his disposition toward skepticism in the face of human misery.[36] As a result, scholarship neglects the racial question in favor of what appears to be the more dynamic issue of gender, such as the substitution of the older Estela (the traditional, spiritual, and moral character who rejected Jorge's marriage proposal) with younger Iaiá Garcia, who is more of a lover of an outward and adventurous life as she conquers Jorge for herself—while Machado remains silent on the predicament of Raimundo as the racial other in *Iaiá Garcia*.

At least three major critical anthologies have addressed the issue of Machado and enslavement, even if in a cursory or clustered fashion. The two perspectives of Duarte and Coutinho, as highlighted previously, are drawn from *Machado de Assis e a Escravidão* (2008), which, on the southern side of the Americas, advances varied perspectives on Machado's stories, including "O Caso da Vara," "Pai contra Mãe," "Mariana," and "Virginus," as well as his novels, including *Iaiá Garcia*, *Memórias Póstumas de Brás Cubas*, and *Memorias de Aires*. On the northern side, Maria Salgueiro's "Machado de Assis: A Keen Look at Nineteenth-Century Brazilian Identity" and Hans Ulrich Gumbrecht's "The Beautiful Form of Sadness: Machado de Assis' *Memorial de Aires*," both of which were collected in *The Author as Plagiarist: The Case of Machado de Assis* (2005), address the problematic issues of slavery, abolition, the Republic, and Brazil's conflicted relationship with its own African heritage. Recently, *Emerging Dialogues on Machado de Assis* (2016) continued the assessment of Machado in the United States. Of the four essays in the section on "Race, Identity, and Society," three address the impact of slavery on identity and social inequalities in Machado: Sidney Chalhoub's "The Legacy of Slavery: Tales of Gender and Racial Violence in Machado de Assis," G. Reginald Daniel's "Machado de Assis: From 'Tragic Mulatto' to Human Tragicomedy," and

Fernando de Rocha's " 'Father versus Mother': Slavery and Its Apparatuses."
Unfortunately, none of these scholars directly engages with the specific
dilemma of Raimundo as a marginalized Black character who is caught
in the double bind of being free and yet enslaved.

In addition, José Bettencourt Machado's *Machado of Brazil* (1962)
draws an astute connection between Machado's life and that of his characters. He describes Luís Garcia, for example, as the author's own alter
ego: "the disenchantment with life so well portrayed in Garcia can also
be found in Machado himself."[37] This detailed description of Machado's
life, as portrayed by the author, provides a rare window into the era in
which *Iaiá Garcia* was written. It was an era in which the Black character
was neither enslaved nor free (especially in the case of Raimundo, who
already had his freedom certificate well before the abolition of slavery in
1888) and thus needed to act in a taciturn manner in order not to invoke
the wrath of the master.

Finally, it is in Earl E. Fitz's *Machado de Assis and Female Characterization* (2015) that a whole, innovative world of research opens
up to scholars of Machado, especially as it concerns the significance of
enslavement, the enslaved, and women in *Iaiá Garcia*. Fitz writes, "the
liberation of an old black man, Raimundo, is paralleled by what the reader
understands as the similarly needed liberation of both the more flexible
younger woman, Iaiá, and the more brittle and battle-scarred older one,
Estela, whose powerful pride is both her strength and her undoing."[38]
Estela was not comfortable with marrying Jorge because she was from
a lower class, but Iaiá was attracted to Jorge for the sake of a personal
sense of fulfillment once she found out that Estela was once pursued in
love by Jorge. For Iaiá, it was enough to conquer Jorge whether the love
was genuine or not. It was about winning. Ultimately, the Raimundo
character, as represented in *Iaiá Garcia*, remains categorically the most
representative character in all of Machado's short stories and novels of
the trope of obscurity and the passivity of the enslaved.

Iaiá Garcia: Invisibility, Docility, and (De-)Humanization of Raimundo

In order to better appreciate the contradictory character of Raimundo,
the web of actions and nonactions needs to be unpacked. Three white
characters, Iaiá (Lina Garcia), Jorge, and Estela, occupy the first plane in

the plot's structure. Iaiá is the young daughter of Luís Garcia, the colonial "master" of Raimundo, who is an ex-enslaved African whom Iaiá inherits from her father. As Iaiá matures into a young woman, a romance develops between Jorge and Estela. Given Jorge's higher-class status and Estela's sense of inferiority due to her lower-class status and her pride (through which she dignifies her poverty), the relationship naturally breaks off. While Jorge struggles to overcome the pain of his unreciprocated love for Estela, Iaiá's passionate energies, pride, and dominant ambition over-power her, and she succeeds not only in falling in love with Jorge but also in marrying him. In a double-edged and double-phased love triangle between Jorge, Estela, and Luís Garcia on the one hand, and Jorge, Estela, and Iaiá on the other, Machado deploys the thesis novel to expose the nineteenth-century belief that people are victims of social determinism, which affects their attitudes and behavior. Beyond the two triangles, the role of antagonist-cum-catalyst falls on Valéria, Jorge's mother, who forcibly inhibits any possible union between Jorge and Estela. She removes Jorge from the family by persuading him to enlist in the Brazilian army in the war against Paraguay. By refusing to marry Jorge, whom she considers to be in a higher social class, Estela consoles herself in the strange pride that material wealth is not as desirable as her own personal dignity. In doing so, she opens an opportunity for the younger and more aggressive Iaiá Garcia, who manipulates the situation to her own advantage by marrying Jorge.

In sharp contrast to the central characters, all of whom are entangled in love triangles and moral turpitudes, Raimundo finds himself obscured by his Blackness and his stature as a "happy slave." In other words, Raimundo is an outsider-insider. He was bequeathed to Luís Garcia while still a toddler, and he is described by Machado, in a demeaning style, as a free slave who chooses to stay on with the colonizing family because he had become "like an external soul of his master," one who had come to accept his submissive status despite his freedom, as if he had no alternative: "Raimundo seemed expressly made to serve Luís Garcia. He was a Negro of about fifty, of medium stature, strong in spite his years, a type of African that was submissive and dedicated. He was a slave though free. Whatever the social and natural differences between the two, domestic relations had made friends of them."[39] The enslaving relationship between Raimundo and his young master, even when humanized by Machado as somehow special and genuine, is endowed with Uncle Tom agency because Raimundo is not in the relationship of his own freewill but rather to fulfill the whims and caprices of the Other. Raimundo's life is monotonous and melancholic: he plays the marimba (African xylophone) to calm his master, he sets the table, he is often nostalgic of his African origins, and he makes the little Iaiá laugh. Regardless of the ambivalent "friendship" Machado evokes between the white master and the Black slave, this relationship is shrouded in a paradoxical pact that, despite the implicit affection, keeps Raimundo in perpetual bondage. While white characters are engrossed in love triangles that focus on social mobility, wealth acquisition, aristocratic living, and future inheritance, Raimundo is condemned to servitude. During a conversation with the master's daughter, Raimundo is humiliated and associated with consumption and exploitation through such expressions as "a saint that's for eating," to which he responds: "Pretty saint! Delicious saint!"[40] His docility and passivity do not allow him to question the racist insinuation of savagery or cannibalism or to interrogate the "innocent" perspective of the child. Machado deliberately evokes these condescending moments for Raimundo as a pretext to his critique of the brutality of slavery. Though supposedly "free," the weight of enslavement continues to hang on Raimundo, hence his implicit obscurity, docility, and subtle dehumanization.

Machado's humanization of Raimundo in the context of the enslaved African's problematic "freedom" calls for a significant revision. Given the Law of the Free Womb of 28 September 28 1871, which demanded that all slaves born on Brazilian soil should be considered as free born (i.e., they are not to face the horrific experiences of their parents), and given that he was issued a certificate of freedom by Luís Garcia, Raimundo's choice to remain an oxymoronic "free slave" may well be a deliberate, creative decision by Machado to question the viability of both the Law of the Free Womb (Lei do Ventre Livre) and the certificate of freedom (carta de alforria) in colonial Brazil. Could the certificate of freedom be another pretext for the slave master to continue to control the freedom of the formerly enslaved by offering them a bogus freedom letter, knowing that most had nowhere to go and that, in all likelihood, many would remain in the service of their master? By psychologically and economically calculating the fate of the formerly enslaved African, the enslaver may have reasoned that there was nothing to lose. In fact, the formerly enslaved African might be so "grateful" for this compassionate masterly gesture as to voluntarily become an honorary "member of the family," without any meaningful authority or say in family affairs, rather than set out on a risky journey to nowhere and potentially be recaptured and re-enslaved by a new master who may not be inclined to follow the laws.

An incident in the life of Iaiá, who is caught in a love triangle between Procópio Dias and Jorge, betrays Raimundo's rebellious though domesticated agency. In the incident, Raimundo refuses to deliver the decisive letter to Procópio Dias that will announce that Iaiá is ready to marry him:

> "Iaiá will forgive me . . . this letter . . . Raimundo doesn't like to speak to that man."
> "Don't speak; all you need to do is leave the letter at his house."
> Raimundo didn't insist. He accompanied the daughter of his former master with his eyes, shaking his head with the same air as before. Then he looked at the letter as if he wanted to guess what was in it. It was only a premonition, but also a conclusion from what he had been seeing those last weeks. They had given him the news of the wedding; it had been discussed every day before Luís Garcia's death.[41]

By not facilitating the impulsive decision of Iaiá to rekindle her relationship with Procópio Dias after she realizes that her stepmother Estela is still in love with Jorge, Raimundo plays a significant role in protecting Iaiá from making the wrong decision and ultimately solidifies the support of Estela for the union between Jorge and Iaiá. In so doing, Raimundo plays the positive "Uncle Tom" role by protecting Iaiá from taking a wrong path in life, rather than the stereotypical role of trying to please his master for the sake of survival.

Conclusion

By comparing Stowe's Uncle Tom to Machado's ambivalent Raimundo, I reach a number of conclusions about Machado that bear on both the celebration and critique of him as a larger-than-life writer, one who deserves to be appreciated despite his subtle and controversial contributions to the discourses of enslavement and abolition in Brazil. First, even though Uncle Tom was enslaved while Raimundo had his freedom certificate, both were still living under the same conditions of oppression, and both lacked true freedom and agency. Second, while Uncle Tom is not entangled in familial or romantic relations like Raimundo, both nurture the colonial daughters to the best of their abilities. Third, both Uncle Tom and Raimundo are faithful and devoted until their deaths. Even though their respective hardships could have brought about an internal revolt, they keep their actions under control and focus their concern on the supposedly real consequences of their actions. Fourth, by enduring both internal and external pain through an appeal to Christian principles of love and compassion for the aggressive Other, both characters are able to forgive the transgressions of their masters. While Raimundo does not experience physical beating, verbal abuse is enough to humiliate him and to subject his dignity to ridicule, especially as an old man. In both cases, the permanent fear of consequence reinforces each character's sense of place. Through humor and sarcasm, Machado questions enslavement but does not openly call attention to it as a shameful system of oppression and exploitation. At best, the esteemed writer's chronicles gave some insights into his contradictory mind, since he was indeed in favor of abolition but could not articulate it until after abolition of enslavement.

Machado, like many writers of his generation, wrote not for the enslaved but for the white establishment that paid his salary and embraced his crafty ambiguity, which ultimately kept the system of oppression intact. Machado obscures Raimundo, despite Raimundo's certificate of freedom, because Machado was never a "protagonist of abolition."[42] In this regard, the Uncle Tom agency is problematic in Machado not because his Black characters avoid this negative stereotype but because Machado himself was not as forthright in advocating for freedom, except in controversial, convenient, and symbolic terms. In sum, Raimundo's predicament in *Iaiá Garcia* as a neither enslaved nor free figure is nothing short of tragic, contradictory, paradoxical, and sublime. While the focus on *Iaiá Garcia* in this essay is a contribution to the process of rereading Machado de Assis as an Afro-descendant, it would be interesting to also revisit his chronicles in a future critical engagement. Since Machado de Assis wrote most of these chronicles anonymously, it would be interesting to tease out the motives and implications of that anonymity. The representation of Raimundo in *Iaiá Garcia* may well be wrought with strategic ambiguities and obscurities on the part of Machado, an attitude that qualifies him more as a bourgeois Black intellectual than a Black consciousness writer; however, the core humanity and African heritage of both writer and protagonist are unquestionable given the contexts of enslavement and impending abolition that caused for celebration then and now. Perhaps to his credit, Machado struggled with the best approach to expose and address the horrors of enslavement with the best weapon of ambiguous criticism that he had at the time of his literary engagement.

Notes

1. "Black Lives Matter" (BLM) was founded in 2013 in the wake of the murder of Trayvon Martin with a demand for the American society as a whole to become more engaged against violence and injustice suffered by Black people for many centuries. Its call for action became even more heightened when George Floyd was also murdered by the police on 25 May 2020. While Machado de Assis was not murdered by the Brazilian police, their continuous assault on the Brazilian underprivileged make the case for revisiting Machado de Assis's Black identity a significant contribution to social justice and activism.

2. See Afolabi.

3. See Farah. The bank's president, Jorge Hereda, while apologizing for the bad taste of the misleading commercial celebrating the bank's 150th anniversary and taking credit for the fact that Machado de Assis was a white man who also kept a savings account with the bank, it took the intervention of SEPPIR (Secretariat of the Promotion of Racial Equality) to oblige the bank to take the remedial action. It was not a voluntary nor ethical self-reflection action on the part of the bank. If this episode happened only a decade ago, who is to say that history will not repeat itself a decade from now? It is a frustrating struggle that has implications for the mental health of the victims of this unwarranted state of affairs in racial relations. See also the actual commercial on YouTube entitled "Branquearam Machado de Assis: Comercial da Caixa Econômica" ("They 'Whitened' Machado de Assis: Caixa Econômica's Commercial"), https://www.youtube.com/watch?v=OboocxKLfRk, accessed 5 May 5 2021 [2.14 minutes].

4. Refers to a state of being fooled, bewildered, or misled. For a film that aptly conveyed this state of mind, see Spike Lee, *Bamboozled* (New Line Home Entertainment, 2001).

5. Fanon 255.

6. The scholarship includes, among other references, Toni Morrison's *Playing in the Dark* (1992), Richard Majors and Janet Billson's *Cool Pose* (1993), Sarah Meer's *Uncle Tom Mania: Slavery, Minstrelsy, and Transatlantic Culture in the 1850s* (2005), J. Reginald Daniel's *Machado de Assis: Multiracial Identity and the Brazilian Novelist* (2012), Adena Spingarn's *Uncle Tom: From Martyr to Traitor* (2018), Marcus Wood's *Black Butterfly: Brazilian Slavery and the Literary Imagination* (2019), and Eduardo de Assis Duarte's *Machado de Assis Afrodescedente* (2020).

7. Sayers 207.

8. Like all the elite characters, Raimundo is simply acting out his subaltern role, to the degree that he is conveniently conditioned. Although Raimundo is

only an actor in a colonial performance, he nonetheless ceases to be an object; as he assumes such a role, he gradually becomes his real person. For a more detailed analysis, see Silva 127.

9. Duarte 2020, 318–19, my emphasis. There is a difference between barely "touching" and directly confronting the issues of slavery and its horrors, which his characters endured but could do nothing transformative or rebellious about. All translations in this essay are mine.

10. For a more in-depth analysis of how the Brazilian press contributed to the debates on abolition through the serialization of Harriet Stowe's *Uncle Tom's Cabin*, for example, see Castilho.

11. Beyond being disguised as a dance by the enslaved to distract colonial censorship, when the expressive art gained popularity in the first decades of the twentieth century, as did the ideology of racial democracy, Capoeira became appropriated and promoted as one of the cultural essences of Brazilian national identity to Brazilians and the rest of the world.

12. Morrison 91.

13. Morrison 90.

14. Morrison 17.

15. Assis Duarte 285, my translation.

16. For insightful perspectives on the art of deception or dissimulation in Machado, see, for example, Gledson (1984) and Silva.

17. Du Bois 2.

18. Sayers 208.

19. Wood 86.

20. Daniel 135–36.

21. The *crônica* was the best genre that allowed Machado to speak forthrightly (even though still with a sense of humor) against slavery, forced labor, and the exploitative conditions of labor after abolition. For a compelling revisionistic reading of Machado de Assis as a writer who was genuinely in favor of abolition but had to wait until the actual abolition in 1888 to state his position and celebrate abolition, see Gledson (2006) and Newcomb.

22. 23. Machado de Assis 28–34.

24. Priester 461.

25. Fitz 1989, 13.

26. For a detailed analysis of the many types (old and new) of Uncle Tom, see Spingarn 107–58.

27. Spingarn 14–15.

28. Stowe 377–78.

29. Sayers 202.

30. Sayers 208.

31. Hartman 107. For more critical insights, see Okeowo (2020) and Samuelson (2009).

32. Duarte 2008, 22–23.
33. Duarte 2008, 19.
34. For more Brazilian critical perspectives questioning Machado's position on slavery and abolition, see Grieco; Magalhães; and Pereira.
35. Coutinho 99.
36. See, for example, José Raimundo Maia Neto, *Machado de Assis, the Brazilian Pyrrhonian* (Purdue University Press, 1994), 52–53.
37. Machado110.
38. Fitz 2015, 100.
39. Machado de Assis 1878, 3–4.
40. Machado de Assis 1878, 7.
41. Machado de Assis 1878, 153.
42. Marotti 122.

Works Cited

Afolabi, Niyi. "Machado de Assis: Uma Teorização da Ambigüidade," *Revista Iberoamericana*, vol. 66, no. 190, 2000, 121–38.

Aidoo, Lamonte, and Daniel F. Silva. *Emerging Dialogues on Machado de Assis.* Palgrave Macmillan, 2016.

Bellin, Greicy Pinto. "The Quest for National Identity in Edgar Allan Poe and Machado de Assis." *International Journal of Language and Literature*, vol. 3, no. 1, 2015, 143–47.

Bernardo, Gustavo, Joachim Michael, and Markus Schaffauer, eds. *Machado de Assis e a Escravidão*. São Paulo: Annablume, 2008.

Caldwell, Helen. *The Brazilian Othello of Machado de Assis: A Study of Dom Casmurro.* University of California Press, 1960.

Candido, Antonio. "An Outline of Machado de Assis." *Antonio Candido: On Literature and Society*, translated by Howard S. Becker, 104–18, Princeton University Press, 1995.

Castilho, Celso Thomas. "The Press and Brazilian Narratives of *Uncle Tom's Cabin*: Slavery and the Public Sphere in Rio de Janeiro, ca. 1855." *The Americas*, vol. 76, no. 1, 2019, 77–106.

Chalhoub, Sidney. *Machado de Assis Historiador.* São Paulo: Companhia das Letras, 2003.

Coutinho, Eduardo de Faria. "A Desconstrução de Estereótipos na Obra de Machado de Assis: A Questão da Escravidão." *Machado de Assis e a Escravidão*, edited by Gustavo Bernardo, Joachim Michael, and Markus Schaffauer, 93–100, São Paulo: Annablume, 2008.

Daniel, G. Reginald. *Machado de Assis: Multiracial Identity and the Brazilian Novelist.* Penn State University Press, 2012.

Duarte, Eduardo de Assis. *Machado de Assis Afrodescendente*: Antologia e Crítica. Rio de Janeiro: Malê, 2020.

―――. "A Morte do Senhor e as Memórias Póstumas da Escravidão." *Machado de Assis Afrodescendente*, 311–29, Rio de Janeiro: Malê, 2020.

―――. "Memórias Póstumas da Escravidão." *Machado de Assis e a Escravidão*, edited by Gustavo Bernardo, Joachim Michael, and Markus Schaffauer, 11–26, São Paulo: Annablume, 2008.

―――. "Machado de Assis's African Descent." *Research in African Literatures*, vol. 38, no. 1, 2007, 134–51.

Du Bois, W. E. B. *The Souls of Black Folk*. Washington, DC: G&D Media, 2019 [1903].

Fanon, Frantz. *The Wretched of the Earth: A Negro Psychologist's Study of the Problems of Racism & Colonialism in the World Today*. Grove Press, Inc., 1961.

Farah, Tatiana. "Caixa Econômica tira do ar propaganda com Macha do Assis branco" (Caixa Econômica pulls commercial with Machado as a white man). *O Globo*, 31 Oct. 2011, https://oglobo.globo.com/politica/caixa-economica-tira-do-ar-propaganda-com-machado-de-assis-branco-2695142.

Fitz, Earl E. *Machado de Assis and the Narrative Theory*. Bucknell University Press, 2019.

―――. *Machado de Assis and Female Characterization: The Novels*. Bucknell University Press, 2015.

―――. *Brazilian Narrative Traditions in a Comparative Context*. Modern Language Association, 2005.

―――. *Machado de Assis*. Twayne, 1989.

Lynn, Alex, Elena Calvo-González, and Marcelo Mendes de Souza. "Whiter Shades of Pale: 'Coloring In' Machado de Assis and Race in Contemporary Brazil." *Latin American Research Review*, vol. 48, no. 3, 2013, 3–24.

Gledson, John. *The Deceptive Realism of Machado de Assis: A Dissenting Interpretation of Dom Casmurro*. Liverpool: Francis Cairns, 1984.

―――. *Machado de Assis: Ficção e História*. São Paulo: Companhia das Letras, 2006.

Grieco, Agrippino. *Viagem em torno a Machado de Assis*. São Paulo: Martins, 1969.

Gumbrecht, Hans Ulrich. "The Beautiful Form of Sadness: Machado de Assis' *Memorial de Aires*." *Portuguese Literary and Cultural Studies*, vol. 13/14, 2005, 307–16.

Hartman, Saidiya. *Lose Your Mother: A Journey Along the Atlantic Slave Route*. Farrar, 2007.

Jackson, K. David. *Machado de Assis: A Literary Life*. Yale University Press, 2015.

Lee, Spike. *Bamboozled*. New York: New Line Home Entertainment, 2001.

Machado, José Bettencourt. *Machado of Brazil: The Life and Times of Machado de Assis, Brazil's Greatest Novelist*. Charles Frank, 1962.

Machado de Assis, Joaquim Maria. *Iaiá Garcia*. 1878. Translated by Albert I. Bagby Jr., 3–4, University Press of Kentucky, 1977.

————. "O Instinto da Nacionalidade," 1873. *Machado de Assis: Crítica, Notícia da Atual Literatura Brasileira*, 28–34, São Paulo: Agir, 1959.

Magalhães Júnior, Raimundo. *Machado de Assis desconhecido*. Rio de Janeiro: Civilização Brasileira, 1955.

Maia Neto, José Raimundo. *Machado de Assis, The Brazilian Pyrrhonian*. Purdue University Press, 1994.

Majors, Richard, and Mancini Billson. *Cool Pose*. Simon & Schuster, 1993.

Marotti, Giorgio. *Black Characters in the Brazilian Novel*. Center for Afro-American Studies, University of California, 1987.

Meer, Sarah. *Uncle Tom Mania: Slavery, Minstrelsy, and Transatlantic Culture in the 1850s*. University of Georgia Press, 2005.

Morrison, Toni. *Playing in the Dark: Whiteness and the Literary Imagination*. Vintage, 1992.

Newcomb, Robert Patrick. "Joaquim Maria Machado de Assis: Six *Crônicas* on Slavery and Abolition." *Portuguese Studies*, vol. 33, no. 1, 2017, 105–22.

Okeowo, Alexis. "How Sadiya Hartman Retells the History of Black Life." *The New Yorker*, 26 Oct. 2020, 1–19.

Passos, José Luiz. *Machado de Assis: O Romance com Pessoas*. São Paulo: EDUSP, 2007.

Paz, Ravel Giordano. *Serenidade e Fúria: O Sublime Assismachadiano*. São Paulo: EDUSP, 2009.

Pereira, Lúcia Miguel. *Machado de Assis*. Rio de Janeiro: Olympio, 1955.

Priester, Paul. "Uncle Tom Syndrome." *Encyclopedia of Multicultural Psychology*, edited by Yo Jackson, 461, Sage, 2006.

Quijano, Aníbal. *Aníbal Quijano: Ensayos en Torno a la Colonialidad del Poder*. Buenos Aires: Del Signo, 2019.

Salgueiro, Maria Aparecida Ferreira de Andrade. "Machado de Assis: A Keen Look at Nineteenth-Century Brazilian Identity." *Portuguese Literary & Cultural Studies*, vol. 13/14, 2005, 285–91.

Samuelson, Meg. " 'Lose Your Mother, Kill Your Child': The Passage of Slavery and its Afterlife in Narratives by Yvette Christiansë and Saidiya Hartman." *English Studies in Africa*, vol. 51, no. 2, 2009, 38–48.

Sayers, Raymond S. *The Negro in Brazilian Literature*. New York: Hispanic Institute in the United States, 1956.

Schwarz, Roberto. *A Master on the Periphery of Capitalism*. Duke University Press, 2001.

Sereza, Haroldo Ceravolo. "Iaiá Garcia e o Antinaturalismo de Machado de Assis." *Variações sobre o Romance II*, edited by Andréia Sirihal Werkema, Maria Juliana Gomboji Teixeira, and Nabil Araújo, 123–39, Rio de Janeiro: Edições, 2018.

Silva, Natalino. *A Estética da Dissimulação na Literatura de Machado de Assis*. Rio de Janeiro: Multifoco, 2017.

Spingarn, Adena. *Uncle Tom: From Martyr to Traitor.* Stanford University Press, 2018.

Stowe, Harriet Beecher. *Uncle Tom's Cabin.* Edited by Elizabeth Ammons, Norton, 2010.

Wood, Marcus. *The Black Butterfly: Brazilian Slavery and the Literary Imagination.* West Virginia University Press, 2019.

Chapter Five

Machado de Assis and the Color of Brazilian Literature in the United States

Benjamin Legg

"Slave Owners, Depicted Uncritically": An Awkward Inter-American Encounter with a Brazilian Master

The momentous first week of June 2020 saw a reckoning with anti-Black violence in the streets of cities across the United States, as well as an intensification of discussions in media, both mass and social, of ways to undo centuries of institutionalized racism. Among the more frequent strategies discussed was the act of reading, both of nonfiction theoretical works defining anti-racism and of literary works by Black authors. People tweeted and Instagrammed lists of Black-authored books, quotes from those works, and websites for Black-owned bookstores. In this environment of radical reading, researcher and translator Flora Thomson-DeVeaux saw her English translation of Machado de Assis's 1881 masterpiece *Memórias Póstumas de Brás Cubas* (one of two that came out in in the summer of 2020), the result of over a decade of work, published by Penguin Classics.

Among the memories Thomson-DeVeaux has of early critical reactions was that of a tweet made in response to a *New Yorker* article about the work. In an interview in October 2020, Thomson-DeVeaux summarized the tweet as well as her reaction to it: "[The tweet said] 'How can you post this when the hero of this book is a slaveowner who talks uncritically about owning slaves' . . . [I thought] I'm curious about this person who is obviously familiar with the content of the novel but did not know much about Machado de Assis" (personal interview). The reason for the translator's curiosity is the fact that Machado was, as Thomson-DeVeaux states in her introductory materials, "the mixed-race son of a humble family, the grandson of slaves" (xviii); in other words, a descendant of enslaved Africans brought to Brazil who, through his work in the Ministry of Agriculture, would have been deeply aware of the situation of the enslaved in Brazil. The tweet itself, posted 19 June 2020, reads: "This Eggers essay was published June 2, 2020, with the reaction to the murder of George Floyd in full swing, and yet there's no mention that the novel's main characters are slave owners, depicted uncritically. A simple prefatory note would suffice" (@FishandBicycles). There was a brief exchange with another poster, a Brazilian with the handle @PedroNakamura, who informed the original poster that Machado was indeed Black.

The whole exchange raises a number of key questions about the reception of Machado and his work, both in his homeland and in the Anglophone world. A recent round of translations by Thomson-DeVeaux and the British team of Margaret Jull Costa and Robin Patterson has once again raised Machado's prominence in the Anglophone reading world, while more than a decade of recent Machadian scholarship in Brazil and the United States has brought the author's racial identity front and center. Nevertheless, general ignorance of Machado de Assis, and Brazilian literature more broadly, outside of Brazil means that the author and his work have been described as "forgotten," "undiscovered," or "underappreciated" for the past seventy years in the English-language press. This paradoxical positioning between Machadian dominance in a national literature context and relative obscurity in the Anglosphere raises some of the most complicated questions that arise when we examine Brazilian contributions to a supposedly global canon of arts and letters.

Through an examination of book reviews and academic articles on the reception of Machado de Assis, I will establish a base of understanding of the ways that Machado has been read in US literary circles, before moving on to discussions of the author in Brazil and the US since 2000. Through these readings, I will focus closely on the way Machado is racialized and the way his work is seen as challenging or supporting systemic racial injustice and the violence of enslavement. By examining these readings, I intend to raise and perhaps answer a number of questions: How does a skeptical pioneer of narrative perspective who beat European avant-gardes by decades fit into a primitivist image of Brazil's contribution to global arts and culture in the mid-twentieth century? Does the growing understanding and acceptance of Machado as a Black creator in Brazil make him more appealing or marginalize him further for US readers? Finally, how important is it for translators and literary critics to focus on Machado's race in their work?

"A Reputation Finally Blooms" (Again): US Reception of Machado from 1950 to 2010

Around the centenary of Machado's death in September 2008, *New York Times* literary critic Larry Rohter published a piece with the headline "After a Century, a Literary Reputation Finally Blooms." This headline may strike a reader well acquainted with Machado as woefully uninformed. Machado, after all, was among the founders of Academia Brasileira das Letras, and his name, reputation, and literary creations permeated Brazilian lives from sambas de enredo to televised minisséries to vestibular college entry exams. A major square in Rio de Janeiro's fashionable Flamengo district was named after him, and his face appeared on multiple banknotes throughout the hyperinflationary 1980s. If anything, a Brazilianist could argue that Machado was too canonical (though it is a credit to his nuanced narratives and literary skill that few ever have). Nevertheless, for the *Times* editor who titled Rohter's piece, Machado's literary reputation was just coming into bloom.

Rohter's article is very much focused on the US reception of Machado, and within the first paragraphs he mentions perhaps the two most commonly cited US literary figures to vouch for Machado's inclusion in a global canon: Susan Sontag and Harold Bloom. Rohter quotes Sontag, who describes Machado as "the greatest writer ever produced in Latin America," as well as Bloom, who claims Machado to be "the supreme black literary artist to date" (B9). His article then goes on to discuss several cultural events focusing on Machado in the tristate area and includes quotations from interviews with Bloom, with Brazilian cultural heavy-hitters Roberto Schwarz and Nelson Pereira dos Santos and with translator Gregory Rabassa. Among the reasons Bloom gives for the apparent delay to Machado's recognition in the Anglosphere is the inadequacy of early translations that was remedied by a newer round of translations in the 1990s, including Rabassa's (B15).

Despite the seeming facility of this explanation, we already find counterevidence when we jump to one of the very sources for the article. Susan Sontag's "early and ardent" admiration for Machado was published in an essay entitled "Afterlives: The Case of Machado de Assis" in *The New Yorker* from May 1990. In this piece, the critic decries Machado's lack of recognition in a paragraph-long sentence:

> Imagine a writer who in the course of moderately long life, in which he never travelled more than seventy-five miles from the capital city where he was born, created a huge body of work—A nineteenth century writer, you will interrupt, and you will be right: author of a profusion of novels, novellas, stories, plays, essays, poetry, reviews, political chronicles, as well as reporter, magazine editor, government bureaucrat, candidate for public office, and founding president of his country's Academy of Letters; a prodigy of accomplishment, of the transcending of social and physical infirmities (he was a mulatto in a country where slavery was not abolished until he was almost fifty; he was epileptic), who, during this vividly prolific, exuberantly national career, managed to write a sizeable number of novels and stories deserving of a prominent place in world literature, and whose masterpieces, outside his native country, which honors him as its greatest writer, are little known, rarely mentioned. (102)

Sontag goes on to write about *Memórias Póstumas de Brás Cubas*, ostensibly introducing the work to a broader Anglophone audience and postulating as to why his work remained so unknown outside of Brazil: "But the impediment is not simply that Machado was not a European writer. Even more remarkable than his absence from the stage of world literature is that he has been very little known and read in the rest of Latin America—as if it were hard to digest the fact that the greatest author ever produced in Latin America wrote in the Portuguese, rather than the Spanish language" (107). We will return to Sontag's piece as well as a particularly strong rebuttal to it by Ilan Stavans later in this chapter. For the time being, it is most important to note that in the essay, Sontag herself attributes her devotion to Machado to a conversation with Cecil Hemley, the editor of her first novel, *The Benefactor*, published in 1963. In 1952, Hemley had been instrumental in the publication of William L. Grossman's translation of the *Memórias Póstumas . . . , Epitaph for a Small Winner*, and he passed a copy on to Sontag, from whence she began her intellectual love affair. What stands out in a reading of Sontag's essay, especially in comparison to Rohter's piece (and later Stavans's) is the lack of novelty in asserting that Machado is underappreciated in the English-speaking world. Sontag states in 1990 what Rohter states in 2008, and Bloom (the second-most quoted source in Rohter's piece) did the same in 2002, when he discussed Machado in his book *Genius*.

To learn more about the longer history of Machadian reception in the United States, we can look to Earl E. Fitz's article entitled "The Reception of Machado de Assis in the United States during the 1950s and 196Cs." In this piece, Fitz gives two explanations for Machado's low profile above the equator that are more nuanced (and specific to a US market) than Sontag's explanation. Among Fitz's most compelling arguments is that Machado's cynical worldview did not mesh well with a sunny, American exceptionalist view of humanity prevalent in postwar years: "Based on what they had accomplished in the war, Americans could be forgiven if they looked at themselves in the mirror and felt they saw success, that their way was the right way and that they should believe in it unquestioningly" (18). Among the downsides of this patriotic sense of exceptionalism was a dismissal of the foreign and a suspicion of cynicism. While cataloging critical responses to the 1952 Grossman translation that so enchanted Sontag, he cites critic SM Fitzgerald, who bemoaned the novel's "cheap nihilism" (Fitz 19), and a piece by Dudley Fitts where the critic comments on the spiritual decay and cultural decadence found in Machado's work (20).

Another motive for the relative lack of critical interest in Machado was the author's incongruence to a preestablished US notion of Brazil's cultural and intellectual value. Fitz writes: "This happened, I believe, because they did not expect to find such subtlety and sophistication in a writer most of them had never heard of, and from a place, Brazil, that they did not associate with high quality literature, as they did such nations as France, Germany, England and Russia" (24). He goes on to compare Machado's lack of success during this era with that of Jorge Amado:

Jorge Amado's *Gabriela, Cravo e* Canela (1958: Gabriela, Clove and Cinnamon, 1962), a novel widely read in the United States and one that seemed to justify American ideas about "progress" and technology while also playing to American stereotypes about "Latin" sex, sun and sand. To Brazilianists interested in the reception of Brazilian literature in the United States, it has always been a source of frustration that Jorge Amado (an undeniably great story teller), and not Machado de Assis (or Clarice Lispector or Guimarães Rosa) has been the one Brazilian writer that Americans tend to know or to have at least heard of, the one writer who, as late as the mid-1980s, is selected to "represent" South American literature in the United States. (25–26)

In other words, it was easier for a US reader most familiar with Brazil as the setting for *Black Orpheus*, the animated Bahia sequence from *The Three Caballeros*, and the sun-drenched seaside romance of the bossa nova boom to digest Amado's colorful Bahia than it was to appreciate an unglamorous nineteenth-century Rio filled with calculating and cynical (albeit deeply human) characters.

An interesting element of these midcentury responses to Machado was the prominence given to his mixed-race background. Hélio de Seixas Guimarães has written on race and Machadian reception. He claims that, at the time of his death, Machado was identified as white by the Brazilian intellectual elite: "as a result of his brilliant career and the recognition he received, Machado was officially white-washed, an unequivocal symptom of prejudice based on color that associates success with whiteness" (12). He then goes on to discuss the way some Brazilian intellectuals in the mid-twentieth century used Machado as an example of the particular genius originating from Brazil's mestiçagem. Around the same historical period, Guimarães notes a tendency in the United States to instead recognize Machado as a Black author: "The internationalization of the figure of Machado de Assis, which gains momentum in the 1950s with the steady and systematic translation of his works into English, particularly in the United States of America, also coincides with the first claims of Machado being a black author, which strains the image held of the writer in Brazil" (20). He gives as evidence Machado's being cataloged as a Black author in the Schomburg Center's catalog in 1962 and 1967, as well as in the catalogs of HBCU libraries at Howard and Fisk (20). In my interview with Flora Thomson-DeVeaux, she points even earlier, to 1952, when translator William Grossman published an article in the NAACP's magazine *The*

Crisis. In this text, Grossman compares Machado to Alexandre Dumas *père*, but he also claims that "[t]o a sophisticated reader Machado is by far the more satisfying" (563). Later in the piece he writes: "We see then that Machado is a Negro writer only in the sense of a writer who happened to be part Negro. He wrote about people as such—their egotism, their hypocrisy, their whole personal inadequacy; in his greatest works racial conflict plays almost no part" (566). Although he highlights Machado's disengagement from discussions on race, the publication of this article indicates that, for Grossman, Machado's race was of paramount importance for the promotion of his translation. Eighteen years later, in 1970, Helen Caldwell also referred to Machado's race starting from the second page of her groundbreaking English-language work on Machado's novels (4). She even makes reference to a Black Brazilian schoolteacher named Hemetério dos Santos, who penned a letter critiquing Machado's own denial of his race (8).

Interestingly, her book also begins with a paragraph that echoes later in Sontag's and Rohter's commentary; Caldwell herself begins her book: "Machado de Assis is no longer unknown among us. Four of his novels and some fifteen or so short stories have now appeared in English and have been greeted with a kind of indignant wonder that this Brazilian author who was born in 1839 and died in 1908 was not even a name to us" (3). In other words, the sense of shock that nobody knows about Machado, as well as a manifested interest in his racial background, have been part and parcel of the US response to his work since it has begun wider dissemination in translation.

Machado's explicit status as a Black/mixed-race author in the limited discussions of his work in US literary circles in the 1950s and 1960s makes sense for a number of reasons. First, there is the long-acknowledged difference between Brazilian and US categorizations of Blackness and whiteness. The legacy of British colonial discourses on racial purity, as well as a slaveholding system where the enslaved had almost no legal means of achieving freedom on their own, meant that mixed-race individuals in the United States were categorized as Black (a nexus of categorization often described as the "one-drop rule"). While the institution of slavery was as violent and dehumanizing in Brazil as it was in the United States, there was a path to manumission for the enslaved, and as such there was a larger population of free people of color than there was in the United States, resulting in racial categorizations more focused on skin color and other phenotypic traits than on bloodlines. This meant that a large number of Afro-descendants, particularly those who climbed socioeconomically like Machado, eventually became "white" in Brazil. In summary, Machado's Blackness made sense to US readers in a country where lighter-skinned Afro-descendants were considered Black. Furthermore, in the 1950s and 1960s, Brazil's image in the United States was very much connected to Afro-descendants and their culture. Among the fruits of Gilberto Freyre's discourses on racial democracy and the lack of de jure discrimination in Brazil—ideas that would become deeply ingrained in Brazil's intellectual and diplomatic circles—was a focus on African contributions to Brazilian culture. US intellectual and artistic circles would have contact with this through works like Canadian anthropologist Ruth Landes's influential 1947 book *City of Women* and French director Michel Camus's 1958 film *Black Orpheus*. Even cookbooks and tourist information aimed at a US audience of the era highlighted Afro-Brazilian aspects of Brazil's cuisine and cultural life (the Brazilian chapter of the Time Life *Food of the World* series book on Latin America is entitled "Brazil: A Touch of Africa") (Leonard 121).

It would make sense, then, that Machado's race would be highlighted in these earlier US encounters with the author in a way that it would not in Brazil. In my interview with Flora Thomson-DeVeaux, she mentioned Grossman's attempt to foreground Machado's race in the discussions of his translation, but she also claimed that "it didn't catch on" (personal interview). What did catch on was more of the idea we first encountered in the opening to Sontag's piece: that Machado's race was a challenge he had to overcome. Thomson-DeVeaux did not want to frame Machado's race as an obstacle in the explanatory materials for her 2020 translation. She listed a group of adjectives frequently used in English-language discussions of Machado: "mulatto, epileptic, poor, stuttering" (personal interview). A great example of this very set of words can be found in Alfred MacAdam's 1998 *Los Angeles Times* review of 1990s translations of *Brás Cubas* and *Dom Casmurro* by Gregory Rabassa and John Gledson, respectively: "In politics as in literature, Machado was an anomaly. Poor, epileptic, mulatto in a caste-ridden society where slavery wasn't abolished until 1888, largely self-educated, he was, nevertheless, no radical" (2). MacAdam's review, one that responded to the newer translations that Harold Bloom (and Larry Rohter) claimed were an improvement on the earlier ones that enchanted Sontag, nevertheless repeats a lot of the common tropes we encounter when reading US responses to Machado. While there have been flurries of excitement around Machado with new waves of translation, one must admit a certain similarity in the discourse. What, then, do we see in discussions around the most recent flurry of Machado translation, which begins in 2018 and includes Thomson-DeVeaux's work? Have evolving conversations around race and around Latin America itself perhaps influenced the reception of these new editions?

Don't "Blunt Its Wickedness": Discussions of Race and Slavery in the Current Wave of Machado Translation

We then arrive to the most recent round of Machadian promotion in US literary circles. Like Grossman and Caldwell in the 1950s and 1960s and like Rabassa and Gledson in the 1990s, there are some key names in this new wave of translations. In addition to the American Thomson-DeVeaux, an independent scholar in Brazilian literature and a researcher for podcasting operation Rádio Novelo, there is the British team of Margaret Jull Costa and Robin Patterson, who have been prolific translators from Portuguese to English over the past decade. Their translation of Machado's complete short stories, a 960-page tome entitled *The Collected Stories of Machado de Assis*, was released by Liveright in 2018 and set off this new cycle of interest in Machado among Anglophone literary circles. As mentioned at the start of this chapter, two translations of *Brás Cubas* were published in the same month in 2020: one, published by Penguin Classics, was translated by Thomson-DeVeaux with a foreword by US novelist Dave Eggers, and the other, published by Liveright, was translated by the British team.

In a comparative review of the two works, Parul Sehgal from *The New York Times* makes the now almost clichéd commentary on Machado being constantly rediscovered by English-language readers: "It's said that each generation discovers Machado anew" (C5). She then goes on to discuss the author's life, bringing up his ancestors' enslavement and avoiding any mention of epilepsy or stuttering. While she claims Thomson-DeVeaux's work is "a gift to scholars," she ends up indicating a preference for Jull Costa and Patterson's translation. That said, an aspect of the American translator's work that she appreciates is the way her notes and introduction allow a US lay reader to understand and appreciate Machado's references to slavery and racial injustice:

> Machado has been described as reticent on race. In fact, Thomson-DeVeaux reveals, his fiction is drenched in references to the slave trade. Modern readers, especially non-Brazilians, just

haven't known where to look. In this novel, these references are seeded into the geography. Take a scene in which Brás Cubas mentions passing through the Valongo neighborhood of Rio de Janeiro. Thomson-DeVeaux writes that Machado's contemporaries would recognize the name instantly as the site of the city's old slave market—once the largest in the Americas. (Sehgal)

In a piece for the website *Electric Literature*, the translator echoes some of her comments on Machado's critique of slavery and systemic racism from the introduction of the Penguin Classics edition. Referencing Sidney Chalhoub's work on Machado's time at the ministry of agriculture, she brings up the author's work helping to implement the Free Womb Law. As for his creation of the character of Brás Cubas, Thomson-Deveaux comments: "And as a non-white man in an overwhelmingly white literary establishment, he constructed a white narrator who can be casually amused by brutal injustice, holding up a grotesque mirror to a nation where slavery was then still legal" ("Introducing . . ."). She also devotes space both in this piece and in her introduction to the challenges of translating a chapter set in the Valongo slave market in which Brás Cubas sees a former slave of his, whom he had violently tortured in his youth, now whipping and torturing a slave of his own. The translator believes that any attempt to expand the chapter through explanation would "blunt its wickedness," one achieved through brevity; she adds: "And yet to leave the sentence as such, without any context, would be to impoverish it immeasurably" (xxiii).

Jull Costa and Patterson also direct their potential readers to the Valongo sequence and other references to the violence of slavery, albeit in a less explicit way than Thomson-DeVeaux does. In a piece in *The Paris Review*, the two translators write: "The subject of slavery is present throughout the novel, but Machado's message is carefully hidden behind cool understatement or apparently blasé indifference—after all Brazil did not abolish slavery until 1888, some eight years after the novel was first published, and Machado himself was the grandson of a freed slave." What is interesting about this new focus on Machado's race and his depiction of slavery in *Memórias Póstumas de Brás Cubas* is the way that it indeed has influenced Sehgal's own reading of the novel(s) and, in so doing, ostensibly the sector of the US reading public that would also read literary reviews in the *Times*. In her review of the two translations, she explicitly mentions the Valongo scene and wonders what it means about Machado's relationship with race and the unjust system so essential to Brazil for over half of his lifetime: "I keep turning this scene in my mind like a Rubik's Cube, wondering at the author's attitude toward his character. Machado plays the scene lightly. He does not linger, and he remains conspicuously fond of Brás Cubas. But I feel Machado wondering, too, as he peers through the eyes of Brás Cubas" (Sehgal).

In Sehgal's article, we see an acknowledgment on the part of a US reader of the complex and subtle critique Machado makes of the institution of slavery. While this new round of translators may be less willing than Grossman was to describe Machado as a Black writer, they more effectively foreground the subtle way Machado contributed to the conversation around slavery and race relations in Brazil during his writing career. When comparing G. Reginald Daniel's book, *Machado de Assis: Multiracial Identity and the Brazilian Novelist*, to Eduardo de Assis Duarte's groundbreaking *Machado de Assis Afro-Descendentei*, Hélio de Seixas Guimarães claims: "The positions of the Brazilian critic and of the U.S. sociologist somehow invert the trends for how Brazilian and U.S. intellectuals were classifying Machado in the 1950s. This is noted in that Daniel, in his very well-documented study on Machado de Assis, seems to adopt more fluid ethnic and racial classifications than those of Duarte" (24). Despite this observation from Guimarães, it is to me quite evident that this twenty-first-century Brazilian tendency to see Machado as a Black writer, or at the very least an understanding of Machado as an author who deals with questions of race and the injustices of slavery, is also present in US discussions of the author.

It is essential to recognize the impact of literary scholar Eduardo de Assis Duarte's work on race and racism in Machado in Brazilian (and Brazilianist) critical circles. Were it not for work like this, one would not find tweets like @PedroNakamura's rebutting the critique of Machado as uncritical of slavery. Assis Duarte published a full book on Machado as an Afro-descendant man, as well as several articles on the topic. Among these is one, translated into English by Thomas Stovicek and published in *Research in African Literatures*, that summarizes some of the critic's key arguments. Duarte establishes the historical consensus, or "reading," of Machado as an author who ignored discussions of slavery and racism, even pointing out an Afro-Brazilian critic, Ironides Rodrigues, who strongly argued against Machado's claim on Blackness (135). The critic then outlines the strong racial prejudices present in late nineteenth-century Brazilian literature and claims that more explicitly abolitionist writers like Aluísio Azevedo, Joaquim Manoel de Macedo, and José Patrocínio "left etched in their writings the characteristic discourse of racial hegemony" (138), a claim that he states "does not apply to Machado de Assis's literary output" (138). Through close readings of Machado's journalistic works, several poems, and short stories and of excerpts from *Memórias Póstumas* . . . and *"Ressurreição,"* Duarte proves that Machado was indeed engaged in conversations on slavery and racism, and he ends the text with the metaphor of the "caramujo," or periwinkle, a creature associated with shyness and introversion in Brazilian Portuguese. He cites Machado's description of his jubilation at the announcement of the emancipation of slaves in Brazil, "sim, eu saí na rua, *eu o mais encolhido dos caramujus* . . . todos respiravam felicidade, tudo era delírio" (150, italics in original), and concludes the article by claiming, "Machado knew how to be a warrior, conscious of his weapons and his targets" (150). For William Grossman, the fact that Machado seemed to address racial conflict infrequently in his work was a sign of his talent as a writer, of his overcoming the limitations of systemic racism and writing about whatever he wanted. From his piece in *The Crisis:* "Machado gives the eternal lie to the notion, apparently held by many American publishers, that a Negro can only produce first-class literature in the realm of racial problems" (566). Duarte's work shows that Machado's true talent was in fact the ability to write about racial conflict and take a stand against the injustices of slavery without alienating a reading public that was deeply invested in those very injustices.

While Duarte's work has left an indelible mark on the study of Machado's work (Thomson-Deveaux's illuminating introduction and footnotes and this very volume being but two examples of its repercussions for English-language readers and scholars), it is far from a monolithic point of view. In this chapter alone, we can point to Caldwell's and even to Duarte's own work as summarizing decades of critique that Machado was not racially engaged enough. We cannot forget Hemetério dos Santos's 1908 letter to *Gazeta das Notícias*, where the Black educator makes deep criticisms of Machado's apparent lack of commitment to abolition (Ximenes). More recent critics continue to debate this new critical turn. A recent article by Alex Flynn, Elena Calvo-González, and Marcelo Mendes de Souza on the short story "Pai contra mãe," among Duarte's most resonant examples of Machado's critique of slavery, argues against the contemporary racialization of the story's characters and conflict: "Duarte, similarly to other scholars (Scarpelli 2004; Dourado 2010; Diogo 2008; Neves 2007; Mangueira 2009; Moraes 2009; Muniz 1996) makes the assumption that

Cândido and Clara are white and that therefore when Cândido's baby is saved from starvation by the delivering of the runaway slave Arminda to her owner, an action that results in Arminda miscarrying, a black child's life has been given so that a white child may survive" (11). The authors comment on the ways this reading of the story has become mainstream by providing images from a comic strip by Célia Lima and J. Rodrigues: "Cândido and Clara are depicted in a manner in which Machado never *expressly* depicts them: they are both white, and to reinforce the point, Cândido even has a somewhat lantern-jawed aspect" (11). In other words, there is still some debate around the racialization of Machado and his work in the field of Brazilian literary studies. That said, it would be neglectful to ignore these debates and discussions when dealing with the author, and even if Flynn, Calvo-González, and Souza debate Duarte's reading, they still give it ample space in their article in order to better engage it.

Such "fortuna crítica" of Machado's work has not necessarily echoed to a US reading public who is not immersed in Brazilian literary circles. A 2018 piece by Ilan Stavans, a Mexican American scholar of Latin American and Latino literature, shows something of a repudiation of this narrative. He structures the piece, a review of Jull Costa and Patterson's "Collected Stories," as a rebuttal to Susan Sontag's claim that Machado was the greatest author ever produced in Latin America. He then goes on to deflate what he sees as an overinflated reputation for the author: "He isn't a great writer at all, though he is good, and sometimes very good. He is also often disturbing, especially in regard to his racist and anti-Semitic views" ("Wrestling . . .") Rather than acknowledging the ample debate around race in Machado, Stavans writes: "He was the son of a mixed-race father and a white washerwoman, yet his views of slavery are invisible. . . . Harold Bloom once misrepresented Machado as 'the supreme black literary artist to date,' when in his work Machado hardly acknowledged his own blackness" (Wrestling . . .). He goes on to specifically critique the story "Pai contra mãe" in its English translation, apparently taking Machado's cold and sarcastic description of slavery—"not all enjoyed enslavement"—as a tacit endorsement of the institution (Wrestling . . .). While many Brazilian critics since Machado's death would agree with this statement, it does not accurately reflect current influential discussions or trends on the subject and rather reads like a dismissal of Bloom's own ignorance of Brazil/Latin America. It also leads to some interesting concluding thoughts on the way race and peripherality impact Machado's reception in the United States.

On "Local Color"

In the same critique, Stavans comments on Machado's lack of a cosmopolitan scope compared to Borges, a Latin American author whom he considers to be a much more likely candidate for "greatness." He cites Borges's famous lecture on "The Argentine Writer and Tradition" and lambasts Machado: "He concentrates on Brazil as if it were his only sphere of influence" (Wrestling . . .). Earlier in the essay, Stavans also decries the fact that "we learn very little about Rio's architecture, its customs, its cuisine," in Machado's work, a complaint that seems to go against Borges's very argument in "The Argentine Writer . . ." that Latin American literature does not need to luxuriate itself in "local color.¹ One could go as far as to see Machado's focus on the inner lives and power struggles of characters in the upper echelons of Carioca society as a radical rebuttal of the need to "nationalize" a peripheral literature. Unfortunately, it appears Machado is too Brazilian and not quite Brazilian enough for Stavans, and this seeming paradox could be key to understanding the repeated confusion at Machado's lack of stature in the United States over the past seventy years.

As I point out at the end of the second section of this chapter, Machado's earliest US translations were published into a market that expected a specific, highly exotic image of Brazil as a nation stamped by African cultures. The content of Machado's work was not reflective of these post-Freyrean explorations of mestiçagem, and perhaps Grossman's midcentury attempt to present Machado as an example of an unsung Black literary figure was a means of bridging that cognitive dissonance for a US audience. While some, including Thomson-DeVeaux in her interview with me, argue that this attempt on Grossman's part did not "catch on," I believe that one could also argue on the contrary. Machado's racial identity, even if not explicitly described as "Black," has been evident in US writings about the author since *The Crisis* article in 1952. Some have used the word "mulatto," while others, like Thomson-DeVeaux, have described him as "mixed-race," but none considered him a white author. It bears reminding that for most of US history and in most US territories, people of mixed race were subject to the types of discrimination used against all Afro-descendants in a regime of bloodline racial categorization. Black cultural products, many of which were produced by people of mixed ancestry, were only considered "mainstream" after their co-optation by artists viewed unambiguously as white. Jazz and the blues become "American" after their distillation into swing and rock and roll. Within this paradigm, whether it is explicitly stated, Machado de Assis's work in the United States would be seen as Black literature.

What has perhaps changed more dramatically is the Brazilian reaction to Machado as a Black author. At the start of his article in the *Review of African Literature*, Duarte comments: "For this reason, not a few have been surprised by Harold Bloom's assertion that Machado de Assis was [the] 'greatest black writer in the history of universal literature'" (134). As Duarte and Guimarães document, and as Hemetério Santos and Ironides Rodrigues bemoaned, Machado had been whitened by the time of his death, whether through his own acts or through those of the Brazilian literary establishment. Guimarães details the ways in which Brazilian literature was (and is) seen as a white endeavor and the inheritor of a European tradition. This configuration of Brazilian society as fundamentally Western resonated through centuries of writings on brasilidade and can be encountered in writers ranging from Eduardo Prado to Sérgio Buarque de Holanda to Vianna Moog and Alceu de Amoroso Lima. While all of these writers maintain Brazil's culture and society as distinct from that of the United States and Protestant Northern Europe, they also all reaffirm that Brazil is the inheritor of a Western, Catholic tradition. In the United States, on the other hand, the stereotyped Brazilian culture imagined in the 1950s and 1960s was decidedly non-Western, a status it would have shared with many US cultural products created by Black artists and intellectuals in the broad popular imagination. Interventions like those of Henry Louis Gates and Paul Gilroy in the 1980s and 1990s challenged this definition of what it is to be Black and Western, and in Gilroy's case they point to transnational Black intellectual experiences as crucial to understandings of modernity. A reading of Machado in light of discussions on global Blackness and Black participation in modern literature could perhaps raise the author's status in literary circles. That said, the current decolonial turn in literary studies, particularly those focused on Latin America, may once again impact receptions of Machado—whose abundant references to the classics and European philosophies, real and imagined—firmly plant him in a literary tradition that is the fruit of European colonialism. As we observe from Stavans's complaint that Machado's work is both too focused on Brazil and lacking in description of that very country, Machado challenges those who wish to categorize him too easily.

This resistance to simple taxonomy reflects broader flaws in US attempts to categorize Brazil, particularly in racial terms. Discussions around Machado's reception as a nonwhite contributor to a Western/global canon are indeed pertinent to understanding how Brazilian intellectuals conceive of their nation within a global context, to debates over systemic racism's role in discussions of whether Brazil should be a player on the world stage, and, finally, to decolonial debates about Western identity. Angharad Valdivia presents the case of blonde, German-descendant television star Xuxa's lack of success in the US in the 1990s as an example of a Brazilian being too white for the US market and for a racialized definition of "Latin" in the United States. At the same time, despite Machado's racial origins, the lack of "local color" in his works made them read as too Western for a critic like Stavans. To deny Brazilian claims of Westernness is to reinforce US and European intellectual hegemony, while to wholeheartedly accept them is to stand in the way of attempts of many Indigenous and Afro-Brazilian creators to decolonize Brazilian culture. In order to fully appreciate the intricacies of Brazil and its vast contributions to world culture, we need to understand the broader intellectual, historical, and political contexts of those contributions. The work of scholars like Thomson-DeVeaux, which aims to contextualize Machado, is invaluable for such deeper understanding.

Note

1. "El culto argentino de color local es un reciente culto europeo que los nacionalistas deberían rechazar por foráneo" (270). "Creo que los argentinos podemos parecernos a Mahoma, podemos creer en la posibilidad de ser argentinos sin abundar en color local" (270).

Works Cited

@FishandBicycles. "This Eggers essay was published June 2, 2020 . . ." *Twitter*, 19 June 2020, https://twitter.com/NewYorker/status/1273825103919316993. Accessed April 13, 2021.

@PedroNakamura. " 'Depicted uncritically,' I guess that's a problem with the English translation then." *Twitter*, 19 June 2020, https://twitter.com/NewYorker/status/1273825103919316993. Accessed April 13, 2021.

Bloom, Harold. *Genius.* Warner Books, 2002.

Borges, Jorge Luis. "El escritor argentino y la tradición." *Discusión*, Emecé Editores, 1957, 267–75.

Caldwell, Helen. *Machado de Assis: The Brazilian Master and His Novels.* California University Press, 1970.

Costa, Margaret Jull and Robin Patterson. "Machado's Catalogue of Failures." *The Paris Review*, 16 June 2020, *The Paris Review*, https://theparisreview. org/blog/2020/06/16/machados-catalogue-of-failures/. Accessed April 13, 2021.

Duarte, Eduardo de Assis. *Machado de Assis Afro-Descendente*. 2nd ed., Pallas/ Crisálida, 2007.

———. "Machado de Assis's African Descent." *Research in African Literatures*, vol. 39, no. 1, 2007, 134–51. *Project Muse*, https://doi.org/10.1353/ral.2007.0033. Accessed April 13, 2021.

Fitz, Earl. "The Reception of Machado de Assis in the United States during the 1950s and 1960s." *Luso-Brazilian Review*, vol. 46, no. 1, 2009, 17–36. *Project Muse*, https://muse-jhu-edu.proxy.library.vanderbilt.edu/article/26894. Accessed April 13, 2021.

Flynn, Alex, Elena Calvo-González, and Marcelo Mendes de Souza. "Whiter Shades of Pale: 'Coloring In' Machado de Assis and Race in Contemporary Brazil." *Latin American Research Review*, vol. 48, no. 3, 2013, 3–24. *Project Muse*, https://doi.org/10.1353/lar.2013.0046. Accessed April 13, 2021.

Gates Jr., Henry Louis. *Figures in Black*. Oxford University Press, 1987.

Gilroy, Paul. *The Black Atlantic*. Harvard University Press, 1993.

Grossman, William L. "A Great Negro Author Rediscovered." *The Crisis*, vol. 59, no. 9, Nov. 1952, 563–69. *Google Books*, https://books.google.com/books? id=vlsEAAAAMBAJ&pg=PA563&dq=a+great+negro+author+rediscovered +william+l+grossman&hl=en&sa=X&ved=2ahUKEwiI0c-t5OrvAhXYWM0 KHbkODGUQ6AEwAHoECAMQAg#v=onepage&q&f=false. Accessed April 13, 2021.

Guimarães, Hélio de Seixas. "Race and Color in the Reception of Machado de Assis" *Luso-Brazilian Review*, vol. 54, no. 2, 2017, 11–25. *Project Muse*–https:// muse.jhu.edu/article/683448. Accessed April 13, 2021.

Holanda, Sérgio Buarque de. *Raízes do Brasil*. José Olympio, 1936.

Landes, Ruth. *The City of Women*. Macmillan, 1947.

Leonard, Jonathan Norton. *Latin American Cooking*. Time-Life Books, 1968.

Lima, Alceu Amoroso. *A realidade americana*. Livraria AGIR, 1954.

Prado, Eduardo. *A ilusão americana*. 1893. Civilização Brasileira, 1933.

Rohter, Larry. "After a Century a Literary Reputation Finally Blooms." *The New York Times*, 13 Sept. 2008, B9. *ProQuest Central*, doc. ID: 433923766. Accessed April 13, 2021.

Sehgal, Parul. "Crossing over to the Other Side on a Hippo." *The New York Times*, 17 June 2020, C5. *ProQuest*, doc. ID: 2413837033. Accessed April 13 2021.

Sontag, Susan. "Afterlives: The Case of Machado de Assis." *The New Yorker*, 7 May 1990, 102–8. *The New Yorker Online*, https://archives.newyorker.com/ newyorker/1990-05-07/flipbook/102/. Accessed April 13, 2021.

Stavans, Ilan. "Wrestling with Machado" *The Yale Review*, 2 July 2018, *Yale Review Online*, https://yalereview.yale.edu/wrestling-machado. Accessed April 13, 2021.

Thomson-DeVeaux, Flora. "Introduction." *The Posthumous Memoirs of Brás Cubas*, by Machado de Assis, translated by Flora Thomson-DeVeaux, Penguin Classics, 2020, xxii–xxvii.

————. Personal interview, 2 Oct. 2020.

————. "Introducing Brazil's Best Classic Writer You've Never Heard Of" *Electric Literature*, 4 June 2020, *Electric Literature*, https://electricliterature.com/introducing-joaquim-maria-machado-de-assis-brazils-best-writer-youve-never-heard-of/.

Valdivia, Angharad N., and Ramona Curry. "Xuxa! Can Latin Americans Be Blonde or Can the United States Tolerate a Latin American." *A Latina in the Land of Hollywood and Other Essays on Media Culture*, edited by Angharad N. Valdivia, University of Arizona Press, 2000, 125–47.

Vianna Moog, Clodomiro. *Bandeirantes e Pioneiros: paralelo entre duas culturas*. Editora Globo, 1954.

Ximenes, Sérgio Barcellos. "A cobrança post-mortem de um professor negro a Machado de Assis pela falta de protagonismo na causa abolicionista." *Medium*, 8 June 2020, https://medium.com/@sergiobximenes/a-cobran%C3%A7a-post-mortem-de-um-professor-negro-a-machado-de-assis-pela-falta-de-protago-nismo-na-adb377c8a37c. Accessed April 13, 2021.

Chapter Six

Black Writer, White Letters?

Machado's Racialized Reception of Identity and Aesthetics

Daniel F. Silva

Though Machado de Assis has become increasingly historicized in contemporary public and literary spheres as a Black writer, his oeuvre continues to be racially codified in complex ways within frayed "world literature" markets as well as in national and global Eurocentric literary historiographies. This essay will thus contend that while Machado's identity has come to be understood in these literary spheres as Afro-Brazilian or Afro-Diasporic, his work continues to be framed and cataloged through Eurocentric paradigms of literary reception that already operated in his lifetime. Paying particular attention to the June 2020 publication of two new translations of *Memórias Póstumas de Brás Cubas*, I shall, moreover, interrogate how the markets and global literary circuitries of transla-tion, consumption, and canonization reproduce problematic and, I will argue, racially influenced divisions of Machado's work between "early" and "mature" phases as well as along lines of genre. What is at stake and what is lost in how Machado and his oeuvre are consumed at this specific moment of reckoning with white supremacy, when certain texts continue to be foregrounded and translated while others are pushed to the margins of his corpus or categorized as part of an "unpolished" phase of literary production? My essay will thus conclude with a reading of existing archives of Machado's reception that propose alternate historiographies of Machado's work, placing it in dialogue with Black literary canons and critical interrogations of racial capitalism.

Racial Capital, Machado's Life, and the Partitioning of His Oeuvre

June 2020 saw a profound and globally coordinated anti-racist activist movement of resistance and solidarity, forged and given a common language by the Black Lives Matter movement, and manifest itself against the ongoing state and state-sanctioned violence against Black life in the wake of the murder of George Floyd on 26 May of that year. Floyd's murder at the hands of police, shown on video across the world, was "only" the latest brazen and brutal killing of a Black person by state power at the service of white supremacist and capitalist economic and political infrastructures. Floyd's death under the knee of white police officer, Derek Chauvin, came on the heels of several other widely reported, and often filmed, murders and executions of Black citizens in the United States, leading to what many observers considered a watershed moment of popular mobilization against institutionalized anti-Black violence with marches and protests taking place in cities around the globe during the COVID-19 pandemic.

That very same month, as millions around the world—especially Black activists and organizers—faced militizarized anti-protest forces and a fatal pandemic in the struggle against systemic racism, another singular and noteworthy event surfaced, though in far different circumstances. For likely the first time in the frayed and complicated history of world literature, two translations of the same literary work were released in the same language in the same month. The piece in question is Joaquim Maria Machado de Assis's *Memórias Póstumas de Brás Cubas* (*Posthumous Memoirs of Brás Cubas*), originally published in 1881 and previously translated into English in 1952 under the title *Epitaph for a Small Winner* by William L. Grossman and again in 1997 under the current title by Gregory Rabassa. The 2020 translations were notably published by two of the largest English-language trade presses, with Flora Thomson-DeVeaux's translation published by Penguin in its Classics series and Margaret Jull Costa and Robin Patterson's translation published by Liveright, a division of W. W. Norton & Company.

Though seemingly unrelated occurrences, the struggle against anti-Black violence and exploitation and the nearly simultaneous release of two translations of the same nineteenth-century Brazilian novel share much historical and material common ground, including the fact that Machado de Assis is of African descent as the grandson of enslaved people. More substantively and broadly, though, both events are inextricable from what Cedric Robinson has importantly termed racial capitalism: "The development, organization, and expansion of capitalist society pursued essentially racial directions, so too did social ideology. As a material force, then, it could be expected that racialism would inevitably permeate the social structures emergent from capitalism" (Robinson 2). Through this framework, we can contextualize the emergence and consumption of Machado's oeuvre within "the complex recursivity between material and epistemic forms of racialized violence which are executed in and by core capitalist states with seemingly infinite creativity" (Melamed 77). This implies a circuiting of various temporalities of racial capital, their diegetic expression in Machado's work, and the material conditions of literary consumption and canonization across periods and geographies.

Firstly, we must consider the material conditions of Machado's life and his rise in literary circles dominated by white Brazilian elites. Machado was born in 1839 in Rio de Janeiro, specifically in the Morro do Livramento neighborhood of the city to Francisco José de Assis, a son of freed slaves, and Maria Leopoldina da Câmara Machado, an Azorean working-class immigrant (Aidoo and Silva 1–2). The family resided in the home of their employer as dependent workers—or agregados. These became his godparents and ultimately helped fund his education. Due to his marginalized and subalternized locale in racial capital, his emergence as a writer, despite his talents, depended upon the relationships cultivated with figures of varying prominence such as journalists, small newspaper owners, and, slowly, with other well-connected writers. Indeed, as Lília Moritz Schwarcz notes, Machado's early life and his early literary career highlight the workings of structural dependency and clientelistic practices that guided the few avenues of social mobility afforded to Brazilians of African descent (15).

In terms of diegetic expression, critical readings can be made of Machado's portrayals of racial capital, its material structures, and the varyingly sordid everyday lives of different subject-positions in pre- and post-abolition Brazil. This rings true across his body of work whether one reads one of Machado's early critiques of slavery, its sexual violence, and its paternalist economies of dependence (as in the 1864 short story, "Virginius"), or the minutiae of bourgeois life of some of his most celebrated characters in his later novels, ranging from Brás Cubas (1881) to Counselor Ayres (1907). As a literary scholar and Machado expert, Nelson H. Vieira argues with regard to Machado's treatment of societal power structures, "Machado was sensitive to the callous daily practices embedded in ruthless behavior during the nineteenth-century period of nation building, when personal and social gains among the bourgeoisie took precedent. As a nation yearning for a nationalist and liberal image of progress, Brazil was critically read by Machado in light of the mad drive to be a civilized society during a period of sociopolitical and financial ambition, yet still dependent on slaves" (viii).

Though I hope to sidestep the pitfalls of pitting Machado's early works against his later works, it is important to note that dominant historiographies of his oeuvre divide it in two periods: his early, more Romanticist-inflected works spanning 1860 to 1878 (including novels, short stories, poetry, and plays) and his later, more Realist-influenced and skeptical works spanning 1880 to his death in 1908. The latter is often referred to as his "mature phase" in which he abandons Romanticist aesthetics—a position he justified and defended in his 1873 essay "Instinto de Nacionalidade" ("Instinct of Nationality"). Here he argues that Romanticist aesthetics could no longer sufficiently articulate national identity and the complexities of national social organization constituted by slavery, problematic notions of progress, and a growing national bourgeoisie made possible by the first two. Following the essay's publication, Machado would go on to publish three further novels that are historicized as making up his so-called early phase—A Mão e a Luva [The Hand and the Glove] (1874), Helena (1876), and Iaiá Garcia (1878). It is important to note that different scholars have challenged this historiography, arguing that many of Machado's later aesthetic traits were already evident in some of his works of the 1860s and 1870s. Vieira, though also arguing that Machado cultivated and perfected a new narrative strategy in the late 1870s and 1880s, perhaps in accord with his 1873 essay, nonetheless contends that "Machado's wry use of narrative point of view to unearth his dissatisfaction with the abuses of the upper echelons of society regarding class, race, and status can also be discovered in subtle intimations permeating his early work" (ix).

Beyond narrative techniques, political concerns—particularly the quotidian violence sanctioned by a racial division of labor enshrined in slavery and its afterlife—were also present in Machado's works of the 1860s and early 1870s. Two short stories of the period come to mind: the aforementioned "Virginius" and "Mariana" published in 1871, both of which have been relegated to the margins of the canonical sector of Machado's oeuvre. Nonetheless, I mention the problematic historiographic division of Machado's work precisely because of what it possibly reveals about his reception and the racial/aesthetic terms of its canonization. To be specific, the supposed historical boundary between his early and "mature" phases is centered on his supposed turn toward skepticism, particularly that which centered on white bourgeois characters, articulating their complexities, contradictions, and abuses. This historiography ultimately fails to grapple with the skepticism and the complex critiques of racial power structures Machado explicitly deposits into his literary treatments of slavery across both supposed phases. In other words, this historiography and reception fundamentally forecloses a charting of Machado's critical skepticism that emerges in his treatment of slavery. By the same token, Machado's literary grappling and, indeed, critical historicization of slavery also finds sustained prevalence in later works, such as the short stories "O Caso da Vara" ("The Cane") (1891) and "Pai contra Mãe" ("Father versus Mother") (1905).

Criticism of Machado's racial politics at the level of literary content, arguing that his work lacked the sustained critiques of Brazilian racial structures of power, have abounded (as we shall further explore ahead), even in his own lifetime. A fellow Afro-Brazilian writer of similar economic background, Lima Barreto (1881–1922) was perhaps the first notable critic of Machado's racial politics (in both public life and literary content), accusing Machado of sidestepping systems of anti-Black racism and the afterlives of slavery in his work, thus leading to his canonization in life and ultimately becoming the founder and first chair of the Brazilian Academy of Letters. Meanwhile, Barreto, whose work "more overtly" and consistently foregrounded the legacies of slavery and the racial materialities of capitalism, became the object of scorn by literary critics and was imprisoned in a psychiatric asylum for alcoholism. Only in the last half of the twentieth century did his work begin to gain critical notoriety.

Barreto's accusations are surely valid to an extent, but the whitening of Machado must also be understood through the trajectory of his work's reception, its dominant historiography, and the concomitant marginalization of certain works in favor of others. In other words, one must account for the racial politics of the literati public and elites of Machado's time as well as the contemporary circuits of consumption and reproduction of his work. Herein lies another important and transtemporal element in the complex relationship between Machado, his oeuvre, and racial capital—the racial materialities of consumption, reception, and canonization. These are processes, by and large, propelled by white bourgeois readerships and agents of the mechanical reproduction of literature, from acquisitions editors to marketing departments at publishing houses. Participation in the dialectics of literary consumption, production, and canonization necessitates participation and immersion in racial capital and colonial accumulation of wealth. Such participation thus operates within the same matrix of anti-Blackness and the afterlife of slavery as the ongoing state-sanctioned violence against Black lives the world over.

The Reception of *Posthumous Memoirs of Brás Cubas* (2020)

Having briefly traced the relationship between Machado's life, his oeuvre, and its readership during his time, I will now return to the recent overlap between the ongoing struggle against anti-Black violence and the double release of *Posthumous Memoirs of Brás Cubas* in 2020. More specifically, we shall turn our attention to what this tells us about Machado's readership and reception in the United States as a writer of African descent, as well as how it operates at the service of ongoing racial capital. This particular relationship between readership and racial capital has been, moreover, a driving force in the mechanical reproduction and consumption of what is known as world literature. An especially complicated category of literary production and consumption, one that has been negotiated in imperial centers, world literature has long had an intimate relationship to empire in the latter's economic and epistemological machinery. As Baidik Bhattacharya theorizes:

> Since the second half of the eighteenth century, through increased interaction with the colonies and through the daily business of governance, cultural practices on both sides of the colonial divide went through radical changes and a set of codes emerged to make sense of this newness. Literature as a recognizable category or even as an object of knowledge—whether as a counter-discourse to modernity or as its extension—was such a code; it was not only fashioned within this global context of imperial cultures, it was indeed designed to reflect this globality in its very organization. The passage from "literature" to "world literature" in the nineteenth century

was thus accomplished within this new condensed visibility of the world and was mediated by colonial histories. (8)

World literature, as a product of imperial canonization, therefore has long partaken in the epistemologies of white supremacy and western universality, with literary products operating for European and North American readers at the level of anthropological texts.

In this regard, the circulation and consumption of literary works from or on the colonized world have served as part of the archiving of non-European life and thus participate in racializing processes. At another level, world literature in its complex participation in signifying time, space, and bodies from diverse subject-positions across global capital (namely those of writers), though filtered through the for-profit dictates of the publishing industry, provides white readers with a comfortable simulacrum of engagement with the history of anti-Black racism through often superficial lexicons that inadequately account for the material life of racial capitalism, the afterlives of slavery, and ongoing coloniality within which the act of consuming a piece of writing by an author like Machado is couched. The investment in reading Machado within the current moment of racial capital, in the material space in which white bourgeois readership and canonization occur and through particular hermeneutic frames that have enveloped world literature, ultimately function as ways of consolidating a misrecognized existence in racial capital itself.

The publication of two translations of the same Machado de Assis novel in the same month (June 2020), and at the same time as anti-racist organizing on a global scale against anti-Black structures of power solidified into visible action, speaks to what I argue to be a racial epistemological dissonance between Machado readerships in the United States and the struggle for Black liberation on national and global scales. The ongoing celebration of *Posthumous Memoirs of Brás Cubas* and its signification as a classic text of literature speaks not necessarily to a whitewashing of Machado's oeuvre, but rather more concretely to white bourgeois understandings of racial power and anti-Black racism, which, despite their acknowledgment of a problem, continue to be at odds with the more robust and materially grounded exigencies of Black liberation movements, past and present.

This dissonance finds an analogous one in the literary treatments of racial capital in Machado's work, between his novels (especially of his so-called mature phase) and his short stories on slavery and its afterlife. As Thomson-DeVeaux and *New York Times* literary reviewer Parul Sehgal point out, Machado's oeuvre, including his most celebrated works, does address racial issues and the legacies of slavery in often subtle fashion. Seghal specifically points out: "In this novel, these references are seeded into the geography. Take a scene in which Brás Cubas mentions passing through the Valongo neighborhood of Rio de Janeiro. Thomson-DeVeaux writes that Machado's contemporaries would recognize the name instantly as the site of the city's old slave market—once the largest in the Americas. This is the backdrop to our aristocrat's leisurely philosophical inquiry and self-preoccupation; this the subtlety of Machado's psychological shading" (n.p.). But what is often most celebrated are formal issues in the novel—the critique of the novel itself and of the white bourgeois literary circles in which he, too, partook. Furthermore, the subtle yet complex evocations of racial violence, capital, and oppression through slavery and its legacies require a set of analytical tools seldom available to and harnessed by white middle-class readerships in the consumptive spheres of world literature, nor are such tools provided in edited translations of Machado's work, though Thomson-Deveaux makes a valid attempt. Beyond editors and translators, one can argue whether it would behoove large multinational presses like Penguin and W. W. Norton & Company to frame works in such a way for world literature readerships economically and ontologically invested in the materialities and metaphysics of racial capitalism.

Even Thomson-Deveaux and Sehgal's perspicacious reading of the above passage can be further unpacked. One can actually read Brás Cubas's frayed philosophizing at the Valongo as a complex superposition of temporalities of racial capitalism in Brazil, with the exploitation fomented and negotiated at the Valongo through the commodification of enslaved Black bodies as instruments and objects of extraction leading to the material conditions that allowed Brás Cubas to access particular forms of economic well-being, institutional privilege, and cultural capital.

From Brazil to the Anglophone World: Machado's Racialized Reception

This partial reading of Machado's treatment of slavery is illustrative of the sorts of readings that have informed Machado's trajectory in the realm of national literature in his lifetime and in the fuzzy terrains of world literature after his passing. It is also illustrative of the many blind spots and the silencing in dominant Brazilian historiographies and national narratives of racial exceptionalism, which have propped up Machado as an example of social mobility in a racial democracy. Indeed, in the time since his death, Machado's life has been archived in hegemonic Brazilian historiographies in ways that have sustained his canonization. As a writer of African descent, his literary acclaim even during his lifetime has come to be signified as an example of a national society in which structural racism supposedly plays a minor part in a subject's life, if at all. Most (in)famously, Brazilian anthropologist Gilberto Freyre—a key intellectual figure in the development of the myth of racial democracy as a project of national historicization—in *New World in the Tropics*, written and published in English for Anglophone audiences, posited both Machado and Lima Barreto as "mulatto writers" (14) who attained social mobility on the road to becoming celebrated writers and contributors to Brazilian literature becoming "second to none in Latin America" (13). Freyre goes on to subtly celebrate Machado for never "expressing himself as a mulatto," while Barreto sometimes "dramatiz[ed] his condition of 'Negro' and 'plebian' in a somewhat un-Brazilian way."

For Freyre, his problematically perceived lack of racial consciousness or denunciation of racism in Brazil in Machado made the latter fit better within dominant fantasies of a racial democratic society, and therefore, within his conception of Brazilianness. Freyre's take on the difference between Barreto's and Machado's racial politics, with a nationalist bent, also bespeaks the comfort with which white Brazilian and subsequently white global audiences have engaged Machado's oeuvre, or at least the dominant historiography and archiving of it and his life (Freyre 13–14). As Hélio de Seixas Guimarães (2017) notes regarding the racialized and racializing receptions of Machado, Freyre helped usher in a celebrated racial reconfiguration of the writer as mixed race starting with his earlier anthropological works of the 1930s. Prior to that, literary critics of the late nineteenth century, like Sílvio Romero, disparaged Machado's writing due, in some measure, to his African descent (1897).

In archiving his life and work across time and space, Machado's readerships have underscored his oeuvre's (particularly of his "second phase") skepticism and narrational and structural innovation, while attention to racial power structures and how they operate in these very works is relegated to a footnote. This is the case with the previously cited Parul Sehgal review in the *New York Times*, but not only: the English translations of Machado's work have been packaged for English audiences in very much the same way since the second half of the twentieth century and as early as the first English translation of *Memórias Póstumas de Brás Cubas* published in 1952. Indicative of the dialectics of literary reception, reproduction, and consumption, this work in particular (notable for its four different translations) has circulated among Anglophone readerships through the reception of celebrated English-speaking white writers. For instance, Thomson-DeVeaux's translation opens with a foreword by decorated contemporary white United States writer Dave Eggers. On the back cover of this edition and others, as well as on bookselling websites, reception of Machado by white writers becomes an advertising technique, with praise and acclaim coming from Susan Sontag, Philip Roth, Harold Bloom, and John Updike, often recycling the same quotes.

Praise has also come in the form of comparison between Machado and the largely white canonized "greats" of world literature. For instance, another piece of praise common to translations of Machado, coming from an undated citation from *The Nation*, compares Machado and *The Posthumous Memoires of Brás Cubas* to Laurence Sterne's *The Life and Opinions of Tristram Shandy, Gentleman* and Xavier de Maistre's *Voyage Around My Room*. This particular comparison has been widely explored in academic criticism of Machado's oeuvre, perhaps most thoroughly by Maria José Somerlate Barbosa and Sérgio Paulo Rouanet. Such comparisons, and others, have become fixtures in the advertising paratexts accompanying Machado's work, in the physical and digital product of the works themselves or in virtual bookshops, large and small. Praise from the aforementioned white writers of the United States can be found on the editorial review sections of Amazon listings, while Mr. B's—an independent bookstore in Bath, United Kingdom—lists Machado among writers such as Cervantes, Joyce, Nabokov, Borges, and Calvino ("The Posthumous"). As Earl E. Fitz points out with regard to this sort of comparison, especially that with Sterne in the 1950s reception of Machado in the United States:

> the continual referencing of Machado's novel with Laurence Sterne and *Tristram Shandy*, had the effect of relegating *Epitaph* [*Posthumous Memoirs*] to the status of a mere imitation of a renowned text from the English novelistic tradition and thus, to dismiss it as inherently inferior. By not taking the trouble to compare the two texts closely and to consider the possibility that Machado's text actually goes further than Sterne's with the

thematic and structural frameworks and doing, finally, for the modern novel something akin to what Baudelaire had done for modern poetry, American critics blinded themselves to the novel's most extraordinary features. (21)

More robust readings of thematic and structural frameworks in *Posthumous Memoires* have certainly emerged since the 1950s and 1960s, as is the case with Sehgal's review in *The New York Times* or Andrew Katzenstein's in *The New York Review*. Nonetheless, a reading that continues to be marginalized in such visible platforms in the public sphere of mainstream United States readership is one that allies Machado's African descent to the novel's engagement with the economic, political, and cultural structures of anti-Blackness in Brazil and beyond. Through Machado's constant deployment of ambiguity allied to irony and skepticism, the reader certainly has a lot of work to do in connecting these dots, but there is a lot that the novel's structure and thematics tell us about racial capital and (the afterlives of) slavery through a narrator who doubles as a satirical character of a mediocre white elite, permitted to be so through the aforementioned structures of anti-Blackness.

While this sort of comparison, emergent from decades of Anglophone reception of Machado, continues to mark the contemporary circulation of his work, the two 2020 translations of *The Posthumous Memoirs of Brás Cubas* attempt to foreground his African descent, perhaps owing to the tumultuousness of the moment of their release. Penguin's publication, translated by Thomson-DeVeaux, introduces Machado as: "The mixed-race grandson of ex-slaves, Machado de Assis is not only Brazil's most celebrated writer but also a writer of world stature, who has been championed by the likes of Philip Roth, Susan Sontag, Allen Ginsberg, John Updike, and Salman Rushdie" (n.p.). Similarly, Jull Costa and Patterson's translation presents Machado as "the son of a mulatto father and a washerwoman, and the grandson of freed slaves" (n.p.) in the edition's accompanying synopsis. Both nonetheless opt for particularly ambiguous racial language in presenting Machado. This may be due in part to the often-cited lack of a public record in which Machado identified as someone of African descent—mixed race or Black—and thus avoids placing onto him an identity that he supposedly never claimed. Moreover, this decision also reflects the long-held disavowal of Machado's Black ancestry by Brazilian and international white literati, during and after his life. There is, moreover, a connection to be drawn between this stance regarding Machado's racial identity and dominant readings and historiographies of his work that shy away from deep readings of racial capital as he grapples with it. Some acclaimed readers of Machado do take clearer stances on his African descent. Harold Bloom's famous assertion, discussed at greater lengths in other chapters in this volume, that Machado is "the supreme Black literary artist to date" is ubiquitous in the paratexts accompanying Machado's works, as is the case with the 2020 Penguin Classics translation by Thomson-DeVeaux. Bloom's assertion regarding Machado's identity is owed arguably to his superficial deployment of US-based racial categories. Moreover, as with other readings by notable authors and critics, Bloom does not celebrate Machado for his treatments of racial capitalism, slavery, and its afterlives, but rather underscores aspects that approximate him to the so-called great writers of the Western canon. Ginsberg similarly compares him to Franz Kafka, while Roth likens him to Samuel Beckett.

Through readings such as these, also present in contemporary reception, Machado's Blackness is either vindicated by or allied to a celebration of his work as participating in Euro-American literary traditions. In this regard, this sort of reception bares resemblance to the trajectories and experiences of other Black historical and cultural figures in relation to white middle-class audiences, in which expressions of deep anti-hegemonic engagement are curtailed or elided altogether, with some figures "sanitized" for comfortable bourgeois consumption or erased largely from the cultural record. The rendering of Machado that persists in dominant US reception, therefore, is one of a writer of African descent that has contributed significantly to the Western literary canon with only "references" to slavery and anti-Black racism in Brazil. There is, however, a sort of parallel archive of Machado's life and oeuvre that centers his African descent in the thematics and structure of his works, while also positing these as potentially radical critiques and revisions of the Western canon.

Black Diasporic Archiving of Machado

The works of Black literary critics and activists in the Americas have performed important engagement with Machado's African descent and his oeuvre in more radical terms, while still grappling with his complex relationship to white bourgeois circles of his time. A watershed moment, though not the starting point, in this archival project of Machado's Blackness came from academic circles, specifically via the work of Afro-Brazilian literary critics like Eduardo de Assis Duarte. In 2007, Duarte published *Machado de Assis Afrodescendente* (*Machado de Assis Afro-descendent*) in Brazil through Editora Malê (the premier press for Afro-Brazilian and Black Diasporic literatures in Portuguese), as well parts of the book in English-language literary journals focused on Africana literatures such as *Research in African Literatures*, thus placing Machado in Black literary histories beyond Brazil and for a broader, albeit academic, audience. In his article in *Research in African Literatures*, Duarte succinctly outlines the main issue of dominant readings and reception of Machado's work and its consequences for how his life and identity have been archived: "The literary profile was made so Western that it would end up leaving its mark not only upon the public image constructed throughout time, but even upon physical appearance, which became transformed into an emblematic effigy of the process of identity whitening that occurred in lands south of the equator" (134).

Years after Duarte's assessment of the public whitening of Machado came a particularly notable and highly visible example of precisely that—one that led to perhaps the most meaningful and public engagement of Machado's Blackness. This came in 2011 when state-owned Brazilian bank Caixa Econômica Federal marked its 150th anniversary by producing and airing a television commercial with whom it called one of its most illustrious accountholders—Machado de Assis. As Afolabi's chapter in this very volume already discussed, Machado is played by a somatically white actor and is portrayed depositing money in his account and mentioning his account number as he writes his will. Here, his manipulated whiteness serves to both consolidate a white supremacist national imaginary by whitening the figure it refers to as "the greatest Brazilian writer" and circuiting that whiteness to the white bourgeois space of the bank itself and to the anti-Black histories of the banking industry. Following a resounding response in opposition to the commercial's casting choice from Afro-Brazilian activists and Brazilian anti-racist organizations, including an official complaint of racism with the Secretaria de Políticas de Promoção da Igualdade Racial da Presidência da República(Secretariat of Policy Promoting Racial Equality of the President of the Republic). This collective response led Caixa to suspend the advertisement and reshoot it with a Black actor as Machado following a statement by Caixa president, Jorge Hereda: "O banco pede desculpas a toda a população e, em especial, aos movimentos ligados às causas raciais, por não ter caracterizado o escritor, que era afro-brasileiro, com a sua origem racial" (The bank extends apologies to the entire population and, especially, to the movements tied to racial causes, for not portraying the writer, who was Afro-Brazilian, according to his racial origin") ("Caixa Tira" n.p.).

Literary scholar João Gabriel do Nascimento Nganga couches the response against Caixa's first commercial as an important moment in Brazilian race relations marked, of course, by white supremacy and racial capital, but also by over a century of post-abolition whitening discourses targeting the short-term and long-term genocide of Black and Indigenous people. More specifically, the collective and swift reaction to the Caixa advertisement represents a small yet important victory against white supremacist hegemony and, namely, its industries of cultural production in Brazil that have long sought to whiten Machado's life and oeuvre (Nganga 79). Referring to the shift in the commercial's casting, Nganga affirms: "se há um branco imposto, há também um negro conquistado, pois, se houve uma retratação por parte desse banco, foi devido à movimentação de sujeitos e organizações da sociedade civil, em especial o Movimento Negro" ("if there was a white man imposed, there was also a Black man reclaimed. After all, if there was a retraction by the bank, it was due to the mobilization of people and organizations of civil society, especially the Black Movement") (84).

In opposing the dominant comparative readings of Machado that have contributed to literary and somatic whitenings of Machado, Duarte's book, as other contributors to this volume explain in further detail, makes deep and detailed literary and historical analyses into how Machado's work rendered counterhegemonic knowledge regarding slavery and racial economic/political structures, as well as how Machado's political life was dedicated to racially pertinent causes, thus performing his own mode of Afro-Brazilian solidarity. Duarte's project thus makes important strides toward rendering public an archive of Machado's literary production and political involvement that posit him in a lineage of Afro-Brazilian and Black Diasporic literatures. Regarding Machado's life, Duarte also dialogues with important historiographic works on this front, including historian Sydney Chalhoub's reading of Machado's political engagement in abolition and public governmental critique as part of a broader endeavor of counterhegemonic historicization.

Nganga importantly centers the role of Afro-Brazilian organizations and mobilization in shifting Caixa's portrayal of Machado. Beyond that particular instance, Afro-Brazilian activism has taken on a broader cultural and public form with regard to figures like Machado, archiving him and his work as Black, racially conscious, and socially engaged. This is in stark contrast to the stance taken by some Afro-Brazilian activists and leaders of late twentieth century who had a significant impact on how Black Brazilians have received Machado. Abdias do Nascimento, in a 1979 publication, famously characterized Machado as one of "the notorious Afro-Brazilians who thought, wrote and acted as mirror-images of the dominant society (white or Aryanoid), and who despite being influential writers, in their work included almost nothing that would identify them in any kind of connection with their African origin" (275). As Alex Flynn, Elena Calvo-González, and Marcelo Mendes de Souza surmise in their analysis of Abdias do Nascimento's stance, it "perfectly reflects the polem-icized and binary nature of the critical reaction toward Machado's body in that Nascimento's tropes of "white" and "black" are placed into a directly oppositional hierarchy, where each category is naturalized and therefore constitutes the other. It therefore allows for Nascimento that Machado's writings can be dismissed as merely an aping of white culture and its values, and that Machado has betrayed his blackness" (9). This dismissal of Machado's Blackness in the last century further underlines the impor-tance of Duarte's reclaiming of Machado and of broader Afro-Brazilian and Black Diasporic re-archiving of Machado's work. Through this sort of reception, moreover, Blackness is not somehow negated by (misread) literary aesthetics, and in the process, meaningful artistic critique by Black cultural producers is allowed to center on the white bourgeois characters to be read in the context of a radical historical and theoretical framework.

It is important to note, moreover, that Afro-Brazilian artistic and activist responses of the second half of the twentieth century to Machado were far from unanimous. For instance, Ironildes Rodrigues, a collabo-rator of Abdias do Nascimento in the Teatro Experimental Negro (Black Experimental Theater), describes Machado as "a white writer who did not feel the least bit of black blood coursing through his heart" (cited in Flynn et al. 256) in his *Introduction to Afro-Brazilian Literature* of 1997. A couple of years prior to the publication of Rodrigues's book, Afro-Brazilian poet Éle Semog (pen name of Luiz Carlos Amaral Gomes) and a close collaborator of Abdias do Nascimento, in a 1995 interview published in the academic journal *Callaloo: A Journal of African Diaspora Arts and Letters*, extolled Machado as an Afro-Brazilian writer who inspired him and who did not shy away from racial issues: "for a writer, reading Mach-ado de Assis is fundamental; it is a journey, a state of being, an idyllic place within literature. Because it is a competent literature, a profoundly ironic literature, a literature impregnated with racial issues, by means of the irony and subtlety of Machado de Assis" (756).

Today, Machado de Assis is received as a Black writer by many Afro-Brazilians thanks to the collective and consistent reclaiming of him as such. In addition to Duarte, other Brazilian scholars/activists have rendered an archive on Machado that places him within Afro-Brazilian literature. For instance, Literafro: o portal da literatura afro-brasileira (Literafro: The Web Portal of Afro-Brazilian Literature), comprised of literary scholars, has significant content dedicated to Machado. His birthday, 21 June, was marked in 2021 on social media by a host of Brazilian and international personalities and organizations, many of which used revised photographs or other images of him that undo the whitening they underwent over the last century.

Outside of Brazil, a similar reception and archiving of Machado into African Diasporic histories has also emerged in Black activist, artistic, and scholarly public and digital spheres. For instance, Machado is featured in the important online reference and archive, BlackPast.org, consisting of over four thousand encyclopedia entries on African American and Afro-Diasporic history, as well as speeches, texts, and other artifacts from prominent historical figures. The multifaceted database was started by historian Quintard Taylor in 2007 and has since become a highly visited resource for nonacademics and academics alike, as well as for students of all ages.

In a June 2021 piece in *Lit Hub* (an online literary review, publication, and network), African American writer Keenan Norris offers an extensive review, critique, and reading recommendation titled "How Black Writers Capture the Comedy and Dark Absurdity of Life in America." In this list of titles, Norris notably includes Machado (and *Posthumous Memoirs*) as a Black writer in dialogue with largely African American writers like George Schuyler, Alice Randall, and Percival Everett in a way that centers the novel's Black epistemology as the vehicle through which Machado carries out his critique of white Brazilian bourgeois and upper-class life. This embracing and integrating of Machado into terrains of Black literary production and consumption as a Black writer, thus revising the racial archiving of his life, identity, and work outside of Brazil, may seem like a recent movement.

While this sort of recircuiting and reinscription of Machado has arguably become more robust in recent years, Machado has been inte-grated, to varying extents, into historiographies of Black literary production since the 1920s, particularly in the United States. This was the case with the anthology *Book of American Negro Poetry*, published in 1922 and edited by distinguished African American poet and writer James Weldon Johnson (1871–1938), whose own work overlapped with and contributed to the Harlem Renaissance. Though the poetic contents of the anthology focus on African American poets (Claude McKay of Jamaica and George Reginald Margetson of St. Kitts are also included), Johnson's preface situates the poetry of the volume in a particularly Black inter-American framework. Most notably, he compares one of the anthology's featured poets, Paul Laurence Dunbar, to whom he regards as the greatest writers of African descent in the broader western hemisphere, including Machado (37). It is worth noting that Johnson includes Machado in his own racial terminology concerning people of African descent of the wider Americas—"Aframericans" (36). The complications of the term notwithstanding, Johnson seems to be among the earliest international readers of Machado to approach him as a Black writer and within Black literary canons and historiography of the Americas.

This sort of international integration of Machado into Black literary canons has augmented since the late twentieth century, for both his own identity *and* his complex and consistent treatment of racial systems of power and structures of anti-Blackness have occurred via important yet underestimated terrains of Black Diasporic solidarity, collaboration, and intersubjectivity. In this regard, substantial efforts have been made by Afro-Brazilian activists and scholars in the revised archiving of Machado's life, identity, and work, while these have been made legible to and taken forward by Black activists and scholars around the world. For instance, when, in 2019, scholars and students at the Faculdade Zumbi dos Palmares (Brazil's only institution openly dedicated to serving Afro-Brazilian students) successfully researched Machado's life toward a more historically accurate visual rendering of the writer—one in which his Blackness is made somatic—news of the new image and its wide (though not unanimous) embrace in Brazil quickly reached international audiences. This was especially the case with online platforms that give digital sustenance to the everyday reproduction of global and local Black collective life. To give a noteworthy example, the London-based Black History Studies—an educational nonprofit founded and operated by Black authors and educators Charmaine Simpson and Mark Simpson—marked the unveiling of the new image of Machado with a Twitter post to its over 128,000 followers, reading: "Brazil's greatest writer Machado de Assis was a Black man, but they whitewashed his image for decades." The post thus both hails and explains the importance of the moment toward revising the dominant historicization of Machado.

Conclusion

To conclude where, or rather when, we began—June 2020—the tumultuous events of this particular month, marked by sustained large-scale global organizing against the structures and practices of anti-Black racism as well as the release of two separate translations of Machado's *Posthumous Memoirs*, indicated the multiple and complex layers guiding his racialized reception in the United States, past and present. On the one hand, mainstream literary reviews of the new translations introduced Machado as a Brazilian writer of African descent, the grandchild of enslaved people. On the other, such reviews also relegated Machado's treatment of racial structures, and racial capitalism more specifically, as important yet marginal to the greatness of his works. The foregrounding of Machado's Blackness in and among United States and Anglophone readerships, moreover, also speaks to the underrecognized work of Black Brazilian scholars and activists in the counterhegemonic re-archiving of Machado as a Black writer, as well as to that of Black scholars and writers from the United States and globally who, as early as James Weldon Johnson in the 1920s, helped shape Machado's reception as a Black writer.

Works Cited

Bhattacharya, Baidik. *Postcolonial Writing in the Era of World Literature: Texts, Territories, Globalization.* Routledge, 2018.

@BlackHistoryStudies. "Brazil's greatest writer Machado de Assis was a Black man, but they whitewashed his image for decades." *Twitter*, 9 May 2019.

"Caixa Tira do Ar Propaganda que Mostra Machado de Assis Branco." *Globo Negócios*, accessed 5 June 2021, http://g1.globo.com/economia/negocios/noticia/2011/09/caixa-tira-do-ar-progaganda-que-mostra-machado-de-assis-branco.html.

Duarte, Eduardo de Assis. "Machado de Assis's African Descent." *Research in African Literatures*, vol. 38, no. 1, 2007, 134–51.

Fitz, Earl E. "The Reception of Machado de Assis in the United States during the 1950s and 1960s." *Luso-Brazilian Review*, vol. 46, no. 1, 2009, 16–35.

Flynn, A., Calvo-González, E., and Souza, M. M. "Whiter Shades of Pale: 'Coloring in' Machado de Assis and Race in Contemporary Brazil." *Latin American Research Review*, vol. 48, no. 3, 2013, 3–24.

Freyre, Gilberto. *New World in the Tropics: The Culture of Modern Brazil*. Knopf, 1959.

Guimarães, Hélio Seixas de. "Race and Color in the Reception of Machado de Assis." *Luso-Brazilian Review*, vol. 54, no. 2, 2017, 11–28.

Johnson, James Weldon. *Book of American Negro Poetry*. Harcourt, Brace, and Company, 1922.

Katzenstein, Andrew. "A Well-Ventilated Conscience: The Digressive, Playful, and Irreverent Machado de Assis." *The New York Review*, 17 December 2020, accessed 15 February 15 2021, https://www.nybooks.com/articles/2020/12/17/machado-de-assis-well-ventilated-conscience.

Melamed, Jodi. "Racial Capitalism." *Critical Ethnic Studies*, vol. 1, no. 1, 2015, 76–85.

Nascimento, Abdias do. "Reflections of an Afro-Braziliano." *Journal of Negro History*, vol. 64, no. 3, 1979, 274–82.

Nganga, João Gabriel do Nascimento Nganga. "O Branco Imposto e o Negro Conquistado: Machado de Assis na Propaganda da Caixa Econômica Federal." *Revista da ABPN*, vol. 8, no. 20, 2016, 74–85.

Norris, Keenan. "How Black Writers Capture the Comedy and Dark Absurdity of Life in America." *LitHub*, 22 June 2021, accessed 24 June 2021, https://lithub.com/how-black-writers-capture-the-comedy-and-dark-absurdity-of-life-in-america/.

"Posthumous Memoires of Brás Cubas." W. W. Norton, accessed on 3 June 2021, https://wwnorton.com/books/9781631495328.

Robinson, Cedric. *Black Marxism: The Making of the Black Radical Tradition*. London: Zed Press, 1983.

Schwarcz, Lília Moritz. "Machado de Assis: Creator and Character in a Troubled Scene." *Emerging Dialogues on Machado de Assis*, edited by Lamonte Aidoo and Daniel F. Silva, 13–26, Palgrave Macmillan, 2016.

Sehgal, Parul. "A Playful Masterpiece that Extended the Novel's Possibilities." *New York Times*, 16 June 2020, https://www.nytimes.com/2020/06/16/books/review-posthumous-memoirs-bras-cubas-machado-de-assis.html.

Semog, Éle. "Éle Semog: An Interview." *Callaloo: A Journal of African Diaspora Arts and Letters*, vol. 18, no. 4, 1995, 756–59.

Machado de Assis, Joaquim Maria. *The Posthumous Memoires of Brás Cubas*. Penguin Random House, 2020, accessed 3 June 2021, https://www.penguinrandomhouse.com/books/618216/the-posthumous-memoirs-of-bras-cubas-by-machado-de-assis-translated-with-an-introduction-and-notes-by-flora-thomson-deveaux-foreword-by-dave-eggers/.

Vieira, Nelson H. "Foreword: Machado de Assis: The Brazilian Master Then and Now." *Emerging Dialogues on Machado de Assis*, edited by Lamonte Aidoo and Daniel Silva, v–xxii, Palgrave Macmillan, 2016.

Chapter Seven

Outsiders Within and Insiders Without

Narrating Race and Identity in Machado de Assis,
Milton Hatoum, and Jeferson Tenório[1]

David M. Mittelman

How should considerations about race and color inform our reception
of Machado de Assis's narrative techniques? Or, what do the formal
peculiarities of Machado's writings suggest about how literary discourse
constructs, reveals, sidesteps, or subverts racialized subjectivities, ideologies,
and institutions? One of the most salient features of Machado de Assis's
fiction is its treatment of the experience and agency of Brazil's precariously
included, the incidentally involved, outsiders who find themselves on the
inside. These characters—including, notably, Helena, Rubião, Capitu, and
José Dias—are plucked from obscure or relatively humble origins to inhabit
the space of the elite, where they struggle to maintain social acceptance
and achieve personal fulfillment. In addition to such characters, Machado
created narrators who position themselves on the boundary of involvement
in the stories they tell: most famously, the deceased author Brás Cubas
and the detached memoirist Conselheiro Aires. The present chapter shows
how this tension between outsider and insider status echoes Machado's
condition as a socially mobile, Afro-Brazilian intellectual at the turn of
Brazil's twentieth century and endures as a legacy that finds expression
in the work of the acclaimed contemporary authors Milton Hatoum and
Jeferson Tenório.[2]

145

It is somewhat difficult to discuss the possible interactions of racialized identity and literary form in the work of Machado de Assis due to the fraught critical legacy we have inherited. Certainly, Machado's own apparent reluctance to explicitly address concerns relating to color is a significant factor that enabled a number of subsequent interpretive tendencies, many of them questionable. Famously, some of Machado's friends and contemporaries insisted that he was, for all intellectual intents, white: socially, spiritually, or whatever else they might have meant.[3] But if Machado could be claimed as white, or at least white enough, by the likes of Joaquim Nabuco, he would also be vulnerable to attack for having been insufficiently attentive to race and color in his writing and/or electing to accommodate himself comfortably at the expense of his fellow Black Brazilians.[4] At the same time, however, he could also be both extolled and excoriated by Afrânio Coutinho, who would devote a book to explicating and in some senses defending Machado's philosophical concerns, as the critic understood them, with reference to the major figures of modern European thought, but only by means of an argument underpinned by a racist analysis of supposed mulatto resentment.[5] Later, with growing critical appreciation for the subtleties of Machado's technical achievements in the development of sophisticated, slippery, socially incisive narratives, and due to the significant influence of Marxist hermeneutics in the Brazilian academy, considerations of race would largely be subsumed within an analysis privileging class-based dynamics and subjectivities.[6] It is only relatively recently, then, that scholars have returned to an attentive appreciation of the possibilities for reading race in Machado. A great many questions therefore still demand critical response, particularly if we consider specific formal patterns and choices within the author's work. Renata Wasserman provides one significant model for this type of work, setting as a starting point in her comparison of the interplay of racial identity and writing in the work of Machado de Assis and Lima Barreto the recognition that "[a] racializing reading of fiction should find, embedded in a text, a suppressed but determining subtext of the power relations between—or among—racial groups" (83).[7]

At the same time, it can be difficult to know how to theorize formal concepts such as point of view in narrative—which is particularly salient for us here, both when considered in relation to the voice of the narrating subject and when taken as an aspect of characterization—in relation to race, racial difference, and racism. Classical narrative theory, largely preoccupied with anatomizing and classifying the components and patterns of narration, had little to say directly about historical questions such as those to do with power, coloniality, domination, marginalization, and liberation.[8] This deficiency has been long noted and there have been many attempts to address it. As early as 1981, for instance, Susan Lanser argued for a feminist theory of narrative point of view that would move beyond earlier formalisms by taking account of, among other things, "the authority, competence, and credibility which the communicator is conventionally and personally allowed," recognizing that "in cases of public communication, the speaker's age, sex, social position, race, class, occupation, etc., are bases for identity status" (*The Narrative Act* 86–87). And yet, although narrative theories are no longer constrained by the supposedly value-neutral typological preoccupations of the structuralist heyday, much narratological theorizing still seems restrictive in its ability to confront concepts like race and coloniality.

Let us briefly take three cases in point. First, it is notable that scholars who are specifically interested in understanding Blackness and narration together have at times had little or no use for classical narratology and its most visible descendants. For example, Heather Russell develops an account of Black modes of narration in the Atlantic world—particularly the Caribbean and the United States—with recourse to a broad theoretical frame of reference that includes little of what is most conventionally termed narrative theory. This seems less than entirely surprising when we notice, in the second place, that narratological theory developed as a domain largely independent of historicized concerns about the relations of power, except perhaps when it comes to gender and sexuality. In a recent collection organized by Lanser with Robyn Warhol, the editors remark that "[w]hat began as a focus on the impact of culturally constructed gender upon the form and reception of narrative texts has broadened to feminist narrative*ogies* that recognize race, sexuality, nationality, class, and ethnicity as well as gender in formulating their theoretical and analytical projects" (*Narrative Theory Unbound* 6). But despite their appeal to intersectionality in presenting the volume, the collection contains but one essay that attends to race and coloniality among the significant categories of analysis, suggesting that the editors do not, in the end, see such concerns as especially central to the theoretical project of building out feminist and queer narratologies.

Similarly, perhaps, in a widely cited essay, Gerald Prince argues that narratology can expand to encompass categories of interest to scholars of (post)coloniality, but his remarks offer only a sketch of a postcolonial narratological theory that "characterizes and articulates narratively pertinent categories and features in order to account for the ways in which narratives are configured and make sense" and that he insists must be considered as distinct from a postcolonial narratological criticism that "uses these categories and features in order to specify the configuration and sense of particular narratives" (379). Setting aside this possibly overstated dichotomy, and although Prince enumerates many interesting considerations about narrative that draw on issues and concepts prevalent in postcolonial scholarship, it is curious that in characterizing the postcolonial he seems to deemphasize categories—such as race, race-based social difference, and (neo)colonial exploitation through direct and institutional violence—that are essential for addressing the cultural legacies of expansionist domination:

> I will sketch a postcolonial narratology which would basically adopt and rely on the results of (post)classical narratology but would inflect it and perhaps enrich it by wearing a set of post-colonial lenses to look at narrative. . . . It is not even bound to a specific corpus or primarily constituted through the study of particular texts and it does not chiefly depend on inductive procedures. Rather, it is sensitive to matters commonly, if not uncontroversially, associated with the postcolonial (e.g., hybridity, migrancy, otherness, fragmentation, diversity, power relations); it envisages their possibly narratological correspondents; and it incorporates them. (373)

At a minimum, then, the linkages between narratological theory and practices of reading that privilege questions relating to racialized identities, colonial and neocolonial violence, and the like remain, at best, weak.

Finally, we cannot escape the glaring invisibility of Brazil (along with other regions, states, and societies defined by the legacies of Portuguese expansionism) within many academic discussions, including literary scholarship and postcolonial theory. Despite having one of the largest Black populations of any nation, despite wide awareness of the depth and richness of Afro-Brazilian cultural expression and creativity, and despite the reputation of innovative proto-modernism that attaches to the name of Machado de Assis, striking gaps and discontinuities abound. Even within scholarship highly concerned with the relations between concepts like coloniality, race and racism, modernity, and aesthetic and intellectual authority—and even when such efforts are specifically interested in Latin

America—it is common for Brazil, its specificities and contradictions, to be elided within the grand theoretical sweep.[9] It is also not surprising that Russell's book, subtitled *Narratology in the African Atlantic*, focuses on texts from the Caribbean and the United States and contains only a passing mention of Brazil as a repository of Candomblé and therefore analogous to other sites of Yoruba-derived religion in the Americas, making no reference to literary writing by Black Brazilian authors. Similarly, it is not altogether unexpected that a major volume written dialectically by five leading narratological theorists, apparently intended to be used as a college-level textbook and definitive presentation of the state of the field at the time of its release in 2012, makes an incidental mention of Machado's *Memórias Póstumas de Brás Cubas*—which gives not only an incorrect date of publication, but also gets the author's name wrong.[10]

Taken together, these challenges substantially complicate critical efforts to read Machado deeply in relation both to the experience of racialization and to the formal constituents of narrative art. In an effort to confront the foregoing difficulties, here is the present argument, in brief: for Machado, the specification of point of view—the vantage from which one witnesses events, the social and discursive position from which one acts—is the crucial question of narrative art, and the answer to it constitutes and animates character, narration, and narrative itself. Moreover, in Machado's texts, point of view is thoroughly racialized or, put differently, racially specified. Therefore, Machado's formal choices regarding point of view, when considered in reference to both a recurring pattern of characterization and the complex development of narrative voice in his later novels, should be understood as racially conscious authorial tactics that set an important precedent for later writers. The second part of this essay will show how Machado's concern for narrative point of view is further adapted by two contemporary writers of Brazilian fiction: Milton Hatoum and Jeferson Tenório.

If the argument as stated appears straightforward, even simplistic, it obviously stands in need of explication. What does it mean to say that for Machado point of view is the central problem of narrative, that it is what constitutes fictional space and the figures and voices that inhabit the literary domain? What does it mean to say that for Machado point of view is significantly racialized? Two familiar passages from *Quincas Borba* are emblematic. In the early chapters of the novel, readers reencounter the eponymous philosopher, who had appeared incidentally in the *Memórias Póstumas de Brás Cubas*, and meet the schoolteacher Rubião, who serves as a caregiver to the eccentric theorist of Humanitismo. Upon declaring himself a disciple of Quincas Borba, Rubião is initiated into the new philosophy, a cavalier and self-serving pastiche of pseudo-Hegelian dialectic, Comtean positivism, and Spencerian social Darwinism, the essence of which is expressed by the famous formula "ao vencedor as batatas." Try as he might, however, Rubião cannot comprehend the philosopher's views:

> —Mas a opinião do exterminado?
> —Não há exterminado. Desaparece o fenômeno; a substância é a mesma. Nunca viste ferver água? Hás de lembrar-te que as bolhas fazem-se e desfazem-se de contínuo, e tudo fica na mesma água. Os indivíduos são essas bolhas transitórias.
> —Bem; a opinião da bolha . . .
> —Bolha não tem opinião. (*Quincas Borba* 649)

> ("But what about the point of view of those exterminated?"
> "Nobody's exterminated. The phenomenon disappears, but the substance is the same. Haven't you ever seen boiling water? You must recall that the bubbles keep on being made and unmade and everything stays the same in the same water. Individuals are those transitory bubbles."
> "Well, the opinion of the bubble . . ."
> "A bubble has no opinion.") (13–14)[11]

Evidently, Rubião, a poor teacher, has difficulty understanding Quincas Borba's metaphors, which only function in retrospect: Humanitas, the only true historical subject, is identified with the victor or survivor of any given conflict. Rubião immediately aligns himself with the loser (exterminado) and is unable to perceive the alleged greatness of Humanitismo in the face of the suffering and annihilation of the weak. Quincas Borba, for his part, has no attention for the (to him) meaningless perspective of the vanquished—for him, the "exterminado" simply does not exist—and he ends up losing control of his own analogy, dismissing Rubião's objection as incomprehensible and declaring that "bolha não tem opinião." As surely as Rubião is incapable of understanding the promised splendor of *Humanitas*, so Quincas Borba fails to grasp Rubião's reservations.

Later, however, when he finds himself the sole heir of the deceased philosopher, Rubião undergoes a psychological transformation:

A memória dele recompôs, ainda que de embrulho e esgarça-
damente, os argumentos do filósofo. Pela primeira vez,
atentou bem na alegoria das tribos famintas e compreendeu
a conclusão: "Ao vencedor, as batatas!" Ouviu distintamente
a voz roufenha do finado expor a situação das tribos, a luta
e a razão da luta, o extermínio de uma e a vitória da outra,
e murmurou baixinho:
    —Ao vencedor, as batatas!
    Tão simples! tão claro! Olhou para as calças de brim
surrado e o rodaque cerzido e notou que até há pouco fora,
por assim dizer, um exterminado, uma bolha; mas que ora
não, era um vencedor. (*Quincas Borba* 656–57)

(The memory brought back the philosopher's arguments, albeit
confused and frayed. For the first time he gave careful consideration to the allegory of the starving tribes, and he understood
the conclusion: "To the victor, the potatoes!" He clearly heard
the dead man's voice expounding the situation of the tribes, the
fights, and the reason for the fight, the extermination of one
and the victory of the other, and he murmured in a low voice:
    "To the victor, the potatoes!"
    So simple! So clear! He looked at his worn drill pants
and his patched waistcoat, and he noted that up until a short
time before he'd been, in a manner of speaking, someone exter-
minated, a burst bubble, but not now, now he was a victor.)
(27)

From this moment forward, Rubião not only sees himself as a victor and
rightful owner of the proverbial potatoes, but he even ceases to appreciate
that the vanquished exist and that bubbles have opinions. After meditating
on the slogan of Humanitismo,

a fórmula viveu no espírito de Rubião, por alguns dias:—Ao
vencedor as batatas! Não a compreenderia antes do testamento;
ao contrário, vimos que a achou obscura e sem explicação. Tão
certo é que a paisagem depende do ponto de vista, e que o
melhor modo de apreciar o chicote é ter-lhe o cabo na mão.
(*Quincas Borba* 657)

(the formula lived on in Rubião's spirit for a few days: "To the victor, the potatoes!" He wouldn't have understood it before the will. On the contrary, we saw that he'd considered it obscure and in need of an explanation. It's so true that the landscape depends on the point of view and the best way to appreciate a whip is to have its handle in your hand.) (27)

The concluding figures Machado's narrator offers here synthesize crucial features that are found dispersed throughout his narratives. But though these lines may seem to be tossed out as an offhand mot juste to neatly close the scene, their implications are more radical than a casual reading might recognize. As others have noted, the appearance of the chicote here serves as an obvious reminder of the domination/victimization dynamic of slavery, suggesting that one's estimation of Brazilian society will vary with one's position in the slavocratic social hierarchy and its post-abolition corollary.[12] Notably, however, Machado's narrator states that the land-scape itself (a paisagem) varies depending on the point from which it is viewed—not simply that one's vision or perception of a scene is defined by a given vantage. In this conception, there is no objective reality of the landscape that could be more or less accurately perceived depending on a favorable perspective. What is there to be perceived at all—what is there to be taken as part of reality—is constituted by the point of view from which it is apprehended.

It is at this point, having slyly offered this radical subjectivism as self-evident, that Machado's narrator equates its validity with another even more unsettling: "o melhor modo de apreciar o chicote é ter-lhe o cabo na mão." This equation, in a move that is as characteristic of the narrating voice as it would be indecorous in the mouths of the characters who enact the narrative, divides the subjects of Brazilian society into victors and vanquished based on whether, perceiving the whip, they face the end of the lash or the butt of the handle—effectively, either enslaver or enslaved. The metonymy of the whip derives its power from two sources: first, the proximity of racial slavery, only recently abolished in Brazil when *Quincas Borba* was published in book form, and our awareness that abolition as it occurred neither intended nor could have engendered an end to the racialized social hierarchy that had preserved legal bondage until 1888.[13] Second, in an instantiation of the subjectivism defined in the preceding clause, what the narrator offers for our contemplation is not the whip as an instrument defined by its function—a means of physical abuse and psychological brutalization—but the whip as an object that one might apreciar: gaze upon with pleasure, admire with aesthetic detachment from its primary uses of inflicting pain and inspiring fear. Only from a certain point of view can the whip even exist as an object of appreciation, and it is toward this position that Machado's narrator shunts the reader, simultaneously hinting at the sting we could feel if we found ourselves cn the functional end of the tool and thereby inviting us to feel embarrassed of our aesthetic standpoint.

Lest we be tempted to think that within this narrative universe the binary possibilities of point of view ought to be understood in s:rictly materialist or economic terms without specific appeal to racialized subjectivities—captive and free labor, class hierarchy, capitalists and dependents—it is instructive to recall that in both early and late wr:tings, Machado put racial difference directly into play. In the 1876 novel Helena, when suspicion mounts regarding the title character's honor and her fitness to remain within the elite family that adopted her in accordance with the will of a deceased patriarch, the young slave Vicente attempts to rescue his mistress from the social danger threatening to engulf her. He approaches the priest Melchior and asks what has gone wrong. When the priest rebuffs him, Vicente recognizes the limits of the confidence into which he might be taken, while insisting that Melchior and the masters stand to lose out if they refuse to listen to what he might have to say: "—Hum! gemeu incredulamente o pagem. Há alguma cousa que o escravo não pode saber; mas também o escravo pode saber alguma cousa que os brancos tenham vontade de ouvir" (Helena 367; " 'Hmm!' the page moaned in disbelief. 'There is something that the slave cannot know about; but the slave might also know something that the white people would want to hear' "; my translation). Vicente characterizes the relevant distinction as between escravos and brancos, identifying the socioeconomic condition of the master class with phenotypic whiteness. Symmetrically, in a novel published over twenty-five years later, the pompous republican Paulo of Esaú e Jacó will declare that "[a] abolição é a aurora da liberdade; esperemos o sol; emancipado o preto, resta emancipar o branco" (Esaú e Jacó 992; "abolition is the dawn of liberty, we await the sun: the Black emancipated, it remains to emancipate the white; Esau and Jacob 91).[14] As Vicente had equated masterliness with whiteness, Paulo identifies servitude with Blackness. The bitter irony Machado achieves with Paulo's remark is due not only to his offensive and opportunistic characterization of the abolition of slavery—which he could have cast as a long-overdue correction to a monstrous injustice that had benefited his own wealthy, mainly white upper class—as a prelude to a political transformation that in the end would also largely benefit people like himself. It is also underscored by an antanaclastic gambit that preserves and deepens the cut of racial difference through the present and into the future by splitting the concept of emancipation in twain: "emancipado o preto, resta emancipar o branco." For Paulo, the survivors of slavery may deserve the legal emancipation granted by the Lei Áurea, but the political emancipation he dreams of is an aspiration for white people—o preto evidently need not apply for citizenship in his republic.

We have seen evidence so far that in Machado's narrative universe the question of subjective point of view is central and that a binary racial division governs subjects' perceptions of themselves and others.[15] It is little wonder, then, that much of Machado's fiction is concerned with perspectives from the boundary between power and powerlessness, portraying characters whose narratives are shaped by their fragile claim to a place within elite society. We have already briefly considered two paradigms of Machado's outsider-on-the-inside characters and the novels built around them: Helena and Rubião. The second case is perhaps simpler, in that Quincas Borba follows the relatively innocent Rubião as he attempts to ride his newfound wealth to power and influence, only to be ruthlessly exploited by more established and sophisticated capitalists, ending up mad, once again impoverished, and, finally, deceased. For Rubião, merely possessing fantastic wealth does not initiate him into the functioning of capital and the ways of its most rapacious stewards. Though his consciousness had been transformed upon receiving his inheritance, Rubião's persistent ingenuousness leaves him ill prepared to act as a full agent of his own actions; the novel becomes at least as much a story of his manipulation by others as it is of his own tragedy.

In Helena, however, the narrative turns from the outset on whether the Vale family can accept as one of their own a young woman possessing every quality expected of an upper-class maiden, except that she was born to the family patriarch out of wedlock—or so she is introduced in the will of the late Conselheiro Vale. In such a position, Helena's graces and talents endear her to some while making her seem inappropriately ambitious to others, and when her identity and origin are called into question, she exclaims that she is powerless to dispel doubts about her integrity. As I have argued elsewhere, the gulf of social prestige between those secure in the power of the master class and all others is great enough to degrade any knowledge the other members of the Vale family (Estácio and D. Úrsula) might think they have of Helena's beliefs and intentions.[16] Be Helena as perfect as she might, without a living patriarch to vouchsafe her place within the family, she can never be secure—and of course Conselheiro Vale had made no move to recognize her while he lived. *Dom Casmurro* constructs a similar trap for the figure of Capitu: the daring attitude that defines her and that the young Bentinho finds so attractive will later be turned against his abandoned wife, presented as a sign of unseemly cunning while the narrator, the avowed curmudgeon Dom Casmurro, incites suspicion against her. This dirty trick that he plays on Capitu, a plainly gendered form of abuse, is underscored by the comic presence of the *agregado* José Dias, another outsider-on-the-inside, whose obvious and often clumsy opportunism is not weaponized against him.

An Afro-Brazilian writer of humble origin who gained access to education and thereby rose to the heights of literary society quite by chance in a slavocracy that invested little in the advancement of poor free people of color, it is difficult to read Machado as having merely an incidental interest in such characters.[17] As David Jackson has put it, "[m]ost notable in Machado are the many contradictions that provided him with an unusual perspective as an outside insider or an inside outsider" (7). Indeed, it is tempting to interpret the repeated occurrence of these figures as successive efforts to sound out the social and discursive possibilities for subjects who, like Machado, though not born into wealth and whiteness, were invited to participate in certain ways and, to a certain extent, in their conjunction. What is at stake in Machado's fiction, from this perspective, is an approach to discourse, social life, and narrative form that is sensitive to a notion that has only in recent years gained widespread currency in academic and literary circles in Brazil, the United States, and elsewhere, but which has antecedents in long and varied traditions of radical thought. Broadly speaking, we can say that Machado's fiction puts into play a *standpoint theory* that recognizes how differences in social power result in different discursive and epistemic possibilities for different people. Under white supremacy, patriarchy, and coloniality, what one is in a position to speak about and what one is in a position to know are not only constrained by one's relative social privilege but also inversely correlated in important ways. As a consequence, those who are most oppressed and least empowered to directly shape political, economic, and aesthetic norms can also, in virtue of their very oppression, gain privileged knowledge not merely of the nature of their own subjugation, but also of the structure of their society and of the subjectivity of their oppressors—a knowledge "privileged" because it is unavailable to the dominant themselves. Drawing on antecedents in Marxist and feminist philosophy, the philosopher Charles Mills has influentially argued that the construction and maintenance of white supremacy as the dominant global political system in modernity depended and continues to rely on what he terms an epistemology of ignorance: "an ignorance, a non-knowing, that is not contingent, but in which race—white racism and/or white racial domination and their ramifications—plays a crucial causal role" ("White Ignorance" 20).[18] Prior to Mills, sociologist and Black feminist theorist Patricia Hill Collins analyzed the distinctive contributions of Black women to knowledge production in general and sociology in particular on the basis of their experiences as what she calls "outsiders within," or marginalized subjects who are provisionally accepted into the spaces or ranks of a more powerful community, as exemplified by experiences as diverse as those of Black domestic workers in white households and Black women social scientists.[19] More recently, citing and continuing the work of numerous Brazilian and other predecessors including Collins and Lélia Gonzalez, Djamila Ribeiro has popularized the term "lugar de fala" as a means of focusing attention on the socially defined standpoint from which subjects intervene in political life and of demanding due deference by the broader society to the standpoints of the oppressed and the experience-grounded insights produced by the subjects who occupy those positions. These contemporary standpoint theories and, in particular, the powerful Black feminist epistemological programs exemplified by the work of Collins and Ribeiro are, in their directness and scope, far more radical than anything we find in the writing of Machado de Assis. Yet, the novelist's frequent narrative use of characters I have called outsiders-on-the-inside—but whom we could also call, with Collins, outsiders within—as well as his own experience in something like this subject position, allow us to place his fiction within a rich tradition that recognizes the complex discursive and epistemic consequences of oppressive economic, sexual, and racial systems.

But there is another sense in which Machado occupied himself with points of view at once inside and outside power, social inclusion, and authorship. In addition to the outsider-within characters like Helena, Rubião, José Dias, and Capitu, the famous first-person narrators from the so-called second phase of Machado's career speak from a position simultaneously proximal to and distant from the events they narrate; they are both on the inside and the outside of their own tales—in a sense, *insiders without.* Brás Cubas, Dom Casmurro, and Conselheiro Aires all exemplify this, though in different ways. Brás Cubas—famously not a dead author, but a dead man who writes—provides perhaps the most obvious example, since his death (his not simply contingent but metaphysical removal from the world of his narrative) is posited as the state of affairs that enables his narration: quite literally a transcendental condition. Freed of the mortal coil, Brás invites his readers to anticipate that he will prove an unusual sort of narrator and, specifically, that he might (at least attempt to) speak truths that a living author could not pronounce. The story Brás tells is his own—his death, his life, his whims, his abuses—but the narrating persona speaks from a position altogether beyond its confines and, were it to have any, its consequences. Dom Casmurro is similarly if less radically removed from the conflicts he relitigates, finding himself largely alone and retired from society in the house he had built in facsimile of his boyhood home. Resigned from the present and divorced from the characters of his story, apparently including his former self, he attempts (or at least claims to be attempting) to reconstruct a lost past and to return somehow to the beginning of things. He has trapped himself in a tale he cannot escape, but within which he no longer lives either.

Conselheiro Aires, narrator-author of both *Esaú e Jacó* and *Memorial de Aires*, exhibits two substantially different behaviors. The primary text of *Esaú e Jacó* largely suppresses its narrator's identity, which would remain difficult or impossible for readers to specify as Aires without the benefit of a paratextual element: the opening Advertência, which states that the tale was found under the title "Último," among but curiously not belonging to the late counselor's memoirs. A reader who believes that Advertência must assume that Aires-the-author went to some pains to create a narrator who, though privy to his experiences, thoughts, and written observations, is supposedly distinct from Aires-the-character. Apparently, Aires, in addition to rehashing the episodes that comprise the novel after having already chronicled them in his *Memorial*, must be read as establishing a cushion between himself and the events he narrates, which he not only observed but in which he evidently played a significant role, even if it was mostly a performance of apathy, detachment, and inaction. Finally, the Aires of the *Memorial*, like the Aires of *Esaú e Jacó*, straddles the boundary between observer and participant in the family drama of the Aguiar couple and their surrogate children Fidélia and Tristão. But this Aires now appears explicitly as a memoirist, writing his narrative merely for his own amusement, with no audience beyond himself in mind. The epistolary form also presumes that its composer is aware, at any given point in the narration, only of events described up to the moment of the composition of a particular fragment—in this case, a particular entry in the memoir. Moreover, as author of the texts that make up the *Memorial*, Aires takes no responsibility for their arrangement into a cohesive or persuasive whole; indeed, the novel's Advertência contains the claim on the part of "M. de A." that what we read is extracted—"desbastada e estreita"—from the raw form in which its author left it (*Memorial* 1096; "pared down and compressed," my translation). In any case, the result is that the Aires of the *Memorial* tells a tale to which he belongs, but which he presents as not really being about himself in a significant way, and in which he both displays and denies substantial interest, since the diary form ostensibly records only his idle observations on the mundane occurrences that make up a small-scale drama.

Against the double bind of social responsibility that afflicts characters like Helena and Capitu, outsiders within who must fend for themselves *and* suffer for appearing to seek personal advantage or benefit, Machado's insider-without narrators use their combined narrative and social authority to enjoy a double freedom. They are active within the stories as participants and protagonists, but as narrators they position themselves at a distance from the events and even from their own agency within them. Brás Cubas, the writing dead, has gone altogether beyond any judgment we might want to make of him; indeed, as he warns his readers, even criticism of his narrative form, to say nothing of moral disapproval of his conduct, will be met only with "um piparote, e adeus" (*Brás Cubas* 513; "a flick of the fingers, and goodbye," my translation). Dom Casmurro, acting as witness, prosecutor, and judge against Capitu, marshals evidence against his wife while moving to absolve himself.[20] And Aires, whether in the novelistic mode of *Esaú e Jacó* or the epistolary mode of *Memorial de Aires*, casts himself as an observer with only detached aesthetic interest in the lives he narrates, despite his evident involvement in their affairs—he is, after all, retired.

In a social, narrative, discursive universe carved sharply at its joints of domination—principally, if not exclusively: white over Black, rich over poor, male over female—the choice of these narrators to position themselves as insiders on the outside, witnesses as well as participants (at times one perhaps wishes to say *perpetrators*), chroniclers as much as characters, can appear only as a gesture of the highest colonial privilege. A move of whiteness, inevitably, in that it assumes an authority not only to express a point of view, not simply to tell a story, but to define the terms according to which the tale will be told and received: the parameters of the discourse, its genre. Machado himself, simultaneously a socially ascendant Afro-Brazilian artist and a formally innovative ironist and social critic, was therefore something of both the outsider-within charac- ter and insider-without narrator. If enacting the double position through narration relies on a claim of privilege and whiteness when performed by Brás Cubas, Dom Casmurro, and Conselheiro Aires, it does so no less for Machado—except with this difference: as both an outsider-within and an insider-without, Machado's stratagem exposes the hypocrisy and corruption of whiteness without too recklessly announcing the fragility of his own claim to perform it in the first place.

Though Machado himself occupied in some ways both the outsid- er-within and insider-without positions, it evidently would have been too much to expect that he combine them in the construction of his major works.[21] Indeed, in his novels, no characters of marginal or secondary social position take up the voice of narration, and many paradigmatic outsiders within meet famously tragic ends: Helena wastes away; Capitu, scorned, also dies young; and Rubião, as we noted, loses his wealth, his reason, and his life.

But this combination of outsider-within character and insid- er-without narrator perspectives is just what Miltom Hatoum attempts in his acclaimed novel, *Dois irmãos*.[22] Drawing also on diverse intertexts including Indigenous narrative traditions and the Bible, Hatoum's tale of fraternal antipathy engages with Machado's *Esaú e Jacó* in multiple ways, extending the productive aesthetic tension between insider and outsider standpoints to the situation of its Indigenous-Lebanese-Brazilian narrator. Structuring their development around the conflicts of twin brothers who have opposite temperaments, the two novels flirt in parallel with national allegory.[23] *Esaú e Jacó* anchors its narrative in decisive historical moments like the passage of the Lei do Ventre Livre in 1871, the signing of the Lei Áurea in 1888, the Baile da Ilha Fiscal and the Proclamação da República in 1889, and the rise of Floriano Peixoto in the tumultuous early 1890s, seeming to mourn the fleeting life of a fast-maturing, modern Brazil that, unable to choose between stuffy conservatism and self-serving radicalism, would ultimately wither and die in the shadow of the Marechal de Ferro. Hatoum's *Dois irmãos* is similarly blunt in tying significant moments in Brazilian history to the life of one family/household: the Lebanese-Brazilian parents Zana and Halim; their twin sons Yaqub and Omar; their daughter

Rânia; and their Indigenous servant Domingas and her son Nael. Told in a complex narration that brazenly obscures its linear sequence by doubling back upon itself, deferring details, and retelling crucial episodes from alternate perspectives, the novel's primary timeline begins shortly after the end of the Second World War, coinciding not only with the end of the Estado Novo and the beginning of the República Populista, but also, as we eventually discover, with the conception of the narrator, Nael, the son of Domingas. Consequently, Nael, having been born around 1946, grows up during the turbulent period of political change and ambitious attempts at modernization and development before reaching majority in the significant year of 1964, when the brutality of the military coup hits home with the arrest and killing of the teacher and poet Antenor Laval, also a friend to Omar. Halim, an immigrant to Brazil whose only dream was to live out his days in blissful seclusion with his beloved Zana, indulging his eternal passion and ignoring all other cares, dies in December 1968, around the promulgation of Ato Institucional 5, the beginning of the most repressive period of the military dictatorship. The final stages of the "biblical" conflict between Omar and Yaqub occur during the succeeding years of authoritarian rule and, again following Machado's model, the bitter endgame of their animosity is played out without explicit references to the historical calendar.

While *Esaú e Jacó* turns in part on the ultimately unresolvable question of whether the maiden Flora, apparently an embodiment of the promise of a modern, post-slavocratic Brazil, will choose as a partner one of two twins—the traditionalist Pedro or the revolutionary Paulo—*Dois irmãos* holds at its heart the puzzle of Nael's paternity: Is he the son of the tempestuous, self-absorbed, appetitive Omar or the reticent, straightlaced, calculating Yaqub? Yet, this is not the only doubt that seeks to govern the narration. Nael begins the novel by narrating the end of Zana's life and her final, desperate question: "Meus filhos já fizeram as pazes?" (*Dois irmãos* 10; "Have my sons made their peace with each other yet?"; *The Brothers* 4).[24] He continues:

> Repetiu a pergunta com a força que lhe restava, com a coragem que mãe aflita encontra na hora da morte.
>   Ninguém respondeu. Então o rosto quase sem rugas de Zana desvaneceu; ela ainda virou a cabeça para o lado, à procura da única janelinha na parede cinzenta, onde se apagava um pedaço do céu crepuscular. (*Dois irmãos* 10)

(She repeated the question with all the strength left in her, the courage an anguished mother finds when death is near. No one answered. Then Zana's smooth, almost unfurrowed face vanished; she merely turned her face to one side, searching for the only tiny window in the gray wall, where a patch of evening sky was gradually going dark.) (*The Brothers* 4)

This opening makes clear enough that we should not expect Yaqub and Omar to ever make peace, even as it poses the nature and causes of their hostility as a central problem to be resolved, or at least deeply addressed. It is not until the fourth numbered chapter, about a quarter of the way into his text and having already sketched in nonchronological sequence a significant portion of his narrative—Yaqub's return to Brazil from Lebanon after the end of the war; some of the early tensions between the brothers before the war; the youth and courtship of Halim and Zana in the 1910s and 1920s; Yaqub's departure for São Paulo in 1950; and Domingas's arrival in the family home two years before the birth of the twins—that Nael discloses his identity as the son of Domingas, the presumed son of either Omar or Yaqub, and therefore the grandchild of Halim and Zana.

When he finally makes this disclosure, explaining that in his early life he knew nothing of his own origins, Nael must therefore also explain his situation within the family home, the spaces he could occupy, the treatment he would expect, and the labor he had performed. Patiently, if somewhat erratically, he unspools his account with suggestive scenes from his youth, engaging in little direct commentary or condemnation of his circumstances. Yet, the tenor of Nael's existence, his role, and his degree of belonging within the house are clear enough from the first lines of his exposition, even before he describes the extent of his responsibilities: "Podia frequentar o interior da casa, sentar no sofá cinzento e nas cadeiras de palha da sala. Era raro eu sentar à mesa com os donos da casa, mas podia comer a comida deles, beber tudo, eles não se importavam" (*Dois irmãos* 60; "I was allowed in the main part of the house, and could sit on the gray sofa and the wicker chairs in the living room. I didn't often sit at table with the family, but I could eat and drink anything they did; they didn't mind"; *The Brothers* 64).[25] Nael, like Domingas and regardless of the fact that one of the twins is his father, is not one of the donos da casa; their cordiality toward him is an expression of their colonial position as settlers—their largesse, but not obligation, fully-fledged care, or reciprocity. He is attached to the family but is not fully a member; he is an outsider-within.

Yet, as a narrator, he will be an insider without as well. Though he poses a question of his own—Who, among this deeply troubled pair, is my father?—when this question arises, it is already in conflict with another that lingers in the narrative atmosphere: Zana's dying, defeated lament, Have my sons made their peace yet? These questions may turn out to be inseparable, since the answer to Nael's question and his ability or failure to discover it will be bound up in the origins, development, and aftermath of the explosive and irreconcilable hatred separating Omar and Yaqub. But they will remain in tension: Which drives the telling of this story? What is this story really about? Whose story, in the end, is this?

This, then, is Nael's condition as a narrator. Not simply that he narrates much of this story as an observer on the margins of the action, seeming to have often been more of a shadow than a presence within the house, a witness to the others' regret, shame, and frustration, but the subordination of his own story to another: the problem of his origin and his relationship to the family he orbits are untellable without diving deep into Zana's question, the hatred between the twins—a tragedy of the dominant. Significantly, his double perspective, quite beyond preventing him from ever referring to his grandparents by any term of endearment, leads him to alternate between mentions of "Domingas" and "minha mãe" throughout his text. He appears unable to fully conceive of his mother and himself outside of their subordination to Zana, Halim, and their children; their subservience within the family home; and their position as colonized subjects tied to and, in this sense, even belonging to the domestic space, but only as specified by the rigid hierarchy of coloniality, only as outsiders within.

It is from this context that Nael's account of the twins' conflict takes its allegorical shape. Like Machado's Pedro and Paulo, Yaqub and Omar seem to represent two incommensurable cultural attitudes in Brazilian development: Omar's passionate and self-indulgent sensualism, his impulsivity, his preference for a sort of jeitinho brasileiro, his disdain for rules and rule followers; and Yaqub's attraction to order and precision, his desire for technological progress, his disgust at what he perceives as backwardness, his willingness to use the coercive powers of the state to impose his conception of order, even at the expense of democracy and fundamental liberties. If this was a choice (the choice?) facing Brazil in the middle of the twentieth century—between, on the one side, a positivist-inspired, technocratic, authoritarian developmentalism and, on the other, a personalistic, sometimes contrarian, anarchic individualism—then it is a choice to be made only from within the colonialist perspective on power and social relations. It is a choice for the sons of successful immigrants, a choice for settlers, but not for Nael and certainly not for Domingas, Indigenous children of the Paranãuasu, as the Rio Negro is known in her native Nheengatu. It is a contest shaped, like that of Machado's Pedro and Paulo, as much by the brothers' mutual bitterness and rejection as by any innate proclivities or their relationships with the other people in their lives. But unlike Machado's twins, condemned deterministically and *ab ovo* to their conflict, having fought each other already within the womb, Yaqub and Omar are parties to a more fully historicized conflict. In Nael's telling, the division between the twins arises from Zana's excessive attachment to Omar and consequent relative indifference to Yaqub. Zana's terror at losing her "caçula," though triggered by Omar's sickliness during his first months, seems to result also from the unhealed trauma of her father's death in Lebanon, an ocean away, when she was but a teenager: a loss of protection, heritage, and identity. Zana's preoccupation with Omar leaves Yaqub in the care of Domingas, herself a child of about twelve years. And Yaqub's affection for Domingas, in some form a reciprocation of her "amor de mãe postiça, incompleto, talvez impossível," is a displaced and perhaps distorted feeling for an absent Zana, which in turn inspires the jealousy of Omar, who, pampered by their own mother, feels entitled to Domingas's attentions as well (*Dois irmãos* 50; "substitute mother's love, incomplete, perhaps simply impossible"; *The Brothers* 51–52).

It is not simply that in Nael's universe, in Hatoum's universe, the violence of the present is dictated by the unclosed wounds of the past; it is not merely that Brazilian modernity is governed by cycles of envy and vengeance that bar any possibility of forgiveness, healing, or hope—as Omar puts it, from his perspective, "Devias ter fugido . . . o orgulho, a honra, a esperança, o país . . . tudo enterrado" (*Dois irmãos* 168; "You should have run away . . . pride, honor, hope, Brazil . . . all buried"; *The Brothers* 186). Rather, for Nael and Hatoum, it is transparent that this violence, the interminable battle to define a modern life for Brazil, remains primarily a colonial problem, a challenge for settlers who gain access to colonial privilege, a problem of making the colony work for those who stand to profit from it. This story, whatever its importance, covers up and at times overwhelms, even if it is unable to fully erase, the colonized experience of Domingas and Nael: their struggle not even to tell their own stories, but to occupy a free and independent role in this one. In the end, Zana's question—Have my sons made their peace?—will overpower Nael's question—Which of her sons is my father?—because Yaqub's love for Domingas arises from Zana's neglect while Omar's assault on Domingas is triggered by his incurable envy of his brother. In Nael's own conception, the most consequential events of his mother's life and of his own are not really about them—at least, not as agents and subjects. In the end, it can hardly matter which of the twins is "actually" Nael's father, since it was their rivalry and competition that first drew Yaqub close to Domingas and led later to her rape at Omar's hands. If anything firm can be said about his parentage, it is that Nael's existence results from the subjugation of his one true parent, Domingas, who is instrumentalized by one twin and abused by the other.[26]

In Machado's *Esaú e Jacó*, Flora is torn between affection for Pedro and Paulo and dreams of unifying them in a magical synthesis, but in *Dois irmãos* only Rânia, the twins' sister, would wish to combine them into one being (73). For Hatoum, the synthetic resolution of the antithetical tendencies of modern Brazil is an incestuous desire within the space of colonial power. It is no choice for his narrator, who, though born of the tension between the twins, will ultimately shun them both. Nael, a son of immigrants and Indigeneity, ought to inherit the promise of the country along with its painful history. Instead, evoking comparison to José de Alencar's Moacir, he inherits only the shack he grew up in, a scrap on the edge of decaying colonial grandeur, and writes, an outsider in his own story, an outsider within what should be his own place, in his own life.

The struggle for belonging and the search for narrative form foregrounded by Machado de Assis and Milton Hatoum continue in contemporary writing, as evinced by Jeferson Tenório's *O avesso da pele*. Visiting the home of his recently deceased father, an Afro-Brazilian student in his early twenties recounts the story of his parents, Henrique and Martha. Though he tells some of his own story, like Nael, Pedro remains by and large on the periphery of the narrative, retelling and reimagining moments in his parents' lives, their conflicts with each other, the abuses they suffered at other hands, and the toll they have paid for the ongoing racism of Brazilian society from the late twentieth century until well into the twenty-first. In Tenório's text, Black Brazilians—especially in the south: Porto Alegre, Florianópolis—continue to find themselves outsiders-within in contemporary Brazil, even when they do everything in accordance with the norms of propriety, even when they try to deal with their own demons, even when they avoid any form of social disruption.

O avesso da pele is particularly noteworthy for its use of second-person narration throughout Pedro's effort to understand his parents, himself, and the world they have all inhabited. Pedro frequently addresses Henrique directly, referring to him as *você*, and although there are passages that do not specifically invoke the second person, the narration suggests no other more likely narratee for those sections of the text. As a result, Pedro appears to be consistently speaking or thinking in apostrophe to Henrique, while also creating for himself and for the text's readers a version of the departed father, who we eventually learn was killed by the police in an absurd and outrageous street stop.[27] Having entered his father's home to find Henrique's ocutá, a stone representing his connection to the orixá Ogum, Pedro finds himself surrounded by the indices of a life he now struggles to comprehend. Pedro's presence among the lingering artifacts of Henrique's existence is, in his own terms, a kind of intrusion, a discomfiting near-encounter reflected in the strangeness of his text, which addresses an absence as he narrates to você scenes from Henrique's life: his exhausting career as an overworked and underappreciated public-school teacher, the violent racism he suffered from the time he was a child, his painful path to racial and social consciousness, the difficulties of sustaining relationships. Pedro's narrative roams widely as he sketches Martha's early life and tribulations, the ups and downs of his parents' intimacy and separation, his own attempt to understand race and relationships, and even, somewhat stunningly, the recurring nightmares and constant terror that plague the unnamed police officer who killed Henrique. At the end, Pedro acknowledges that he has created his narrative for himself, expressing what he could not communicate to Henrique previously and inventing events that might fill in some of the gaps in what he knows of his parents' lives. His narration is a ritual of closure and continuity, a complement to his retrieval of the *ocutá*, which he intends to release into the waters of the Guaíba.

In some respects, the world Tenório shows us in *O avesso da pele* could seem to invite a more naturalistic presentation. Although the characters created in Pedro's narration are poignantly realized as individuals with specific personalities, attitudes, and trajectories, the novel is permeated by a sense of the typicality of their struggles, the mundaneness and inexorability, above all, of the pervasive, crushing racism that is overwhelmingly determinative in the lives of Henrique and Martha. The utter banality of racial injustice: the crude jokes Henrique hears among a girlfriend's family; the sexual fetishization of racial difference that briefly colors before souring a mixed-race relationship; an employer's straightforwardly racist declaration that he does not like negros, but that Henrique is a good one; Martha's subjugation by a mother-in-law who appropriates her labor and demeans her sexual agency; the bare violence of the state—police harassment unto death. But Tenório does not limit his project to pointing out and describing the intractable forces and persistent patterns that leave Henrique and Martha "apenas duas pessoas quebradas" (27; "just two broken people").[28] As Pedro declares, "Não acho que devemos lidar apenas com a lógica dos fatos" (183; "I don't think that we should only deal in the logic of facts")—this novel cannot be simply a diagnostic litany of social ills, as deterministic and insurmountable as these might seem, as objective as their denunciation might appear. By employing the narrative second person and risking the awkwardness inherent in a discourse that seems to tell its addressee what he either already knows or else might be an invention he could know to be false, Tenório's narrator opens a space of powerful tension. Since Pedro's supposed audience is not just contingently but essentially absent, one can think of his narration as directed as much to the emptiness where his father should be as it is to Henrique himself. And because we know that Henrique, or the space that Henrique left behind, can offer no response to Pedro's address, the dense silence of the null narratee becomes a position to be occupied by a suitably disposed reader, as if lying down within his outline on the sidewalk.

And yet, if it is a somewhat facile assumption that second-person narrative may be particularly apt for engaging the affective involvement of a reader, and if Tenório's narrative architecture is highly effective in creating opportunities for readers to empathize with Henrique, as he is constructed by Pedro, as well as with Pedro himself and his other significant characters, *O avesso da pele* aims for something even more than this. As a novel that foregrounds the experience of Black Brazilians while participating in a literary culture historically and, to a large extent, currently dominated by the politics and aesthetics of whiteness, this text makes insiders of outsiders and outsiders of insiders. It is not only that readers who have lived the racialized oppression experienced by characters like Henrique and Martha will easily "relate to" or "identify with," in some indistinct sense, the events and interactions narrated by Pedro. But by narrating in the second person, despite the specificity of the actions and qualities ascribed to *você*—inevitable reminders that the supposed narratee of the text is Henrique, or at least Pedro's idea of him—Tenório also ensures that some of his narrator's enunciations will turn out to be largely or even entirely true, quite literally, for certain readers. Consider, for instance, Pedro's accounts of how Henrique might have absorbed the quotidian racial aggressions of supposedly cordial social relations:

> Até aquele momento você nunca havia sofrido racismo, assim, tão descaradamente, não que você se lembre. Mas você não se chocou, pois uma espécie de inércia tomou conta do seu corpo, você não sabia reagir. Na época, você nem sabia muito bem o que significava ser negro. Não havia discutido nada sobre racismo, nada sobre negritude, nada sobre nada. Naquele momento você era apenas um corpo negro. Mas no fundo sabia que estava diante de um escroto. Mesmo assim você não reagiu. (20–21)

> (Until that moment you had never experienced such racism, so openly, not that you could remember. But you weren't shocked, as a kind of inertia took hold of your body, you didn't know how to react. At the time, you didn't even really know what it meant to be Black. You had never discussed anything about racism, about negritude, about anything. In that moment you were just a Black body. But deep down you knew that you were dealing with an asshole. Even so you didn't react.)

> Acontece que, em pouco tempo, você não só passou a ser o negão da família, como também passou a ser uma espécie de para-raios de todas as imagens estereotipadas sobre os negros pois disseram que você era mais resistente à dor, disseram que a pele negra custa a envelhecer, que você deveria saber sambar, que deveria gostar de pagode, que devia jogar bem futebol, que os negros são bons no atletismo. *Você não corre?* Que os negros são ruins como nadadores, *já viu algum negro ganhar medalha olímpica na natação? Agora, olhem lá nas corridas. Vocês ganham tudo. É porque desde cedo aprendem a correr dos leões na África, não vê como aqueles quenianos sempre ganham a São Silvestre?"* (29, italics in original)

> (It so happens that, within a short time, you didn't just become the family negão but you also became a kind of lightning rod

for all the stereotyped images about Black people since they said that you were more tolerant to pain, they said that Black skin doesn't age so easily, that you must know how to dance samba, that you must like pagode, that you must be good at soccer, that Blacks are good at track. *Don't you run?* That Blacks are terrible swimmers, *have you ever seen a Black person win an Olympic medal in swimming? Now, look at track races. You all win everything. It's because you learn from a young age to run from the lions in Africa, don't you see how those Kenyans always win the Saint Silvester?*)

Or, the recurring terror of racial profiling and harassment by police:

Enquanto você conferia a hora no seu relógio, dois policiais, em motocicletas, da Brigada Militar se aproximaram de você e perguntaram o que fazia ali parado. Você demorou alguns segundos para responder, na verdade queria se recusar a responder, pensou em confrontá-los, perguntar por que estava sendo abordado, mesmo que já soubesse a resposta. Você estava cansado daquilo. Cansado de ter que dar explicações para a polícia. (142)

(While you were checking the time on your watch, two policemen, on motorcycles, from the Military Brigade approached you and asked what you were doing standing there. You took a few seconds to respond, in truth you wanted to refuse to respond, you thought of confronting them, asking why you were being stopped, even though you already knew the answer. You were tired of it. Tired of having to give explanations to the police.)

Você estava novamente cansado, com sono. Não via a hora de chegar em casa. Então você viu as cores vermelhas de uma sirene se aproximarem. Você rezou para não ser abordado mais uma vez. No entanto, sua reza não funcionou. Eles desceram de arma em punho, não apontaram para você, apenas mandaram você se virar e pôr as mãos na cabeça, perguntaram para onde você estava indo. (150)

(You were tired again, sleepy. You couldn't wait to get home. Then you saw the red colors of a siren approaching. You prayed that you wouldn't get stopped again. Nevertheless, your prayer didn't work. They got out with guns drawn, didn't aim them at you, they just ordered you to turn around and put your hands on your head, asked where you were going.)

Truly quotidian for some, frequent and predictable for others, merely hypothetical for the rest—the thoroughly generic, terribly routinized slights and atrocities of a racist society cannot strike all readers in quite the same way, with quite the same force. While the myth of Brazilian racial inclusiveness continues to hold currency in much of white and middle-class society, Black Brazilians and other attentive observers know that in addition to day-to-day degradations, official, quasi-official, and other racist violence is lethal and pervasive. Since the publication of *O avesso da pele*, numerous cases of such violence have captured national and international media attention, including the 2020 murder in Porto Alegre of João Alberto Silveira Freitas, a forty-year-old Black man, by two white security guards employed by the Carrefour supermarket chain; the 2022 murder in Rio de Janeiro of Moïse Mugenyi Kabagambe, a refugee from the Democratic Republic of the Congo, after he demanded payment for back wages; and the two most deadly police interventions in Rio since at least 1989: the massacres in the communities of Jacarez-inho, where twenty-eight people were killed in 2021, and Vila Cruzeiro, where twenty-five people were killed in 2022. Yet, though there have been mobilizations for racial justice and protests against anti-Black violence, Brazilian society at large has not embraced calls for systemic change, and right-wing politicians have continued to call for more arms and more policing.[29]

Tenório's second-person poetics quite plainly *speaks to* its readers differently, depending on our color and racial consciousness, whether we have lived the oppression of structural racism and state violence, or whether we have not—whether we require an act of imagination to contemplate how subjects might be formed, duped, inhibited, coerced, subjugated, and ultimately struck down in the street by the power of this prejudice. In so doing, this aesthetic politics of negritude inverts the historically racialized assumption regarding not only who is likely to write literary fiction, but in fact, perhaps even more profoundly here, who reads literary fiction.[30] Tenório's novel carries forward the questioning project of Machado de Assis and Milton Hatoum, asking not only who is inside power and who is inside narration, but now: Who is in the audience? To whom and for whom is this tale told? Who can make up an audience worth addressing?

Playing on the indeterminacy of the audience, the second person of *O avesso da pele* asks not just who reads novels, but also who reads *this* novel, a text of Blackness, of literatura negro-brasileira. The text carries a sense that for some readers, this narration tells them what they already know, recognizes them, even as it is an invention of a certain version of familiar experiences. And it simultaneously creates for other readers a potentially jarring challenge: Can you place yourself within this *você*? What are the bounds of your compassion, your concern, your solidarity? If this text does not speak *to you* in the way it addresses others, if it is not in this sense *for you*, will you reject it or will you embrace it?

Tenório's novel lays bare how the racial boundaries that differentiate us as agents and authors inevitably differentiate us as readers too. By positioning the traditional insiders of literary reading as outsiders and bringing the historical outsiders of literary culture into the center of his project, Tenório enacts a part of what is required for building an emancipatory aesthetics out of the ruins of our heritage. His novel reminds us that the persistent dualities of modernity do not simply disappear or lose their force when recognized as artificial or historical or constructed, but rather they but must be confronted. And this confrontation must be guided by our acceptance that the historical hierarchies of power, however spurious, however trumped-up, have placed some on the inside and others on the outside—have made us truly if contingently different to one another. Perhaps, Tenório suggests, if we grasp and respect the reality of *this* difference, we can construct together an aesthetics and politics of justice and liberation, marching forward as Pedro does, intoning as he pursues a future he does not yet even envision: "tenho Ogum em minhas mãos, e ainda me sinto perdido, mas a palavra continua não sendo essa. Vou em frente, na direção do Guaíba. Tenho Ogum em minhas mãos porque agora é a minha vez" (180; "I have Ogum in my hands, and I still feel lost, but that is still not the right word. I'm going forward, toward the Guaíba. I have Ogum in my hands because now it's my turn"). By challenging and reversing the positions of outsider and insider, not only in characterization, not only in narration, but also in readership, Brazilian authors continue Machado's struggle for emancipatory form.

Notes

1. In honor and memory of Anani Dzidzienyo.

2. The views expressed are those of the author and do not necessarily reflect the official policy or position of the Department of the Air Force, the Department of Defense, or the US government. PA#: USAFA-DF-2021-287.

3. In an oft-quoted letter, Joaquim Nabuco chided José Veríssimo for referring to the author in print as mulatto, further insisting that as far as he himself was concerned, Machado was white. For discussion of what inferences might or might not be appropriate regarding Machado's own sense of identity on the basis of this and similar surviving documents, see G. Reginald Daniel.

4. Abdias Nascimento, for instance, problematizes Afro-Brazilian writing and intellectual production by noting the presence of "notorious Afro-Brazilians who thought, wrote and acted as mirror-images of the dominant society (white or Aryanoid), and who despite being influential writers, in their work included almost nothing that would identity them in any kind of connection with their African origin" (275), counting Machado among these. More recently, Niyi Afolabi has pointedly extended this criticism of Machado, emphasizing the author's failure to approach his work from a perspective of aesthetic and political negritude: "Yet, to Afro-Brazilians, those I consider his 'neglected people,' he is nothing but a cowardly traitor whose self-centeredness, alienation, and reliance on the so-called 'mulatto escape hatch' combine to disqualify him as a deserving contributor to the cause of black liberation, especially during the era of the abolition struggle" (26–27); "Machado seems too cautious to articulate any opinion that will set him at odds with the dominant white elite. Even if caution, tact, and diplomacy were his intentions, they are ideologically misplaced and compromised" (30); "In avoiding the problem of slavery, Machado does not eliminate it; rather, he succeeds in displaying his indifference and confirming his status as a coopted writer within the prejudiced Brazilian society of his time" (32). Afolabi's contribution in this volume revisits but does not disavow this assessment of the author's project and its limitations.

5. Coutinho relied heavily and uncritically on Gilberto Freyre's contentions regarding mestiço psychology in *Sobrados e mocambos*, combined with similarly prejudiced conjectures regarding the psychological impact of Machado's epilepsy. Here he pronounces on racial politics in Brazil and the resentment of mixed-race Brazilians, an attitude he thinks has legitimate origins, but which is ultimately misplaced and inappropriate: "É admirável a facilidade de acesso que a sociedade brasileira favorece às classes inferiores. Esta é sem dúvida uma das soluções ao problema das relações entre classes, e não o acirramento da luta ou o alongamento das distâncias. Mas esse fenômeno não se tem processado de modo normal, do ponto de vista da psicologia social, o seu mecanismo tem sido cheio de tropeços e entraves por causa da defeituosa e falha psicologia do mestiço, consequência do seu desejo de subir e dos resíduos da escravidão" (Coutinho 146).

6. The work of Roberto Schwarz, as well as that of his principal acolytes and interlocutors, is representative. For critics like Schwarz, Alfredo Bosi, John

Gledson, Regina Zilbermann, and others, the institution of slavery and its funda-mental role in ordering economic relations in colonial and imperial Brazil figure large, but their approach has little place in the main for Blackness, whiteness, or other concepts of racialized identity and power as terms of analysis.

7. To be frank, I think Wasserman's choice of "racializing" here is some-what infelicitous. The critic evidently does not mean to refer to a reading that invents and imposes racial categories not otherwise in evidence in the political and aesthetic context of the work and its reception, but instead to an approach to interpretation that begins from a location of specific sensitivity to the racial (and other) categories operative in the discursive history of the text. In other words, it is not the reading that is racializing, but the systems of power operative in modernity; Wasserman convincingly calls for a reading that responds to histories and experiences of racialization.

8. Consider, paradigmatically, Gerard Genette's *Narrative Discourse*.

9. Consider, for instance, the influential work of decolonial theorists like Aníbal Quijano and Walter Mignolo.

10. Herman et al., *Narrative Theory: Core Concepts and Critical Debates*, 21–22. In Brian Richardson's section of the introduction, the novel is dated to 1888 (!) and the author is named as "Antonio Machado de Assis."

11. Translations from *Quincas Borba* are by Gregory Rabassa.

12. Earl E. Fitz notes incisively that the metaphor "melds the theoretical question of how a person reads a literary text (but, in truth, any text or set of signs) with the all-too-real issues of slavery, power, and violence" (98).

13. In fact, *Quincas Borba* was first published serially beginning two years prior to abolition and was significantly revised before its publication as a book in 1891.

14. Translations from *Esaú e Jacó* are by Helen Caldwell.

15. Alex Flynn, Elena Calvo-González, and Marcelo Mendes de Souza argue that critics have too eagerly "colored in" Machado's characters, as in the reception of "Pai contra mãe," and that because the author sets this sort of trap for incautious readers, a careful reading of his work may warn us off endorsing a binary concep-tion of racial identity since the either-or—either Black or white—choice may lead us to further naturalize racial difference and thereby further rarify and empower whiteness. Although their reading of the short story and their admonition about coloring in Machado and his characters is well argued, their conclusions attacking racial mobilization under the banner of Blackness are much less persuasive. For one thing, despite the complexity and even at times apparent fluidity of racial identity, the fundamental division inherited from the modern construction of race seems ineluctably two-fold: the graced, the acceptable, the good enough (white, white enough, near white, favored mixtures, etc.) and the inferior, the others, the rest (Black, Brown, disfavored mixtures, etc.). The category of whiteness is inherently exclusionary, deriving its value only from its nonuniversality, its scarcity. So the

contention that one might attack the dominance of whiteness by preempting the identity alignment of Black and Brown subjects appears incoherent.

16. "Training Skeptical Readers in Machado de Assis's *Helena*," *Chasqui*, vol. 48, no. 1, 2019, 37–55.

17. Consider how Lúcia Miguel Pereira describes the young Machado haunting the halls of the school for which he worked, selling the sweets prepared by his stepmother: "Certamente, nas horas de folga, procurava ouvir trechos das lições dadas ás meninas ricas, pescar aqui e ali uma noção, um esclarecimento. Não seria possível ao baleiro penetrar nas classes, mas os moleques têm mil manhas, sabem escutar ás portas, esgueirar-se pelos corredores, esconder-se nos desvãos escuros. Imovel, o coração batendo de susto, emquanto esperava o taboleiro das quitandas, Joaquim Maria ouvia as aulas que não lhe eram destinadas" (36).

18. On the necessity of white supremacy to obscure its own construction of racial inequality and, consequently, to keep its interpellated subjects ignorant of the conditions that make it possible, see Mills's *The Racial Contract*.

19. Collins first developed the "outsider within" concept in her widely cited article "Learning from the Outsider Within: The Sociological Significance of Black Feminist Thought." A number of the arguments presented in that article later received more extensive treatment in Collins's very influential *Black Feminist Thought*.

20. See, famously, Helen Caldwell's defense of Capitu (*The Brazilian Othello of Machado de Assis*) and Silviano Santiago's dissection of Dom Casmurro's abusive exercise of lawyerly rhetoric ("A retórica da verossimilhança").

21. It might be possible to construct a counterexample based on a reading of *A casa velha*, a text whose narrator participates in the story while maintaining some detachment and whose social position is somewhat less insiderish than the more paradigmatic Brás Cubas or Aires. And yet the basic point stands: it is hard to imagine a Machadean novel narrated by a social aspirant or outsider within like Helena or Rubião.

22. Hatoum is surely not the first Brazilian writer or even canonical author to attempt this. For instance, Lima Barreto, so often compared favorably with Machado in terms of their respective treatments of race and racism, might be read as developing the combined outsider-inside character and insider-outside narrator in *A vida e morte de M. J. Gonzaga de Sá*.

23. The notion of allegory, and within its sphere the concept of national allegory, is somewhat vexed, potentially raising theoretical considerations far beyond the scope of this discussion. It is worth mentioning in passing, however, some significant points of reference. First, Frederic Jameson's contentious claim that under late global capitalism "third-world" literature necessarily performs national allegory as its mode of representation has been roundly critiqued as totalizing and reductive; see especially Aijaz Ahmad's influential rebuttal. Considerable controversy and debate around this topic have continued since the late

1980s. Indeed, the apparent inevitability of national allegory as a category for understanding "third-world" cultural production seems to be not only a consequence of occupying a "first-world" critical position, but moreover, as Ahmad argues, it is a result of insisting on an inflexible, essentializing tripartite division of "world" subjectivities. And yet, Jameson seems to be on to something, in that national allegory does appear to have been, and to remain, a seductive approach to aesthetic creativity in traditions such as Brazil's. In addition, to say that a text seems to invite national-allegorical interpretation is not necessarily to imply that the work must be read as endorsing one specific set of associations or that it therefore stands to be decoded in such a manner as to yield a univocal mapping of its events, characters, and other constituents onto determinate national-historical referents. For more on the complexities, challenges, and limitations of reading national allegory in Machado's *Esaú e Jacó*, see Jobst Welge's "Machado de Assis' *Esaú e Jacó* and the Problem of Historical Representation" and my own "Machado de Assis and Euclides da Cunha, Interpreters of an Inexplicable Nation."

24. Translations from *Dois irmãos* are by John Gledson.

25. Gledson's otherwise apt translation perhaps obscures some significant overtones for the point I am trying to make here. The phrase "podia comer a comida deles" could be rendered more directly, "I could eat their food"; more bluntly even, Gledson's translation has the narrator say that he rarely joined "the family" at the table, but Nael actually refers to them rather coldly as "os donos da casa" — "the owners of the house."

26. One might object to this interpretation on the grounds that there seems to have been genuine mutual affection over the years between Yaqub and Domingas. This is true enough, but there is no indication that Yaqub ever did anything that could have led to emancipation, independence, or any form of self-determination for Domingas. His generosity toward her and toward Nael, such as it is, is more patriarchal largess: at best a way of making them more comfortable without actually changing their prospects, at worst a means of co-opting their participation within an oppressive system of relations.

27. The notion that second-person narrative can be read as apostrophe is due to Irene Kacandes. For an interesting criticism of the theory, see Rolf Reitan.

28. All translations from *O avesso da pele* are my own.

29. See, for instance, reporting by Camargo and Sperb; Rocha; Barbon; Palhares; and Nogueira, Rizzo, and Sassine.

30. This approach to second-person narrative is prefigured by Brian Richardson's now classic essay "The Poetics and Politics of Second Person Narrative," in which the theorist briefly discusses the work of Jamaica Kincaid as an example of narrative produced from a position "painfully aware of the antithetical communities of reception, as well as the ideological codes that typically encase notions like the model reader. The assumptions that white middle and upper class audiences bring to the act of reading are thus foregrounded and exposed—particularly the

insidious assumption that they are, 'naturally,' the universal you addressed by the text" (324). However, Richardson does not see so far as to imagine a situation of narrative reception in which not only the assumption but also the reality of a primarily white and wealthy audience are directly contested.

Works Cited

Afolabi, Niyi. *Afro-Brazilians: Cultural Production in a Racial Democracy*. University of Rochester Press, 2009.

Ahmad, Aijaz. "Jameson's Rhetoric of Otherness and the 'National Allegory.'" *Social Text*, vol. 17, 1987, 3–25.

Barbon, Júlia. "Operação policial na Vila Cruzeiro já é a 2ª mais letal da história recente do RJ." *Folha de São Paulo*, 24 May 2022.

Barreto, Lima. *Vida e morte de M.J. Gonzaga de Sá*. São Paulo: Revista do Brasil, 1919.

Bosi, Alfredo. *Machado de Assis: O enigma do olhar*. São Paulo: Editora Ática, 1999.

Caldwell, Helen. *The Brazilian Othello of Machado de Assis: A Study of Dom Casmurro*. University of California Press, 1960.

Camargo, Cristina, and Paul Sperb. "Homem negro morre após ser espancado por seguranças do Carrefour em Porto Alegre." *Folha de São Paulo*, 20 Nov. 2020.

Collins, Patricia Hill. *Black Feminist Thought: Knowledge, Consciousness, and the Politics of Empowerment*. Second edition. Routledge, 2000.

———. "Learning from the Outsider Within: The Sociological Significance of Black Feminist Thought." *Social Problems*, vol. 33, no. 6, 1986, S14–S32.

Coutinho, Afrânio. *A filosofia de Machado de Assis e outros ensaios*. Rio de Janeiro: Livraria São José, 1959.

Daniel, G. Reginald. *Machado de Assis: Multiracial Identity and the Brazilian Novelist*. Penn State University Press, 2012.

Fitz, Earl E. *Machado de Assis and Narrative Theory: Language, Imitation, Art, and Verisimilitude in the Last Six Novels*. Bucknell University Press, 2019.

Flynn, Alex, Elena Calvo-González, and Marcelo Mendes de Souza. "Whiter Shades of Pale: 'Coloring in' Machado de Assis and Race in Contemporary Brazil." *Latin American Research Review*, vol. 48, no. 3, 2013, 3–24.

Freyre, Gilberto. *Sobrados e mocambos*. 2 vols., Rio de Janeiro: Livraria José Olympio, 1961.

Genette, Gérard. *Narrative Discourse: An Essay in Method*. Cornell University Press, 1980.

Gledson, John. *The Deceptive Realism of Machado de Assis: A Dissenting Interpretation of Dom Casmurro*. Liverpool: F. Cairns, 1984.

Hatoum, Milton. *Dois irmãos*. São Paulo: Companhia de Bolso, 2006.

————. *The Brothers*. Translated by John Gledson, Farrar, Straus, and Giroux, 2002.

Herman, David, et al. *Narrative Theory: Core Concepts and Critical Debates*. Ohio State University Press, 2012.

Jackson, K. David. *Machado de Assis: A Literary Life*. Yale University Press, 2015.

Jameson, Frederic. "Third World Literature in the Era of Multinational Capitalism." *Social Text*, vol. 15, 1986, 65–88.

Kacandes, Irene. "Narrative Apostrophe: Reading, Rhetoric, Resistance in Michel Butor's 'La Modification' and Julio Cortázar's 'Graffiti.'" *Style*, vol. 28, no. 3, 1994, 329–49.

Lanser, Susan S. *The Narrative Act: Point of View in Prose Fiction*. Princeton University Press, 1981.

Machado de Assis, Joaquim Maria. *Casa velha*. Chapecó: Editora Grifos, 2000.

————. *Esau and Jacob*. Translated by Helen Caldwell, University of California Press, 1965.

————. *Dom Casmurro. Obra completa*. Edited by Afrânio Coutinho, vol. 1, 3 vols., Rio de Janeiro: Aguilar, 1962.

————. *Esaú e Jacó. Obra completa*. Edited by Afrânio Coutinho, vol. 1, 3 vols., Rio de Janeiro: Aguilar, 1962.

————. *Helena. Obra completa*. Edited by Afrânio Coutinho, vol. 1, 3 vols., Rio de Janeiro: Aguilar, 1962.

————. *Memorial de Aires. Obra completa*. Edited by Afrânio Coutinho, vol. 1, 3 vols., Rio de Janeiro: J. Aguilar, 1962.

————. *Memórias póstumas de Brás Cubas. Obra completa*. Edited by Afrânio Coutinho, vol. 1, 3 vols., Rio de Janeiro: Aguilar, 1962.

————. *Quincas Borba*. Translated by Gregory Rabassa, Oxford University Press, 1999.

————. *Quincas Borba. Obra completa*. Edited by Afrânio Coutinho, vol. 1, 3 vols., Rio de Janeiro: Aguilar, 1962.

Mignolo, Walter. *The Darker Side of Western Modernity: Global Futures, Decolonial Options*. Duke University Press, 2011.

Miguel-Pereira, Lúcia. *Machado de Assis: Estudo critico e biografico*. São Paulo: Editora Nacional, 1936.

Mills, Charles W. "White Ignorance." *Race and Epistemologies of Ignorance*. Edited by Shannon Sullivan and Nancy Tuana, 13–38, SUNY Press, 2007.

————. *The Racial Contract*. Cornell University Press, 1997.

Mittelman, David M. "Machado de Assis and Euclides da Cunha, Interpreters of an Inexplicable Nation." *Brasil/Brazil*, vol. 33, no. 64, 2020, 139–61.

————. "Training Skeptical Readers in Machado De Assis's *Helena*." *Chasqui*, vol. 48, no. 1, 2019, 37–55.

Nascimento, Abdias. "Reflections of an Afro-Braziliano." Translated by Elisa Larkin Nascimento. *The Journal of Negro History*, vol. 64, no. 3, 1979, 274–82.

Nogueira, Italo, Marcel Rizzo, and Vinicius Sassine. "Aposta em armas e ausência de ação nacional marcam segurança pública sob Bolsonaro." *Folha de São Paulo*, 13 Sept. 2022.

Palhares, Isabela. "Marcha da Consciência Negra em SP critica Bolsonaro e relembra vítimas da pandemia." *Folha de São Paulo*, 20 Nov. 2021.

Prince, Gerald. "On a Postcolonial Narratology." *A Companion to Narrative Theory*, edited by James Phelan and Peter J. Rabinowitz, 372–81, Wiley-Blackwell, 2005.

Quijano, Aníbal. "Coloniality of Power, Eurocentrism, and Latin America." *Nepantla*: 1.3 (2000): 533–80.

Reitan, Rolf. "Theorizing Second-Person Narratives: A Backwater Project?" *Strange Voices in Narrative Fiction*, edited by Per Krogh Hansen et al., 147–74, Berlin: De Gruyter, 2011.

Ribeiro, Djamila. *O que é lugar de fala?* Belo Horizonte: Letramento, 2017.

Richardson, Brian. "The Poetics and Politics of Second Person Narrative." *Genre*, vol. 24, 1991, 309–30.

Rocha, Matheus. " 'Continuaram batendo mesmo depois da morte,' diz tio de Moïse." *Folha de São Paulo*, 1 Feb. 2022.

Russell, Heather. *Legba's Crossing: Narratology in the African Atlantic*. University of Georgia Press, 2009.

Santiago, Silviano. "Retórica da verossimilhança." *Uma literatura nos trópicos: Ensaios sobre dependência cultural*. São Paulo: Editora Perspectiva, 1978, 29–48.

Schwarz, Roberto. *Ao vencedor as batatas: Forma literária e processo social nos inícios do romance brasileiro*. 2nd ed., São Paulo: Livraria Duas Cidades, 1981.

———. *Um mestre na periferia do capitalismo: Machado de Assis*. São Paulo: Livraria Duas Cidades, 1990.

Tenório, Jefferson. *O avesso da pele*. São Paulo: Companhia das Letras 2020.

Warhol, Robyn R. and Lanser, Susan S. *Narrative Theory Unbound: Queer and Feminist Interventions*. Ohio State University Press, 2015.

Wasserman, Renata R. Mautner. "Race, Nation, Representation: Machado de Assis and Lima Barreto." *Luso-Brazilian Review*, vol. 45, no. 2, 2008, 84–106.

Welge, Jobst. "Machado de Assis' *Esaú e Jacó* and the Problem of Historical Representation." *Luso-Brazilian Review*, vol. 52, no. 2, 2015, 19–36.

Zilberman, Regina. *Estética da recepção e história da literatura*. São Paulo: Editora Atica, 1989.

Afterword

A Conversation between Friends

Vanessa K. Valdés and Earl E. Fitz

Vanessa K. Valdés: To begin this conversation properly, I want to thank you first for inviting me on this journey with you, and when I say "this journey," I not only mean this book but also for being instructive in my learning about Machado de Assis. For our readers, I want to make transparent our relationship, yours and mine, and my relationship with this writer. You were my introduction to Brazil, full stop. I started graduate studies at Vanderbilt University in the fall of 1999, dropped the semester due to a family emergency, and began again in the spring of 2000. Somewhere in my first year, you asked if I intended on studying Spain or Latin America; hearing my choice of the latter, you emphasized that I needed to study Brazil. I knew very little about the country, other than that the national language was Portuguese, and because you made a good argument about needing to understand continental South America as a whole, rather than just Spanish America, I agreed. Studying Brazil changed my life: I learned about Black history there, and started seeing similarities, not only with a history of enslavement, but in themes and motifs in literatures across the hemisphere. I took a Portuguese-language class taught by Cacilda Rego, and that Carioca's accent reminded me of the Puerto Rican Spanish with which I had grown up, and I took to it. I started piecing together my understanding of diaspora, and in taking your Comparative Methodologies class, you gave me the tools to be a

179

comparatist, which I have attempted to apply in all of my work, beginning with my dissertation. All to say, again, thank you.

When did you learn about Machado de Assis? Do you remember your first encounters with him and his work?

EARL E. FITZ: I first encountered Machado in the fall of 1970, when I had the great good fortune to take a graduate seminar at the CUNY Graduate Center with Greg Rabassa on Brazilian literature. We read the *Memórias Póstumas de Brás Cubas*. I knew immediately I was in the presence of greatness, both with Greg and with Machado's novel.

VKV: What was it exactly about Machado that struck you in those terms?

EEF: I was dazzled by Machado. And, before the semester was over, I had reread the novel twice, each time seeing more and more about how he did what he was doing. Not entirely ignorant of world literature masterpieces, I realized this great Brazilian writer, egregiously unknown outside of his native country, was doing things no one else had done. He was breaking all kinds of new ground, not just about the novel form but also about our reigning theories of narrative. I knew there was a lifetime of work there. My problem was that I was also being dazzled by other Luso-Brazilian writers, Fernando Pessoa, from Portugal, and Guimarães Rosa and Clarice Lispector, both from Brazil. I would end up teaching and writing about these and other Luso-Brazilian writers, but I made sure I read, taught, and wrote about at least some Machado every semester. I never failed to learn more and more about his art, things that I had never seen before. His novels and stories are an inexhaustible well of information about how language works and about the nature of narrative. Machado is a genius, especially when one considers his circumstances and all he had to overcome.

VKV: I wholeheartedly agree with you about him being a genius; the first time I read him—and *Memórias Póstumas* was also my introduction to his oeuvre—I couldn't believe that this Black man was writing in this way in the nineteenth century. I thought I was reading a contemporary novel, having by then learned about postmodernism and the unreliable narrator and all of that. I was holding evidence of Black genius. I know critics reading this conversation may chafe at my defining him as a Black man and will accuse me of looking at him with US eyes, as someone raised in the United States and therefore as someone tied to the legacy of the one-drop rule and hypodescent. I *was* born in the United States, to Puerto Rican parents who, if we are going to go by Brazilian culture, or Puerto Rican culture for that matter—if we are going by the legacies of Iberian colonization, my parents were both mulatos, which means I'm a mulata. Neither my parents nor I ever used that term, much less embraced it—that was never our reality. In fact, I remember a moment about a decade ago when I understood mulatez within our cultures in a visceral way, rather than simply intellectually. Someone commented on how they liked the color of my skin and called me "mulata." I hadn't ever experienced that in Puerto Rico or other places in Latin America, but in that moment, something clicked. I understood that in that moment the proximity to whiteness had just been delineated, as had a distance from Blackness. But mulatez does not equal whiteness, by any stretch of the imagination; it didn't a decade ago, when I had that exchange, and it definitely didn't in nineteenth-century Brazil. And so for me, it has always been impossible to believe that Machado was not aware of himself as a man of African descent. He may not have said "sou negro" or "sou pardo" in public, may not have written it, but there is no way that the awareness of his heritage did not fuel all of his actions. I look at the reality of his life and the historical context of his life, in which Black human beings, free and enslaved, were heavily surveilled and monitored, particularly in the capital city of Rio. I find it almost comical to think he sidestepped his heritage. The very invention of categories to designate "not white" within white supremacist regimes is an indication of difference rather than synonymity. Machado is a genius not in spite of his heritage but, in fact, precisely because of it.

Machado de Assis has been the subject of several of your books. Can you describe that journey, how you thought about him and his work toward the beginning of your career and how that has evolved, perhaps, over the years?

EEF: In the beginning, as I've said, I was dazzled by what Machado was doing. I was being overwhelmed by true greatness, and I knew it. I thought at the time that it must be like how defenders in the 1950s and 1960s had to have felt when they tried to control Pelé and Garrincha. You put into use all you know or can do, but it's not enough. I also knew, in my dim kind of way, that if I really wanted to understand Machado enough to properly appreciate his brilliance, and I did, I would have to spend the rest of my life studying his work. So that's what I did. That's why I wrote in my book about his new theory of narrative that the road to the modern novel must now run through Machado de Assis.

So, I would say that while in the beginning I knew that with Machado I was, though quite overwhelmed, in the presence of genius, and a funny, iconoclastic one at that, I also knew that further readings would reveal more to me, more of his greatness. And his uniqueness. Again, like Pelé and Garrincha. And that's where I am today. I know more about Machado than I did when I started, but there's a lot I'm still discovering. That's why a writer like Machado de Assis benefits from gaining new readers through time. I'm still learning, too.

VKV: It's true, one can always come back to these books and see something different, find another dimension. That's a hallmark of greatness in and of itself, isn't it, the room for the different interpretations? Given that this is a study about the reception of Machado's work here in the United States, how do you think considerations about race and color inform our reception of Machado de Assis's narrative techniques?

EEF: Considerations of race and color have to be part of anyone's reception of Machado de Assis. He was a writer part of whose ancestors were Black. And he lived and worked in a culture where slavery was still practiced. I hope, however, that such considerations do not overshadow Machado's genius as a narrative iconoclast, which is where I think his true greatness lies. But when I contemplate his reception here in the United States, a culture that has long struggled with both racism and the place of Black writing in its literary canon, I am not comforted, since it would be all too easy for critics here to reduce Machado's innovative work to matters of melanin. A better route, I think, is to appreciate Machado as a great writer, one who is Black and fully aware of all this means.

VKV: Yes, absolutely. You rightly point out that the issue is not him and his work but who is reading him and how *we*, his readers, are interpreting him. When we read the bibliography of literary criticism focused on Machado, what calls my attention is how Black critics have read him both here and in Brazil, and for many, how he addresses, or doesn't address, racism is a flashpoint. What do you make of Machado's decision to avoid openly addressing racism?

EEF: Machado certainly could have commented overtly about the racial situation in his Brazil. But he didn't. On the other hand, his novels and stories, and especially his post-1880 novels and stories, are full of references to the poisons of slavery and racism. We can assume Machado had a reason for treating these issues as he did. My guess is that he saw himself as a writer more than anything else. A writer, I would add, who demanded the active participation of the reader in the creation of his texts' meaning. In the first of his "new novels," *The Posthumous Memoirs of Brás Cubas*, Machado has his deceased narrator/protagonist, Brás Cubas, trying to help his befuddled reader to understand the meaning of an earlier sentence. In chapter 138, entitled (in one of the now multiple English translations of this wonderful novel, or anti-novel) "To A Critic," a finally exasperated Brás declares something like this: "Good God, do I have to explain everything?" For me, this line serves as a window into how and why Machado, and especially the late Machado, wrote as he did. I think he resented being expected to have to explain everything to the reader, and so he didn't. The astute, engaged reader—like the astute, engaged citizen—knew perfectly well what the racial situation was in Brazil and did not have to be told. I remember well when, in the 1960s, Irving Howe chastised Ralph Ellison for not being as militant in his work as Howe thought he should be, and I do not want this to be the fate of Machado and his reception here in the States.

Vanessa, why do you think Machado's references to the toxins of slavery and racism are presented by Machado as they are?

VKV: I think he was brilliant and ambitious and understood the society in which he lived. I suspect he knew he was one of the smartest people in any room into which he walked, and his most incisive commentary comes at the expense of the white middle and upper classes of Brazil, in all of their bourgeois pretensions at being modern and building that modernity on a foundation of genocidal violence. The capital of Rio de Janeiro was at the very center of the endeavor of slavery in his country: it is an understatement to say Machado would not have ascended within Rio society writing against enslavement. Rather, he made a series of choices with which we may or may not agree, creating works that appealed to a white Brazilian elite and bourgeoisie that, for decades, looked to Europe—to France in particular—for its cultural cues. It doesn't mean he disavowed his African heritage; it means he was strategic in determining when and how he could write about Black life and culture for his audience.

For me, reading Machado recalls Paul Laurence Dunbar's "We Wear the Mask": "We wear the mask that grins and lies, / It hides our cheeks and shades our eyes." Dunbar was three decades younger than Machado but their lives overlapped, and so for me, looking at the work of his African American contemporaries here in the US lends insight. In both Brazil and the US, during the nineteenth and early twentieth centuries, politicians and intellectuals, white and Black alike, were facing existential crises in trying to define these countries while struggling to figure out how to incorporate populations of African descent into their body politic, if at all. African Americans lived through the promises of Reconstruction, only to see those destroyed with the rise of Jim Crow and the construction of whole political, economic, and social systems that were defined explicitly by anti-Black racism and discrimination, and yet they developed strategies by which they lived and thrived: they wore the masks. The artists developed strategies by which they offered their criticisms but in ways that are easily missed. I absolutely agree with Eduardo de Assis Duarte, who, as we reference in the introduction, names what Machado employs as a poetics of dissimulation.

What we see over the course of his career is Machado consistently pointing out the hypocrisies of living within the empire that Brazil was at the time, as it lurched toward supposed modernity. But because he includes these satirical observations from the perspectives of his white protagonists, certainly in his most famous narratives, his criticism can look to be muted on one hand, rendering it all the more effective. I remember first encountering his work and thinking, "Wait, he got away with this?" But of course he did, because his compatriots didn't realize that they were the objects of his contempt. There's a fair amount of rage in his novels, from my perspective, relatively thinly veiled, but his sleight of hand is so effective that it's easy to miss. Machado demands that we read in ways in which we are unaccustomed, particularly when it comes to Blackness. He includes signs and codes that much of his reading audience did not notice because they did not see a whole segment of their population as having a capacity for intelligence.

Let's return for a second to your mentor: Could you say a bit more about renowned translator Gregory Rabassa and what he meant to you?

EEF: Greg and I hit it off right away. His first question to me, in early September of 1970, was, "In Iowa, do they say 'crick' or 'creek?' " I thought to myself, "Damn, I haven't been here twenty seconds and I'm already about to fail a test." I screwed up my courage and replied, 'Well, in my part of Iowa a crick is what you get in your neck and a creek runs through your back forty. But if you have a little stream at the bottom of a hill, you might call it a crick." "Good," Greg said, a little enigmatically, with a grin. Later, I would find out he loved language, regionalisms, and accents. And clear answers. He also loved puns, the more outrageously interlingual the better. That was another thing we had in common.

As a teacher, Greg was demanding. He brooked no nonsense or carelessness. He was a veteran of World War II—a survivor, he often said—and he took learning as a rare and privileged opportunity, one not to be squandered or wasted. He expected us to do our jobs, which was to read, to connect things, and to meet deadlines. All good habits to get into.

I thrived in that environment. Greg prized close, careful reading and he loathed jargon, which he regarded as a sign someone didn't know what they were talking about. Perhaps that's why I regard it in the same way. Greg's advice was, "Have something to say, and then say it. Be clear and concise." I remember once on a paper for him I had made some vague reference to a "whirling dervish." In the margin, he wrote, "Don't they all?" From Greg, I learned to think about what I was saying and how I was saying it.

We became very close in the years that followed graduate school and would talk on the phone almost every afternoon at 5:30 Eastern Standard Time. About everything and nothing. About "cabbages and kings," as he liked to say. A lot of stories. Using his best old New Englander accent, Greg loved to tell tales of growing up in rural New Hampshire, people in his family, his dogs, and his friends. He also liked to reminisce about his experiences as a soldier in the war and the people he met. There were also a lot of puns. And a lot of politics. A lot of laughing. All in all, I think maybe what I learned from Greg is this: Be good enough at your work that you can put pretentiousness on the shelf, where it belongs, and have some fun with what you do. And be a good citizen. Think of others and not just yourself. Stand up for what's right. By the way, Greg was a committed integrationist and an advocate of equal rights. If he were here right now, I think he'd say something like this: "We fought the damn war to make discrimination against people impossible!"

VKV: Let's talk a bit about that specific lesson from fighting the Second World War in relation to the birth of this study: you approached me about this subject in the summer of 2020, when the world was exploding, between the pandemic and calls for justice and equity swept the United

States and then encompassed the world. What about that moment inspired a Machado project?

EEF: Yes, it was in the summer of 2020, when the United States was again exploding over still unresolved questions of social injustice and racial prejudice, that I wrote you about the question of Machado's reception in the US and the rest of the Americas. As a longtime advocate of Black writers here in the States, and as someone interested in comparative studies involving Brazil, the United States, and the rest of the Americas, it occurred to me that it might be useful, to readers here in the US and to readers in Brazil, if we put together a book that explored Machado's reception here in the States. Specifically, I wondered if Machado, a great writer of African descent and one fully aware of living in a racially charged place and time, would be read here as a Black Writer, as that term is understood in the United States. And if this line of interpretation were suggested, would Machado be criticized for not presenting us with texts that illustrate what that categorization means to us? Or would he be read in some other way? The question of reception is of immense importance in global literary studies, and I wanted us to consider Machado in that context.

In Brazil, as you know, Machado, until very recently, has been thought of, by the establishment intelligentsia, as a Black writer who wrote as though he were white. While Machado's reasons for writing the way he did are not entirely known, there is considerable evidence that he thought of himself as an artist, not as a social activist. As Henry James would do in the United States, Machado wanted to cultivate the art of fiction. And to bring it to new levels of sophistication and seriousness. He did that, and more.

But there is also considerable, text-based evidence that Machado was keenly aware of race and its ills in Brazil and that he did, in fact, build many examples of this into his work. Especially his post-1880 fiction. In *The Posthumous Memoirs of Brás Cubas* (in Rabassa's brilliant rendering of this novel), for example, we have the case of Prudêncio, the former childhood slave whom a young Brás mistreats and who grows into an adult who mistreats his own slaves. The pernicious cycle of slavery repeats itself. *Quincas Borba*, published some ten years later, depicts the demotion of a Black cook simply because the newly rich white man, who employs him and even likes him because they both hail from the same part of Brazil, is told by false friends he needs a white, European cook if he wishes to fit into higher echelons of society (a fact which, in and of itself, is an indictment of said society). In a racist society, Machado shows us, skin color trumps talent. And in the powerful story, "Father versus Mother," which recalls for US readers our own shameful experience with the Fugitive Slave Laws, the abject cruelty of slavery is skewered, as is the capitalist system that benefits from it and that forces moral people to do immoral things. And in Machado's final novel, *Counselor Ayres' Memorial*, a young Brazilian woman, who clearly represents the future of a more progressive and just nation, inherits a lucrative plantation and, instead of seeking to make money off it and off the slaves who run it, gives it to the Black men and women themselves, to own and to operate. Machado's work, his novels and stories, but also his less well-known poetry and plays (comedies, mostly), contain other examples not just of his racial awareness but his anger at *all* forms of bigotry and oppression, including that directed at women. Yet it is true that his fiction is not like that of his also marvelous, but more racially militant contemporary, Lima Barreto, who was open and upfront about his rage at the stupidity of racism.

Right now, moreover, there is, in Brazil, a movement that wants Machado to be recognized, and hailed, as the Black man he was, and as a Black Brazilian man who is also a master of world literature. This movement will prevail, I predict, because it has right on its side and because we are slowly progressing to a point when our conception of "greatness" in literature does not have to be tethered to skin color. It's past time we did so.

VKV: Yes, absolutely; in fact, the hesitation on the part of many scholars to incorporate Machado's Blackness in these conversations about genius has always called my attention. He was innovative with the form of narrative, he was ironic, he was all of the things that has attracted the notice of intellectuals the world over, seemingly in spite of his Blackness—as if one thing had nothing to do with the other. And that discomfort called out to me. Having studied him and the field for longer than I have, to what do you attribute such discomfort?

EEF: The "distress" you note, Vanessa, in reading the scholarship on Machado and finding little commentary on his Blackness is valid. It's an odd lacuna, isn't it? But it generates the still unanswered, and maybe unknowable, question: Why? To answer it, I'll have to go way above my pay grade, but I'll try. One reason Machado was not, for a long time, more written about as a Black writer is that his work does not generate that particular reading. But that doesn't mean his concerns are not there, does it? Machado was the grandson of freed slaves. He lived in poverty. He was fully cognizant of Brazil's history of slavery—he was forty-nine years old an established writer when, in 1888, slavery was finally abolished in Brazil!—and he knew what racism was, having undoubtedly experienced it himself. And he would have seen others suffer from it as well. So why didn't Machado attack racism, front and center, in his work? That's the question, isn't it? As you know, his stories and novels especially are larded with examples of it. But they are not the focal points of his work. Should they be? I'm not so sure. At the same time, I do think Machado's Blackness is an aspect of his art that needs to be elucidated more than it so far has been. It's there, and we need to understand it better.

A second reason, closely related to the first, could be that Machado's texts, complex, multifaceted, and laced with irony as they are, lead scholars to see his concerns with race and racism as parts of the larger human condition, which I believe is Machado's real subject. We have met the enemy and they are us. We're our own worst enemies. I think Machado would be nodding his head in agreement.

On the topic of race, to read Machado is to have a very different experience than one gets reading, say, Richard Wright, LeRoi Jones, and James Baldwin. It has always seemed to me that Machado's case is more analogous, in many ways, to that of Ralph Ellison, who, like Machado, was a Black man trying to be an artist in a time and place that demanded more bare-knuckled activism. Wasn't it a white critic, Irving Howe, who denounced Ellison for not being militant enough? But Machado's insistence on equal rights for all people, regardless of skin color, gender, or sexual orientation, as an absolute condition for a democracy, or a democratic Republic, to fully realize itself puts him in the company of Baldwin as well. The outrage I associate with Jones's poetry I do not find in Machado's work—though I suspect that, in private, Machado might well have felt a kinship with Jones as well.

A third possible reason for the dearth of studies about Machado's Blackness is that Brazil's largely white elite has sought, historically, to promote him to the world as a white writer. This concern would have been particularly acute in the segregated United States of 1952, when Machado was first translated into English and marketed in the US and the English-speaking world.

A deeply mixed society, biologically and culturally, Brazil and its power brokers have long been sensitive about the faces they present to the world. And they followed carefully what was transpiring in the United States of the 1950s and 1960s, especially as regards race. This may help explain why Brazil's leaders, also mostly white, for too long made Machado appear to be lighter skinned than he really was. It was as if a Black man, or one of mixed racial heritage, could not be celebrated as Brazil's greatest writer. Or exported to the rest of the world. Could Machado have received a fair hearing in the United States in that era? Can he get one now? We're about to find out.

VKV: Yes, we are. You mentioned his poetry and his plays—why hasn't the fullness of the body of Machado's work been studied to a greater extent? Do you believe that solely to be a question of translation? Do you think there's a certain level of resistance to learning that he was even *more* of everything that people already think he is? And here I'm thinking of the still mostly white Brazilian elite.

EEF: I tried to say something useful about his poetry and his plays in my first book on Machado, called, cleverly enough, *Machado de Assis*. What I thought then I still pretty much think now: Machado was a good poet and dramatist, and sometimes an excellent one, but he was never, in these genres, the genius he is in narrative. That's his true métier, the one where he's like Pelé or Garrincha with the ball at their feet running loose in the open field. Only a handful of his poems have been translated into English. And, unless I've missed it, none of his plays have been translated. This all needs to be done. His poetry and his plays, in the main one-act comedies, all have merit on their own, some much more than others, but they all contribute to his brilliance as an innovative and genre-blending writer of short stories and novels. That's the key thing. I've always thought part of his skill at creating such wonderful scenes in his narratives must come from his work as a dramatist. And that his lifelong interest in poetry led directly to his sense of language as a self-referential semiotic system in which individual words mean something only in relation to the other words in their system. I think Machado antedates Saussure on this matter.

VKV: One more question: What do you hope this study does? Is it in keeping with what you hope for with any of your work? Thinking of my own projects, my intention is to make room for more of this work. I remember in college and in graduate school, I would go to the stacks and later, databases, certain that someone had written up the particular thought I had. And I started seeing that there were whole opportunities to keep writing, to be in dialogue with others, as together we promote the work of Black artists, writers, intellectuals from throughout the hemisphere. For me, the more I write, the more I'm learning, and so I continue asking questions. How do you think about your own work?

EEF: My hope is that this study will facilitate a more complete appreciation of Machado here in the United States and in the Americas generally. I also hope it will help us finally put an end to prejudice based on skin color and allow us to celebrate greatness when we encounter it. I hope for this as I also hope we can do the same with our prejudices about gender and sexual orientation.

I see this book as contributing to my interest in the mechanisms of influence and reception and to my longtime advocacy of inter-American literature. For me, this all began back in October of 1967, when I was a student at the University of Iowa. I was taking a class on early Spanish American literature with Professor Oscar Fernández and, while reading *La Araucana*, it came to me that applying the comparative method to our several American literatures, and including our Indigenous ones, might be an interesting new approach to what the greater American experience entails. And using Latin America as the platform from which to launch it. Oscar and another great Iowa professor, Mary Lou Daniel, encouraged me to pursue this line of thought. And so I did. I had not yet read Machado de Assis at that point, but once I had, the various pieces of the inter-American project began to fall into place. Machado was not a part of the wrenching debates over race, racism, and art taking place in the US at that time. Perhaps, with this book, he now will be, inasmuch as the same debate is still with us.

As for my own work, I like to think that I've helped a bit to gain for Brazilian literature the respect it deserves, in Latin America, in the Americas more broadly, and in the world. I also like to think I've been useful in showing the excellence of Spanish American and Brazilian literature to comparative literature as a global discipline. Overall, I give myself a solid B as a grade, albeit one that has, on occasion, stumbled into the B+ or, more rarely, A- range. Mostly, though, I hope my work has not misled anyone, hindered their progress, or muddled their thinking.

VKV: You've done so much better than you will acknowledge, and at the risk of embarrassing you, I want to thank you, not only for inviting me to this project but also for your mentorship and encouragement throughout these years, more than two decades now. Thank you for modeling how to be human in this enterprise known as academia, fully human. I remember marveling as you shared with me how you would wake up early, before your family had arisen, in order to write and then would be a partner to your beloved Julianne and fully take part in getting your children ready for school in the mornings. Any student of yours knows that you have cared about your teaching as much as you have cared about your scholarship, and this too was important for me to see as I was coming into this world. I may not get the chance to do this in print ever again so please know this has been one of the highest honors of my life, collaborating on this book with you, particularly because we are studying a man to whom you've dedicated years. There's so much work left to do.

Contributors

Niyi Afolabi is a professor of Portuguese and Afro-Brazilian studies in the Department of African and African Diaspora Studies at the University of Texas at Austin. He is the author of *The Golden Cage* (2001), *Afro-Brazilians: Cultural Production in a Racial Democracy* (2009), *Ilê Aiyê in Brazil and the Reinvention of Africa* (2016), and numerous articles and edited volumes on transatlantic migrations and the African Diaspora.

Regina Castro McGowan is a senior lecturer of Portuguese, Spanish, and Black studies and the director of Lusophone studies at The City College of New York (CUNY). Dr. Castro McGowan's teaching and research focus on Luso-Afro-Brazilian literature, historiography, and film. She has been awarded national and international grants for archival research at the Biblioteca Nacional de Portugal, Brazil's Fundação Biblioteca Nacional, and the Bibliothèque Nationale de France. Her latest published works include the bilingual critical edition of previously unpublished poems by Portuguese poet Nita Lupi and the article 'Whose Place of Speech?' Brazil's Afro- and Queer-Centric *YouTube* ahannels and the Decentralization of *TV Globo's Telenovela* Discourse."

Paulo Dutra is an assistant professor of Portuguese and Spanish at the University of New Mexico. He specializes in the intersections of race and artistic and cultural production in Luso-Brazilian/Latin American contexts with an emphasis on conducting independent approaches to literary and cultural production that present alternatives to mainstream practices. He is the coeditor of the special issue of *Machado de Assis em linha* that explores race and slavery in his works and worked as a consultant for Editora Todavia's collection "Todos os livros Machado de Assis" published in 2023 and sponsored by Itaú Cultural. He is the author of a short story collection, *Aversão oficial: resumida* (Malê, 2018), and a poetry collection, *ablliterações* (Malê, 2019), semifinalist of Oceanos Prize in 2020.

Earl E. Fitz is a professor of Portuguese, Spanish, and comparative literature at Vanderbilt University. He has pioneered the application of comparative methodologies to the study of both Brazilian and Spanish American letters, the use of literature written in Spanish and Portuguese to comparative scholarship, and to the establishment of a new PhD track concentrating on inter-American literary study. Professor Fitz also encourages a comparative approach to the literatures of Spain and Portugal and to the development of comparative Iberian studies as an emerging field. He is the author of a number of articles and books, including *Rediscovering the New World: Inter-American Literature in a Comparative Context* (1991); *Ambiguity and Gender in the New Novel of Brazil and Spanish America: A Comparative Assessment* (coauthored with Judith A. Payne, 1993); *Sexuality and Being in the Poststructuralist Universe of Clarice Lispector* (2001); *Brazilian Narrative Traditions in a Comparative Context* (2005); and *Translation and the Rise of Inter-American Literature* (coauthored with Elizabeth Lowe, 2007). Professor Fitz's most recent projects involve the completion of a comparative history of inter-American literature, a study of the Borges translation of Faulkner's *The Wild Palms*, and an essay on Machado de Assis, Borges, and Clarice Lispector that offers a new, more comparative evaluation of Latin America's renowned "New Narrative."

Benjamin Legg is a principal senior lecturer of Portuguese at Vanderbilt University, where he coordinates Portuguese language instruction. He researches twentieth- and twenty-first-century Brazilian literature, film, and popular music; national identity-building in Brazil and Lusophone Africa; and cultural perception's role in the development of Brazil–US relations. His work has appeared in *Letterature d'America* and *Portuguese Literary and Cultural Studies*, as well as in edited volumes on Brazilian performance and global food studies. An active translator, he has had translations of Brazilian poetry and film criticism published in anthologies. His most recent project explores Lusophone African national identities in a global context.

David M. Mittelman is an associate professor of Portuguese at the United States Air Force Academy, where he teaches courses in Portuguese language and Afro-Luso-Brazilian cultures. His work on Brazilian literature and cinema has appeared in *Romance Quarterly*, the *Journal of Lusophone Studies*, *Brasil/Brazil*, *Chasqui*, and other venues.

Daniel F. Silva is an associate professor of Luso-Hispanic studies and Black studies at Middlebury University. He is the author of four monographs: *Embodying Modernity: Race, Gender, and Fitness Culture in Brazil* (University of Pittsburgh Press, 2022); *Empire Found: Racial Identities and Coloniality in Twenty-First Century Portuguese Popular Cultures* (Liverpool University Press, 2022); *Anti-Empire: Decolonial Interventions in Lusophone Literatures* (Liverpool University Press, 2018); and *Subjectivity and the Reproduction of Imperial Power: Empire's Individuals* (Routledge, 2015). He is also the coeditor of four volumes: *Migrant Frontiers: Race and Mobility in the Luso-Hispanic World* (Liverpool University Press, 2023); *Lusophone African Poetry and Short-Stories After Independence: Decolonial Destinies* (Anthem Press, 2021); *Emerging Dialogues on Machado de Assis* (Palgrave Macmillan, 2016); and *Lima Barreto: New Critical Perspectives* (Lexington Books, 2013). He is the coeditor of the book series *Anthem Studies in Race, Power, and Society* with Anthem Press and has published scholarship in numerous edited volumes as well as in journals such as *Hispania*, *Chasqui*, and *Transmodernity*.

Vanessa K. Valdés is an independent writer, scholar, speaker, and curator. She is the former associate provost for community engagement and professor of Spanish and Portuguese at The City College of New York (CUNY). Her research interests focus on the cultural production of Black peoples throughout the Americas: the United States and Latin America, including Brazil and the Caribbean. She is the editor of *The Future Is Now: A New Look at African Diaspora Studies* (2012); *Let Spirit Speak! Cultural Journeys through the African Diaspora* (2012); and *Racialized Visions: Haiti and the Hispanic Caribbean* (2020). She is the author of *Oshun's Daughters: The Search for Womanhood in the Americas* (2014) and *Diasporic Blackness: The Life and Times of Arturo Alfonso Schomburg* (2017). With David Pullins, she is the coauthor of *Juan de Pareja, Afro-Hispanic Painter in the Age of Velázquez* (2023), which accompanied the exhibition of the same name on view at The Metropolitan Museum of Art from 3 April to 16 July 2023.

Index